THE ARCHANGEL

PUBLISHED BY: Mark Anthony DiBello

PUBLICATION IS AVAILABLE BY WRITING THE PUBLISHER –

OR AT: www.MarkAnthonyDiBello.com

PUBLISHING ACKNOWLEDGMENT:

Anthony Francis DiBello, God bless you.

PUBLISHING ACKNOWLEDGMENT – IN MEMORY OF:

Mrs. Dorothy Leona Burek DiBello, God bless you.

ADDITIONAL PUBLISHING ACKNOWLEDGMENTS:

Mrs. Helen Burek Krill, God bless you.

COVER AND WEBSITE PRODUCTION:

Mark Anthony DiBello

PHOTOGRAPH & IMAGE ACKNOWLEDGMENT:

The photograph and image used in this book were created by and used with the authority of Mark Anthony DiBello.

Mark Anthony DiBello
86,543 words
www.MarkAnthonyDiBello.com
All Rights Available
310.717.2440

THE ARCHANGEL

Written by
Mark Anthony DiBello

THE ARCHANGEL - INTRODUCTION

Life: The meaning of life for Long Island, millionaire wanna-be Michael Angelo Roman is money. Until, in a divine dream, the archangel commands that his namesake *actually* save a life— Michael's only hope for saving his own.

I am Mark Anthony DiBello, the writer of *The Archangel*. This is how the book: *The Archangel* came into existence. It is based on three true stories...not one, not two, but three true stories.

One day, in the 1970s, God spoke to me. It was through His archangel Michael that the Creator of the Universe said: "You are to write an action-adventure version of the Bible..."

The Archangel is inspired from the true story of the Bible. Michael is God's messenger; and life's savior has been *The Archangel*.

Hebrews 12:7 "You have made him a little lower than the angels. You have crowned him with glory and honor, and have set him over the works of Your hands."

"...*Him?*" Life has a higher
Savior: God Himself. *The
Archangel* is the story of the
Bible; but *The Archangel* is also
the true story of Jesus Christ.
John 14:6 "I am the way, the
truth, and the *life*."

The millennium is here and the
work of *The Archangel* is complete.
In prayer...I recalled that very
first time God spoke to me: "You
are to write an action-adventure
version of the Bible...that will
be the meaning of *your* life."

And this is how the third and
final true story begins...

THE ARCHANGEL - CHAPTER OUTLINE

<u>DAY ONE</u>
IN THE BEGINNING...

*In the beginning...a
lifeless, foot-long, rainbow trout
lies prone on a sandy-brown,
kitchen cutting-board and
countertop. Encamped around it
are a woven, wooden basket of
apples and uncut bread loaves, and
a glass chalice of water and one
of wine. A singular, vase-less
flower symbolically completes the
setting.*

MICHAEL

THURSDAY, EVENING - APRIL 13, 2000

The Archangel's main divisions
(chapters) are eleven days in the
life of Michael Roman. *MICHAEL* is
the initial subdivision. By
listing the day, date, and
relative time, the book reads like
a journal; and the incidences in
Roman's life serve as a "blueprint
for life."

Michael Angelo Roman is the main
character. We learn of his
inborn, sinful nature in a
flashback to his christening. In

this portion of the book, we also meet his sexy wife Magdalene. Her background is also divulged in a flashback. The backgrounds of the supporting characters in *The Archangel* are also revealed using this technique.

DAY TWO
1ST DREAMS & VISIONS

FRIDAY, 3:00 A.M. - APRIL 14, 2000

In the bedroom, the air is serene and peaceful. Roman and Maggie are each sleeping. They lay face down—dead to the world. Roman rolls over. In moonlight, his countenance basks in an inexplicable prolonged stillness. In his sleep, he hears his own voice in his head: **"I am Michael."**

Michael receives his initial calling from his namesake angel.

More meaningful, to the true-life nature of the book, is this scene:

At 3:00 A.M., in a different bedroom, a man's silhouetted, moonlit image appears to be Michael Roman. However, this man is lying alone. The bedroom furnishings are decidedly different: less costly, more pious and homey. A portrait of Jesus

Christ guards over the headboard.
A palm plant grows housed on a
windowsill. A simple wooden chair
rests bedside; a pen and a tablet
of paper are positioned there.
Awakened abruptly, the man leans
over and lights the candle. He
scribbles a few sentences on the
paper.

DISCIPLES & BETRAYERS

In this subdivision, we're
introduced to the supporting
characters; two of whom serve to
help Michael. The others plan
their diabolical schemes to betray
him.

DAY THREE
2ND DREAMS & VISIONS

SATURDAY, 3:00 A.M. - APRIL 15,
2000

Michael encounters the angel a
second time. The angel's identity
becomes clearer.

THE ARK

In this subdivision, we meet Noah
Muhammad. He is the third
supporting disciple or "good guy"
character. Noah introduces the
reader to the biblical figure on

whom he is based. Noah (Islamic)
also represents one of the
thirteen major religions described
in the book. For each religion:
the doctrines, prophets,
relationships to angels, and moral
codes on human life are outlined.

In the latter stages of this
division, a scene where Roman's
racehorse is injured reflects the
betrayers, if you will, handling
of the three major subplots in the
story. Here is an excerpt:

    *Judy interjects, "It's a sin
and a crime to have to kill'em—but
let him put him to sleep."*
    *Maggie implants upon him, "He
can't race and can't reproduce—
it's a sin to lose that money."*
    *Lincoln takes his shot.
"It's a crime—but the horse is
worth more dead than you are
alive."*
    *Roman ordains, "Everybody
listen! It's my decision, my
choice, my verdict...let's see if
first he can be saved."*

DAY FOUR
3RD DREAMS & VISIONS

SUNDAY, 3:00 A.M. - APRIL 16, 2000

    *In Roman's bedroom, again
there is an eerie stillness.*

Roman and Maggie are asleep. An omnipresent light is again present.

> *On his stomach, Roman rolls over. His eyes are closed shut.*

"I am Michael...The Archangel, Michael...save a life..."

THE SPIRIT

Michael (the character) exhibits his mortal disdain for life. His hatred reaches its pinnacle when he gratifyingly kills his horse. He is termed, "*...an addictive killer with a fix.*"

Later in this subdivision, Roman interacts with Noah and is given detailed information on the realities of Noah's homelessness. Having been homeless myself, this is a very insightful portion of the book.

At this juncture in the book, Michael Roman consults with the Reverend Mark Anthony character. Their stories start to intertwine. In the classic literary format, the Reverend is the mentor and comedic trickster for the hero Michael Angelo.

The final two stanzas of *THE SPIRIT* subdivision, lead to the first "plot point" (again, in keeping with classical storytelling).

The dramatic conflicts involving Maggie's unwanted pregnancy choice and Judy's influence on Aunt Mary's assisted-suicide decision; unfold here. Also, the discovery of supporting character Lesliannas Von Adolf's death penalty ordeal is detailed.

At this point, the subplots and the sinfulness of Roman reach a breaking point. A visit by the Holy Spirit miraculously changes Michael's life forever. He is determined to "save a life." Michael calls on God in an originally written prayer. The book contains many original and biblical prayers; not to mention original poetry, song verses, catch phrases, and a plethora of Bible quotes and notations.

<u>DAY FIVE</u>
LIFE

MONDAY, SUNRISE - APRIL 17, 2000

Roman's lifeless hand buoys in the shimmering water. The

bandage has disappeared and the burn has healed. He lies faceup in the rowboat. His eyes are sealed shut. Bearded, his long hair drapes him. A black Bible rests in the opposite hand of his dangling arm. His eyes burst open—they are full of life!

The book now takes on its episodic format covering the subplots. Michael informs Judy and Lincoln of his godly plans. He also attempts to rescue Maggie from an abortion clinic. Included, is the Reverend and Ernie Goldstein's goal to form a Christian church.

DAY SIX
WORKS

TUESDAY, DAWN - APRIL 18, 2000

The day begins at the backyard pond. This is a passage between Michael and Maggie:

Michael remarks, "This is a great book." He mandates, "You should read this second Gospel... this story is definitely too good, not to be true."
"When Hell freezes over. For Christ sake, what's up with you Michael Angelo?"

BORN AGAIN

Throughout the book, the BORN
AGAIN subdivision involves
Maggie's abortion choice and the
contrasting arguments she and
Michael make. Maggie demands
their house. Michael submits on
the grounds Maggie does not abort
the child and "saves this one
life."

TRIALS & TRIBULATIONS

Lincoln's first interview with the
accused Von Adolf is covered. Her
story is a complex cross between
the murder of a fellow inmate's
unborn child and the link to the
death penalty. This "story within
a story" resembles an infamous
1960s court trial, and
prophetically, a highly
controversial 1998 Texas capital
punishment case as well.

THE JUDEO-CHRISTIAN CHURCH

The use of Roman's donation to
construct the Universal Church of
Angel's, Life, and God is
chronicled. The writing
incorporates Mark Anthony's goal
to unite Judaism, Catholicism, and
all of Christianity with a
universe of angel believers.

SOS — SUICIDE OR SELF-DESTRUCTION

The Aunt Mary Frances and Judy "fictitious" characters are in Mary's religious art shop. The characters are based on persons of the Bible; Judy is the blatant portrayal of Christ's disciple Judas, and Aunt Mary represents both Christ's mother and the biblical man Job. This euthanasia story line is patterned after the Book of Job.

SERVICE PART I
"Entertain"

The Reverend's church is a storied reality. The liner notes from the theme song are intermingled with the highlights of the church's opening.

WORKS II

DAY SEVEN
WORKS II

WEDNESDAY, MORNING - APRIL 19, 2000

Wednesday is divided into two sections. The initial section covers the day's events before noon and the latter after 12:00 p.m.

BORN AGAIN 1

At an abortion rally, prominent
speakers address biblical and
humanitarian concerns over the
abortion debate. Maggie has
chosen to abort, despite the
"deal" with her husband.

TRIALS & TRIBULATIONS 1

At California Superior Court,
Lincoln has gone on the defense.
His strategy is to prove, by a
systematic comparison of
conflicting statements, that his
client is indeed innocent. There
are three distinct inconsistencies
that determine whether Von Adolf
or her foe is telling the truth.
All the while, Lincoln undermines
his efforts because of his
personal beliefs on the
constitutional justice of capital
punishment. This segment reads
like a detective novel.

*SOS – SUICIDE OR SELF-DESTRUCTION
1*

Aunt Mary Frances and Judy discuss
Mary's terminal illness issues
with Mary's overly critical
friends. Life affirming,
Christian ethic is derived
directly from the Book of Job.

BORN AGAIN 2

Maggie confronts Michael after being denied access to the clinic.

Throughout *The Archangel*, recurring themes present themselves in a multitude of subliminal, background, and symbolic situations and stories. The theory: "What comes around goes around" is literally consistent. The book, like life itself, is cyclical in nature.

SERVICE PART II

Drama, action, mystery and comedy...yes, comedy; *The Archangel* possesses clever dialogue, situational comedic "funny stories," and a written comedy monologue that appears at the fictional halfway point.

Within the context of the story, this comedic routine is the second phase of the Reverend's church service. The Reverend sees humor in the hypocrisy of some human beings with regards to a death sentence:

"*Then from death row, you take that last walk. I love the way they always put you in a ton*

*of shackles and handcuffs—that's
in case you try to escape back
into regular prison."*

THE JUDEO-CHRISTIAN CHURCH 2

Reverend Mark, Ernie, and Michael
Roman philosophically discuss war,
death, and Christ. Mark gives a
biblical interpretation.

TRIALS & TRIBULATIONS 2

Lincoln, enticed by further
financial gain, intensifies his
defense of Lesliannas. His
written case studies, anecdotes,
and data are outlined in orderly
fashion.

*SOS – SUICIDE OR SELF-DESTRUCTION
2*

The Archangel: Saint Michael is
the leader of God's angels. To
better understand the nature of
angels, one must have experiences
with these spiritual beings.
Through the written words of Aunt
Mary, the vast manifestations of
angels are documented; this is an
excerpt:

*Judy asks, "Enlighten me?
Why on Earth, for God's sakes, do
angels appear so only you can see*

*them? Why is it, when people have
an angel sighting, no one else is
ever around to see it?"*

*"Because Judy...the angel
Raphael once landed on my head,
healed and enlightened me with the
answer. The incredible reason why
angels appear alone is not because
I, myself, wouldn't believe it;
but because human hearts and minds
are weak and angels are aware that
the viewer of the angel might end
up believing you, the non-
believer. God's angels know some
people believe other people,
instead of believing angels—that's
why."*

*Judy says cynically,
"Amazing."*

Later in this subdivision, the
dialogue revolves around Mary's
idol: Elvis Presley. Judy's
arguments surrounding "The King's"
death finally persuade Aunt Mary
Frances to seriously consider
suicide.

Elvis, Abraham Lincoln,
Michelangelo, da Vinci, King
David—these are just some of the
references made to God's great
human beings.

APOCRYPHA

The writings and prophecies of
Jeremiah, Isaiah, Ezekiel, and
Moses are as appropriate for
today's thoughts on life as the
teachings centuries ago. When
applied to Maggie's decision, the
consequences of her abortion
choice can be horrific.

<u>DAY EIGHT</u>
JUDGMENT

THURSDAY, DAWN - APRIL 20, 2000

God gives us all free will. In
each of the subplots: Maggie, a
modern-day woman; Mary, a
contemporary Christian; and
Lesliannas, a repentant sinner;
willfully participate in the fate
of their lives.

SERVICE PART III
"Enlighten"

The Reverend Mark Anthony closes
the church service by preaching a
summation; biblical,
revolutionary, and revealing truth
and conviction merge with
Christianity and literary fiction.

CHURCHES: CHAPTERS 1-14

In the final part of the church
program, thirteen church members
share their biographies, a Bible
passage, a personal problem, and
the dogma of a baker's dozen of
worldwide religions (from Buddhism
to Hinduism, and Protestantism to
Zoroastrianism). These
testimonies each follow the
Apostle Paul's New Testament
letters.

TESTAMENT

The Reverend's concluding speech
inspires Michael to present
himself as a born-again believer.
"The service has ended, go in
peace."

<u>DAY NINE</u>
SALVATION

GOOD FRIDAY, 8:01 A.M. - APRIL 21,
2000

At Denver International Airport,
peace gives way to an earthquake.

Michael must physically save a
life. A countdown of possible
passenger rescues begins...20...
10...5...Michael endeavors through
fourteen stages to the point where
he and one man remain.

<u>DAY TEN</u>
DEATH

HOLY SATURDAY - APRIL 22, 2000

One man has survived. The other
man has died.

<u>DAY ELEVEN</u>
IN THE END...

EASTER SUNDAY, SUNRISE - APRIL 23,
2000

The dead man reappears...or does
He?

MANKIND NEEDS A SAVIOR...

THE ARCHANGEL

Mark Anthony DiBello

D A Y O N E

IN THE BEGINNING...

In the beginning...a lifeless,
foot-long, rainbow trout lies
prone on a sandy-brown, kitchen
cutting-board and countertop.
Encamped around it are a woven,
wooden basket of apples and uncut
bread loaves, and a glass chalice
of water and one of wine. A
singular, vase-less flower
symbolically completes the
setting.
   In a man's hand; an expensive,
primeval, kitchen cleaver rotates
like a propeller. The shining,
silver blade ceases spinning. A
guillotine, the razor-sharp
implement slashes down beheading
God's first creature.

MICHAEL

THURSDAY - APRIL 13, 2000

EVENING

In the Bethpage, Long Island, New York house of Michael Angelo Roman, in the dining room, by a vigil of candlelight, the dining table bears the footprints of the man and woman's celebration feast. There are two untouched glasses of water, two empty chalices of wine, a remaining loaf of bread and the bony skeleton of the fish.

Native New Yorker, Michael Angelo Roman has just returned home from work. He's handsome, with chiseled facial features and a ponytail of long black, lightly graying hair. He appears much younger than a man who is celebrating his fiftieth birthday dinner.

His wife, Magdalene "Maggie" Hagar Roman, is exotically beautiful. She's nineteen-years-old, a fair-skinned Greek and Egyptian girl. She was created sexy. Skinned in a three-quarter-length mink coat, she slithers on the tabletop to her man. Like a ship cutting glacial ice, she melts her way with the flicker of a small heart-shaped candle she

2

guides. The inscription reads: "I love you."

Her long fingers uncoil. She plucks a juicy, red apple from the basket. Her luscious lips and pearl-white teeth prepare to chomp on the fruitful delight. In the blink of an eye, a simple housefly is unearthed. Magdalene spots the teeny, winged creature and commands—"Jesus Christ, Michael. Kill him!"

Instinctively, Roman lunges for the fly swatter close-by. As if in slow-motion, Roman beats the bejesus out of the fly. Roman subconsciously flashes back to a morning in 1950....

Inside a cathedral in New York City, New York; an exquisite, floor to ceiling, stained-glass window streaks the proceedings with a prism of color. It's a work of art, with seven vertical panes of angels, centered by a sword-carrying Michael. A larger pane of Christ and the disciples rises above it.

The baby, Michael Angelo Romano, is being christened. Present at the altar is Michael's father, Giuseppe Romano, and Giuseppe's brother Vincenzo, who serves as the infant's Godfather. Giuseppe's wife Maria is flanked by her two sisters: eighteen-year-old, Mary Frances, and twelve-

year-old Clare. Mary Frances is
fairer in complexion, less Italian
in appearance. The men, an
associate, and their accompanying
four bodyguards, are all classic
Mafiosi.

Father Giovanni Baptisté
delicately holds the whimpering
baby over the baptismal pool.
Only the infant is aware of the
enlightening angelic presence
illuminating him. It emanates
from a pristine statue of a cherub
(baby angel).

Father Baptisté blesses the
child in the melodic Latin hymn—
"*In Nomine Patris, et Fíllii, et
Spirítus Sancti.*"

In his broken English,
Giuseppe whispers to his
associate. "*Mio padre difamiglia
Romano*, he'a loved his life...he
spent it dying. He'a died poor.
Id'a rather live rich."

The church window becomes
darkened, the way a passing cloud
might cause. Smash! Shatter! A
team of seven, black-hooded,
assassins breaks through. They
barrage the altar with gunfire.
The bodyguards, the associate,
then Vincenzo Romano are shot
dead. The sword-wielding leader,
flailing his weapon, slices Mary
Frances' forearm. She dips it in
the bath. Giuseppe is slain by
the sword through his heart. The

4

wailing baby is dropped into the
sacred water. He is immersed in
the blood red sea.

Maria Romano bellows,
"Clare!" The women cling together
and are spared. They shriek in
tragic despair. Instinctively,
they worry for the lives of the
priest and the child. Mrs. Romano
cries out, "Father Giovanni!"

An assassin's pistol is
placed point-blank at Father
Giovanni. The assassin, from
behind the hooded veil,
commissions, "No man lives." The
trigger is pulled, as if in slow-
motion.

The baby, for the first time,
has stopped crying. He's held
like a bloody newborn from the
womb.

This evening, back in the
dining room, the birthday candle
brightens Roman's face. Magdalene
kneels on the table. She is both
alluring and playful. She
presents the first portion of her
gift to him in an originally
composed song. While perhaps not
the most gifted songstress, she is
a sensual siren. She slips him
the candle's directions.
Uneducated herself, she sings
fluently but struggles reading.
"These are 'The Directions.'" She
sings:

5

*"1. should keep this
candle close-by,
like love, handle with
care all of the time.
2. get the candle to
light, find the
perfect match.
3. ways this candle
ignites...
A. person with the fire
inside, should not
B. afraid of love's
unknown.
When you cannot...
C. with your eyes,
hold the candle in the
dark.
4. you will never be
lost, if you look
for your love with the
feelings in your heart."*

Magdalene subconsciously flashes back to a night in 1980....

Backstage, at an indoor concert in San Francisco, California, sixteen-year-old Jezza Hagar (soon-to-be, Magdalene's mother) is nineteen weeks pregnant and looks beyond her years. She is, more or less, a notch below a prostitute and a notch above a groupie. Jezza, a bit high on grass, is euphoric to be here. However, a serious issue still plagues her.

A black-leathered, hard rock band is wrapping an encore. The music is loud and cutting. The stage steams like a dark cloud from a sewer grate—lights in a firestorm hue of red and flaming oranges. An announcer is heard on stage, "That was Harlot, ladies and gentleman! Give it up California for Harlot!"

The audience, in ovation, screams out, "We want the Harlot! We want the Harlot!"

As the song whines down, lead-singer Hadley Harlot makes his way offstage. He immediately swills whiskey, pops some prescription pills, and takes a hit from a joint. He looks devoutly demonic, and yet desperately destroyed. His manager confronts him. "Hey man, if you're trying to kill yourself— it won't be long now."

Jezza says, "Hey Hadley that was supernatural man."

Hadley intonates, "Hey, what's up? Where you been baby?" He asks a fellow band member about Jezza, "Hey, remember this number?"

"Yeah, ain't that the bitch you pumped the life outta' once?"

Jezza is angry, anguished, and ambitious. She tells the band member, "It's Jezza Hagar to you asshole.... Yeah Hadley, I'm

pregnant. First time I fucked up
and forgot that goddamned pill.
So let's do it...Vegas tonight...
you and me. You owe me that
much."

The audience continues to
chant. The band is going back on.
The audience erupts.

Jezza screams, "Do it
now...or you'll pay when it's
born!"

Hadley licks a bandanna
through his mouth. "LSD
man...long live a life of sin and
death." He disappears into a
black cloud of smoke—an eternal
darkness. The audience cries out
a devilish crescendo of death.

This evening, back in the
dining room, Magdalene stands
before Roman. She slowly unravels
her coat. Her inviting lips ask,
"So, what did you dream for on
your fiftieth birthday?"

"To be a millionaire by the
time I'm fifty.... And to have a
sweet, young wife take off the
$5,000 mink coat I just bought for
her and reveal to me her priceless
body."

"Then your dream has come
true. Feast your eyes on this
Michael Angelo Roman. I'm your
work of art...your masterpiece."

Maggie has a model's body.
She wears trendy, new lingerie
with the price tag still purposely

affixed. It's purple and scarlet,
silk and lace. She appears
resplendent in bracelets, a
diamond horse-head necklace, and a
strand of pearls. Maggie offers,
"Why don't you make l-o-v-e, love,
to me you animal?" Roman pulls
her close by the dangling price
tag. By design, it strips the
garment away.

LATE EVENING

     In Roman's bedroom, together
in bed, by the glowing
candlelight, wafting incense
smoke, and billowing silk sheets,
the couple appears like a Greek
god and goddess. Roman's body is
also in incredible condition.
Their muscles ripple; the sinew
shines with the glint of oil.
Roman's skin is a golden pseudo-
tan; Maggie's gleaming porcelain
white. The couple makes intense,
passionate, animalistic love.
There is a forceful diversity in
their carnal delights. Each
demands, on occasion, a particular
pleasure position. They
communicate by touch, sense, and
experience. Maggie moans, "Fuck
me you stallion. Don't forget to
use protection...the last thing I
need on Earth is a fuckin' b-a-b-
y, baby."

D A Y   T W O
―――――――
1ˢᵀ DREAMS & VISIONS

FRIDAY - APRIL 14, 2000

3:00 A.M.

In the bedroom, the air is
serene and peaceful—a dramatically
different scenario. Roman and
Maggie are each sleeping. They
lay face down, dead to the world.
Roman rolls over. In moonlight,
his countenance basks in an
inexplicable, prolonged stillness.
In his sleep, he hears his own
voice in his head:

"I am Michael."

His eyes open.
At 3:00 A.M., in a different
bedroom, a man, in his vision,
sees a cookie jar. The man's
silhouetted moonlit image appears
to be Michael Roman. However,
this man is lying alone. The

bedroom furnishings are decidedly
different, less costly, more
pious, and homey. A portrait of
the Lord guards over the
headboard. A palm plant grows
housed on a windowsill. A simple,
wooden chair rests bedside. On
it: a pen, a tablet of paper, a
candle, and stick matches are all
positioned there. Awakened
abruptly, the man leans over and
lights the candle. He scribbles a
few sentences on the paper.

DISCIPLES & BETRAYERS

In Roman's bedroom, Roman
arouses Maggie from her sleep.
"Magdalene...Maggie...wake up.
Did you see or hear something?"
"No."
"Did you feel something?"
"No, Michael...you must be
dreaming. Go back to bed."
Unable to resume sleeping, a
nude Roman smokes a cigarette and
stares out the window. From
Roman's vantage point, overlooking
the acre, or two, of stately
backyard property, the refracted
moonlight spotlights an empty
rowboat, floating unattended for
years, on the small pond. The
glow seems to give the small

wooden vessel a life of its own.
Dawn awakens.

DAYBREAK

Michael Angelo Roman begins
every day with a ritualistic,
morning routine. An avid antique
weapons collector, he will put one
primordial weapon to the test.
Today, he selects his favorite: a
slingshot.
He walks to the rear of the
mini-estate. The enclosed wooded
area might be picturesque were it
not devoid of other vegetation.
The meticulously kept grounds
present a steely, rather than
scenic, landscape. The grounds
appear like a corporate picnic
area or smoking lounge. The sole
life may come from the single
stable at the rear of the acreage.
Beersheba, a thoroughbred
racehorse, an exquisite equine
specimen to some, is nothing more
than a serious investment for
Roman.
Roman doffs his Stars and
Stripes, 1972 Olympic jacket. He
stretches his taught, and
vascular, back and arms. He
straps a heavy weight to his
waist. With the help of wrist
straps, he does back pull-ups and
chin-ups from a wooden crossbeam.
Powerful and strong, this regiment

he's kept devoted to since his days as a silver medalist in archery at the Munich games.

A series of dead or dying trees, with brightly displayed targets nailed into the trunks, are his prize. Using the slingshot, he strikes them with increasing proficiency. Hungry for a kill, he sets his keen eye on his premiere pet project. He pulls a stone, from a pile in an unused birdbath, and places it in the stick and pouch. In one shot, the sacrificial squirrel he spotted takes its final breath.

Returning to his abode, he notices a pigeon has marked its territory on the pane of a cathedral style, smoked glass window outside the house. Obsessively disturbed, he wipes the droppings from the side of his wooden castle and off the cement walkway. "Pigeons—I'll kill'em if I ever get my hands on 'em!" Roman doesn't notice the nest of colored eggs tucked neatly there.

MORNING

In the Roman house, in an area next to the kitchen, the sun beams a smile on Elizabeth, the noticeably pregnant Hispanic cook, and maid. She clutches the gigantic crucifix hanging from her

neck, a gesture to thank her Maker
for the day. She's vacuuming,
performing her weekly task of
cleaning the Roman's house.
Maggie, in a revealing maid-type
outfit of her own, is up
uncommonly early.

Elizabeth greets her, "*?Cómo
está usted.* Good morning, Señora
Roman. Juan and I say *óla.*"

Maggie says halfheartedly,
"Good morning, Estrellita."

"It's Elizabeth."

"I know."

In the kitchen, the vixen,
with the dexterity of a magician,
lights a cigarette. The flame
seems to torch her face. This
task she's rehearsed numerous
times, but the breakfast she
attempts to prepare for her
husband, she has not. The egg
she's holding drops and breaks.
"Christ Almighty." Her anger,
hopelessness, and frustration
manifest themselves when she spots
a common housefly innocently
traveling between an unbroken egg
and a jar of honey. "Fuckin'
horse." She reaches into a
cabinet and grabs a hand-held
vacuum fly remover. As if in
slow-motion, the housefly is
vacuumed up the clear tube leading
to the handled portion of the
deadly device.

14

Roman, having changed, enters
the kitchen wearing a dapper suit
and jewelry. Maggie, almost
remorseful, remarks, "I can't c-o-
k in the kitchen, but that doesn't
mean I wasn't cooking last night."

"Why do you think I hired you
and married a cook? Shit...you
know what I mean. That's why I
hired a cook." Always a physical
man of touch, he pinches her
dragon-tattooed backside before
embracing her.

"Michael, I hate to ask, but
can I have a little allowance?"

"Sure, but what do I get in
return?"

"Me and my l-o-v-e."

"I love you."

"I love you, too."

LATE MORNING

In the cul-de-sac, outside
the Roman residence, although it's
an unseasonably warm day, the tar
dumped from a pavement company
truck steams on the front yard.
Roman is having a good portion of
nature's green carpet paved into a
mini-parking lot. The handful of
minority workers labors away.

Roman's sharp 1999 red JAGUAR
XK8 convertible is parked on a
patch of healthy grass. His wife
Maggie's red Land Rover Discovery
SE7 (license plate: ROMANS)

remains in the garage. Roman
enters his auto and lowers the
top.

Immanuel, the Hispanic head
laborer, approaches from near his
truck. The truck's tank reads:
MANNY'S—"LIFE IS A FREEWAY—IF YOU
DON'T FOLLOW THE ROAD GOD MADE FOR
YOU—IT'S YOUR OWN ASPHALT."

"Hello, Señor Romano. I'm
Immanuel, the boss. Did you want
us to take out that tree—that
tombstone of Adam and Eve...and do
over there too?" Their attention
is directed at the wooden monument
of nature.

Roman responds, "Get rid of
it."

"Then we got to fix the cost
a bit...okay?"

"Listen, 'Immanuel Labor'...
I've already given you bums enough
dinero...you're not sucking any
more money outta' me." Roman
springs out of his "Jag," rips off
his jacket, and proceeds to the
garage. Immanuel walks with him.

"Señor, Mister...you know the
ground is soft in some spots—maybe
we wait? Besides, you do a lot of
paving, no good when it rain."

Roman, using an old ax, chops
down the tree. "Who's paying who?
I want this done before summer
gets here and stuff starts
growing...showers and flowers and

16

all that crap." He tramples the
last flower on the property.
He sinks back down in his car
seat. In a rush, his car torches
the grass beneath its tires as he
speeds off. (His auto tag reads:
EMPIRE.)

MIDDAY

Inside the Manhattan, New
York City, high-rise office of
Michael Roman, the techno-posh
office looks more like a *Sharper
Image* catalog showroom than a
workplace. Just as in his house,
the only plant life is a macabre
abundance of Venus flytrap plants.
The only clue as to how he makes
his living—may be the
inconspicuously seen, but large,
complicated sketch of a six-
pointed star, within two circles,
framed on his wall.
His best friend's arrival is
announced, on the desk intercom,
by Lucy his secretary. "Abraham
Lincoln Peters to see you sir."
Lincoln Peters is thirty-nine
years of age. He is a hardened
New Yorker with dark features and
a medium build. He enters the
office. He totes his trademark
blood-red umbrella. He smokes
cigarettes like a fiend. Lincoln
greets Roman, "Welcome back."

"Lincoln...got the umbrella huh?"

Lincoln jabs the air, and pokes the floor, with a playful prod and a voracious violence, explaining, "Muggers and bums." He opens up a daily tabloid and proudly displays an inside page for Roman.

Roman reads it aloud, "'THE PERSECUTOR' SCORES ONE FOR CAPITAL PUNISHMENT." Roman condones. He and Lincoln exchange a high five. "All right! So how is New York City's number one prosecuting attorney?"

"The Constitution is God. I'd like to fry that asshole marching out front for crapping on my right to bear arms amendment—nail'em up on a stake—serv'em up like a kabob...you know...shit on a stick." Lincoln sits. Lincoln subconsciously flashes back to a summer evening in 1976....

On the patio, in the upper-class neighborhood, young, fifteen-year-old Lincoln is seated on the synthetic green outdoor carpet. It's difficult to distinguish if he is wearing a religious or military school uniform. He sits, alone, in a trance.

Only adults are present at the catered, political fund-raiser. Senator Peters, slightly

18

intoxicated, is speaking. An inebriated Mrs. Peters smokes profusely. She pays little attention to her husband or to her son.

A female cocktail guest initiates the conversation. "Senator...tell us about education?"

The senator states seriously, "Teachers are just as important as parents...parents can only do so much."

A male guest asks, "Senator Peters, tell us about the party?"

The senator quips, "Party? Yeah, I enjoy a good party. Hey, this is 1976 and still there are only two things that will never end in this life—death and taxes.... So whoever it was that said: 'Give to Caesar that which is Caesar's,' didn't know how to spell IRS for Christ's sake."

Lincoln is mesmerized by the amount of flies, resting in pieces, beneath the bug zapper. As if in slow-motion, a stricken housefly flickers and fries on the grated cage. It makes an unmistakably morose sound.

The senator rambles, "I am a public servant. I care for the lives of my people. I love this country. So when my public speaks to me on the issues...goddamn it, I listen; whether it be taxes and education, or capital punishment and abortion; for I am a man of the people, a leader. For in the end...a leader is a follower who knows where he is going. And you can quote me on that!"

The heat lightning from the sky creates an amazing effect as the bolts momentarily appear in the form of an angel. The surge of electricity strikes the zapper knocking Lincoln back.

Today, back in the office, Roman rises from his chair. Lincoln and he make their way to the door. Lincoln recalls loudly, "For Christ's sake—goddamn it!"

Roman rebukes him, "I thought you didn't believe in God?"

"I don't. It just makes for good swearin'—the name really gets the point across.... I almost forgot...here, I got you a present." From his jacket pocket, he hands Roman an automobile bumper sticker.

Roman reads it aloud, "IF YOU CAN READ THIS..."

Lincoln hands him a second bumper sticker.

Roman reads it aloud, "...YOU DIE!" He says, "I'll put it on Maggie's car.... How 'bout meeting tomorrow at Aqueduct? My horse is racing."

"Is the Pope Catholic? Does a bear shit in the woods? Come on—

I'll let you buy me lunch and a
lap dance for your birthday."

APPROXIMATELY 4:45 P.M.

     In his office, Roman is
seated at his desk wrapping the
weeks work. He waits for a
monetary addictive fix. Roman
beckons into the intercom,
"Lucy...tell Ernie Goldstein to
get in here with my weekly
report."
     Goldstein has been waiting
outside. He's a forty-one-year-
old, rotund, Jewish fellow with
dark brown hair. Goldstein is
loving and meek, very religious.
He is humorous by nature, a bit of
a goof. "Welcome back. Ernest Sy
Goldstein at your service." Ernie
subconsciously flashes back to a
late evening in 1968....
     In an old fashioned bedroom,
in a middle-class home, ten-year-
old Ernest Goldstein is seated
bedside in the godly and trinket-
filled room. His very elderly and
wise grandfather Abel Goldstein,
Bible in hand, speaks his peace.
"I want to read you something.
This is Isaiah, chapter 40, verse
3: 'Prepare the way of the LORD;
Make straight a highway for our
God. Every valley shall be
exalted and every mountain and
hill brought low; The crooked

places shall be made straight And the rough places smooth; The glory of the LORD shall be revealed, And flesh shall see it together; For the mouth of the LORD has spoken.'"

Ernie asks, "What does it mean Grandpa?"

"You will understand when you are old like your Grandpa Abel." Abel presents him with a cherished heirloom, an antique model train caboose. "You are to build a set from the last to the first, from the old to the new...7:14 'Therefore the Lord Himself will give you a sign: Behold, the virgin shall conceive and bear a Son, and shall call His name Immanuel, God-with-us.'"

Grandpa Abel takes his last spoonful of oatmeal. He refers back to the Bible: "It has been written...'Death and life are in the power of the tongue, And those who love it will eat its fruit.' Proverbs 18:21. In the course of your life Ernest, when you speak in terms of life and death, I want you to add another train car...it will give you wisdom." The sheer white curtains blow lightly from the sliver opening of the window. "The wind reminds Grandpa he must sleep now son. Before you go to bed, I want you to read Exodus 20:13 for Granpa.... Yahweh loves

you...okay? Don't forget your
choo-choo."

The boy nods his head
agreeably. He takes the treasured
gift.

"I will read you this last
one from the Old Testament. This
is from the Book of Daniel...
chapter 12: 'At that time Michael
shall stand up, The great prince
who stands watch over the sons of
your people; And there shall be a
time of trouble, Such as never was
since there was a nation, Even to
that time. And at that time your
people shall be delivered, Every
one who is found written in the
book. And many of those who sleep
in the dust of the earth shall
awake, some to everlasting life,
some to shame and everlasting
contempt...'" The curtains gust
an incredible wind. They billow
and wave like angels' wings.

Back in the office, Goldstein
continues: "'...Those who are wise
shall shine like the brightness of
the firmament, And those who turn
many to righteousness, Like the
stars forever and ever.'
...Thankfully, he was blessed to
pass away in his sleep—the great
way to die—when most die because
of life.... It was his time, God
needed him."

"Goldstein...you're
daydreaming—the report."

Goldstein hands Roman an
easy-to-read copy. Goldstein gets
a paper cut and a smear of blood
on the page. Goldstein reads,
"The total personal assets of
Michael Angelo Roman—Friday, April
14, 2000...

"From top to bottom—Empire,
the business: $333,000. Home and
property on Bethpage, Long Island:
$250,000. Thoroughbred racehorse:
$200,000 even, [NOTE: Value of
insurance not applicable].
Automobiles—1999 Jaguar XK8
convertible: $74,128. Two year
lease on Land Rover Discovery SE7,
[minus final payment sent today],
net price: $37,040, ownership
papers pending. Total of both
autos: $111,168. Continuing—
weapons collection, including 1972
Munich Olympics silver medal in
archery: $65,6-6-6. Shall I go
on?"

Roman insists, "As always."

Goldstein submits, "Clothing
and jewelry belonging to Mrs.
Magdalene Hagar Roman including
new fur coat and $350 sales tax:
$25,350."

"Any cents?"

"Exactly!...Savings and
checking, Chase Manhattan Bank:
$13,650,00. Lucy reports petty
cash of: $41.75...and lastly..."

Roman counts the cash in his
trousers pocket. "Five hundred

dollars...and...here Goldstein..."
Roman tosses him a quarter. "In
case of emergency."

"...And zero debits."

"And I don't owe anybody
anything. What's the goal of life
if you don't own anything in the
end...huh? What's the grand
total?"

"$999,376.00 exactly....
Chances are sir, by this time
Monday—you'll be a millionaire."

"I was aiming for my birthday
yesterday...but tomorrow will do
just as well."

Goldstein, not remembering
Roman's day, "That's right.
Mozltov! Happy Birthday."

"See Goldstein—dreams can
come true. I guarantee I'll be a
billionaire by the very day I'm a
hundred."

"'When a person's earthly
dreams cross with God's heavenly
will—then Earth and Heaven,
Creator and creation—shall be as
one.' ...My minister at church
said that."

"What's a Jew like you doing
in church? Isn't church against
your religion?" Roman rises and
gathers his belongings, including
a metallic briefcase. He and
Goldstein prepare to depart.

Goldstein imparts, "I'm
always learning—I love Jews and I
love Christians—the common

25

denominator is love, not
religion.... Mr. Roman, would you
like to be my guest at church
tomorrow?"

Roman nods negatively.
"Thanks, I'll be at 'The Big A,'
Aqueduct.... You like horses,
Goldstein?"

"I think they're one of the
Lord's most beautiful creations.
I always wanted a pony when I was
a kid..."

"It's 'cause you got a big
caboose." Roman pats him on the
hind-end.

As they reach the door, Lucy
the secretary enters. "Mr. Roman,
your wife called. She wanted to
remind you to be home early; your
cousin will be here this
evening.... And this registered
letter arrived late for you."

"Give it to Goldstein."
Roman quickly exits.

Goldstein opens the letter
and reveals the contents to Lucy.
"Unbelievable. There's what I
call a perfect coincidence...
Romans 6:23 'The wages of sin is
death.' His final check from that
course he'd been teaching—$623."

Lucy shakes her head in
disbelief. She returns to her
work.

Alone, Goldstein is
astonished by the numerology. He
matches the letter with Roman's

ledger sheet. The total is:
$999,999. He assuages, "Poor guy.
Who would believe it? Now that's
what I call, *a day late and a
dollar short.*"

LATE AFTERNOON

　　In a health club, a small
video crew is adjusting the
lighting around a treadmill
machine. The privately owned gym
is run by Jordan. He is in his
early thirties. He's dark-
skinned, short and stocky, with a
crew cut.
　　Roman inquires at the front
desk. "What's this?"
　　"I don't know—some Christian
guy is shooting a workout video."
　　Reverend Mark Anthony is
thirty-nine years of age. He is
tall and muscularly lean, in many
ways, an incarnation of Michael
Roman. In his New York accent, he
flies by, commenting to Roman, "I
love that about people...they tell
you they don't know and then they
give you an answer.... Hey
Jordan, tell that guy not to stand
next to me; I don't like to be the
second best-looking guy in the
joint." Mark asks Roman, "What's
up, 'Brother?'" Mark Anthony
races to the treadmill. He speaks
in the direction of the video
camera lens. "GOD'S GIFT—THE

CHRISTIAN WAY TO A HEALTHY AND
HOLY BODY, MIND AND SOUL. I'm
Reverend Mark Anthony..."

Mark Anthony kneels and prays
on the treadmill. He sees the
video lights. He subconsciously
flashes back to 9:14 P.M.,
December 18, 1960....

In an operating room in Glens
Falls, New York; Monica is the
pretty, twenty-four-year-old,
fair-skinned brunette in labor.
Six large lights focus down.
She's in danger and excruciating
pain. Monica cries, "Oh God! Why
me dear God?! God, why me?!"

Doctors, nurses, an
anesthetist, and a priest are
present. The doctor tells her,
"Try to relax Monica." He tells
the anesthetist, "Get ready the
anesthesia."

The priest prays: "'A man of
God came to me, and His
countenance was like the
countenance of the Angel of God,
very awesome; but I did not ask
Him where He was from, and He did
not tell me His name.'"

Monica begs, "Oh my poor
baby! Let me die! I will not
betray my baby's life—you do all
that you can to keep this child
alive! How can I live with myself
if I let you take my baby from
me?!"

The doctor says, "We're going to save you both."

The anesthetist says, "Monica, the pain will end—start counting backwards."

Monica cries out, "My God!"

The anesthetist says, "Count Monica—count the lights."

Monica counts out, "7... 6...5...4...My God... 3...2...1."

She draws the line on the EKG machine. A white sheet is drawn over her head.

Back in the gym, envisioning his mother's angelic face, Mark is on the run. He's spirited by some *Aerosmith* music.

Roman, wondering, asks, "What's he doing?"

Jordan ponders, answering, "I don't know—he's into spirits and angels or some nonsense—who knows with him?"

Mark is in maximum overdrive; his arms wave and motion upward. Roman exits.

EARLY EVENING

On the neighborhood street outside Roman's house, Roman is returning from the gym. Three children: Jessica, age-ten; Britni, age-seven; and David, age-five; each with fair-complexions, attend to a wounded-legged kitten.

Britni begs, "Mister, help—it got runned over."

Roman asks, "Where's its mother?"

Britni and Jessica answer, "We don't know."

"Well, give it to me—I'll take it to a vet and have him put to sleep."

Jessica tells him, "But it's not sleepy—it's hurt."

Roman responds, "Go ask your parents—it's humane."

Britni asks, "Jessie, what's humane?"

Roman interjects, "It's what a human does. It's just an animal kids—it doesn't have a brain."

Jessica spouts out, "But it's got a heart."

Britni scolds Roman. "If your mom saw you with a broke't leg—you wouldn't want to go to sleep."

EVENING

In the living room of Roman's house, Maggie proudly shows the backyard view to Roman's cousin Judy Christabella. Judy is forty-one-years-old. She has dark hair with spider web gray strands. She's plump, well endowed, and boisterous. She eats, she drinks, she smokes and she gambles—that's Judy. She has a beer bottle in hand. "Nice spread Maggie. I'll bet you a million bucks you never get Michael in that lake. Our aunt says he won't even walk by a pool."

"Or have about as much a chance of him shedding a tear."

Judy asks, "Not much of a crier, huh?"

Roman walks in the door.

"Michael," says Maggie.

"Hi, Honey." Roman sees his cousin. "Judy Christabella..."

"Hi, Michael...What's it been, a G-D eternity? What, since we were puppies? You look beat for God sakes. You kids up late on the hobbyhorse, huh?"

Roman explains, "I couldn't get to sleep last night...How'd you get...Why are you here?"

"I was telling your little missus—I had to take the train down from Albany. My friggin' car's in the shop and I'm short on coin." She tells them, "After this weekend, I'll hit A-C for a day—shoot some craps, you know roll them bones, baby needs a new pair'a shoes..." She zones back in. "But anyways, I wanted to tell you firsthand, in case she didn't reach you herself, it's Aunt Mary Frances..."

Maggie thinks, Michael has never mentioned her. Judy reads it like a poker face. She says,

"Me and her is his only livin'
relatives." She goes on to
explain, "Well anyways—we were on
the porch at my place last night,
but I knew I was leavin', so I
went to check on her this morning
at the store—you know she sleeps
in that god-awful place?" Judy
subconsciously flashes back to
8:45 A.M. this morning....

     The quaint religious art
shop, in Albany, New York, is
replete with gifts and icons of
the Lord, angels, and even a few
of Elvis. Mary Frances Killion-
Wilder is a sixty-nine-year-old
poetry buff. She has light-
colored hair and a soft, angelic
face. She is meticulously dressed
in *K-Mart* fashions. She kneels
behind the counter; her joyful
countenance refracted in the glass
case of angel figurines, her back
to the open and empty cash
register. "'One day when the sons
of God came to present themselves
before the LORD, Satan also came
among them.'" She clutches her
chest in pain, but habitually
conceals it.

     Judy enters from the curtain
divider in the rear. "S.O.B's—
broke in again right? Just the
kitty?"

     "Oh! You almost frightened
me half to death child." Aunt
Mary Frances swishes away a winged

intruder. "Shoo fly." She instructs Judy, "It's just money—perhaps they needed it more than me?"

An ill-tempered Judy notices the smashed door window. Judy asks, "When are you going to bar the windows?"

Aunt Mary Frances replies, "Bars keep people away. All are welcome here."

"How the hell are you ever gonna get ahead in this life? It's too damn short to waste it all away in here."

"Judy love, I'm needed here. I just haven't had the time."

"Forty years you've been here. Forty...Forty years and you don't take even a Sunday off. Nowhere—no Vegas—no nothin'. All your life you've preached about wanting to see 'The King'—King-this, King-that; if it wasn't Christ the King—it was that dead-as-stone Elvis. Stop with the God, stop with the angels—it's time to get a life and start living!"

Aunt Mary Frances continues tidying up. She toys with a favorite Elvis. Judy hurls it out the broken window. "There! Now Elvis has left the building! And I don't care if God punishes me for being angry!"

Aunt Mary Frances clutches her chest, but is no longer adept at concealing it. Judy asks, "It's your chest again isn't it? That's the third time this week. I'm taking you to a doctor if it's the last thing I do."

Aunt Mary Frances says, "If God wants me—I'm His."

"Don't hand me that, what comes around goes around, give'n take Scripture."

Aunt Mary Frances brushes the housefly away. She quotes: "'Naked I came forth from my mother's womb, and naked shall I go back again. The LORD gave, and the LORD has taken away; blessed be the name of the LORD!'"

Judy lunges, behind the counter, at the fly. "To Hell with the fly!" Judy, as if in slow-motion, uses a forty-year-old canister of bug spray and poisons the housefly to death.

Back in the living room, Judy says, "That's when she said if the pain of this life got to be too much—she knew she could trust in Michael to save her. Those were her exact words."

Maggie says, "And?"

Judy answers, "I virtually had to beg her to get to a hospital. I know for fact she's never seen a doctor—thinks she can pray everything away." Judy gets

emotional. "It's breast
cancer...spread everywhere.
Doctor said, she's terminally ill,
said, it's a miracle she's stayed
alive this long...could be a
day...a week...Lord only knows."

Maggie asks, "Is there any
chance for recovery?"

"Odds are about one in a
million—but *I* doubt it. But, with
all her spiritual stuff...doctor
said, it's been known to happen."

"So what do you want Michael
to do?"

"I don't know?" Asking,
"Michael, you tell me?"

Roman says cold-heartedly,
"I'm tempted to say, there's
nothing anyone can do—let her die
in peace as they say."

D A Y T H R E E

2ND DREAMS & VISIONS

SATURDAY - APRIL 15, 2000

3:00 A.M.

In Roman's bedroom, Roman and Maggie are asleep. There is a supernatural aura in the room. A spot of moonlight, coming from behind a cloud, peering through the window, seems to cause Roman to roll over and lie face up. In his sleep, he speaks:

"I am Michael: The Archangel."

Roman's eyes dart open immediately. He rolls over to see if his wife perhaps touched him. She is sound asleep.
Unable to again fall back to sleep, he walks, towel around his waist, to the window overlooking

36

the yard. From his vantage point,
he stares aimlessly at the
rowboat. Dawn arrives.

THE ARK

DAYBREAK

     In the backyard, Roman
appears more weary than usual.
He's neglected shaving this
morning. He carries with him, his
choice weapon for the day:
boomerangs. He stretches for a
brief moment. He attaches the
weight, but forgets the wrist
straps. He does his chin-ups, but
weak, does only a few. He tosses
the boomerangs at the tree targets
and a couple of archery targets as
well. He still strikes the
bull's-eye with regularity.
     The horse van carting
Beersheba to Aqueduct backs into
the stable. The van's logo reads:
ANGÉL'S AIR N' GROUND EQUINE
LIMOUSINE SYSTEM—"IF YOU SEE A
HORSE FLY—IT MUST BE ANGEL'S."
     Angél is in his late
twenties. He is the well-bred,
Hispanic, driver and groom. He
works to load the 3-year-old colt.
He hollers, "*Buenos Días Mr.
Roman*, it's Angél. The Man gave

us a great sunrise this morning didn't He?"

Roman only waves. Closer to the wood line, Roman misses a foolhardy attempt at a rabbit.

Angél apprises Roman about *Beersheba*. "He's shown promise in the morning works. He'll be coming from the clouds at the finish. Hopefully, God-willing, you'll have a winner on your hands."

Roman hardly acknowledges. He heads back to the house. He notices the pigeon droppings on the walk (not the wall) beneath the window. He empties the rocks from the birdbath and positions the bath to catch the bird's remains. He grows angrier.

Angél hops in the truck. He shouts to Roman, "Good luck—God bless!"

MORNING

In front of the house, the new driveway is yet unusable. In his car, Roman, rushing, exits perilously close to the sidewalk. The three neighborhood children are playing a safe distance away. Roman, however, does not see the good-sized, blonde, retriever he accidentally hits. That terrible sounding thump is followed by the awful shrill of the wounded dog's

cry. Roman is anxious. He gets
out. The dog starts limping away.
The children come rushing over.
Roman fights to find compassion,
for an instant, he holds the hound
like a baby. But like a
frustrated parent, he cannot cope
with the helpless wailing. "He's
hurt pretty bad kids—I don't think
he's gonna make it. Go see whose
dog it was and tell'em I took'em
to the vet and I'll take care of
it...Okay? Go."

Jessica says, "Brit—go tell
your mom that the mean guy hit
Joshua with his car by mistake."

Roman's unaware of the
adolescent's appraisal of his
character.

LATER THAT MORNING

In the health club, Roman is
diligently working out on
equipment adjacent to a leg
machine Mark Anthony's on.

A pretty girl struts by. She
says to Mark, "Hi, how are you?"

"Terrible, how are you?"
Mark answers satirically.

She smiles.

Olympic athlete, Daniel
"Zoro" Mazda, inquires congenially
of Mark, "I've been watching you—
you're pretty confident of
yourself aren't you?"

"I'll tell'ya—my ego needs a spotter. I'm confident 'cause I got it—but humble 'cause I know where it came from."

Roman asks Mark, "You're in your own little world aren't you?"

"What's up handsome? Yeah, but that's good—I can always find a parking space."

Roman asks, "What are you on?"

"Life, God man—He's the best."

"God?"

"Yeah, God's cool."

Mark makes his way to the front desk. He asks about Roman, "Hey Jordan, where do I know that guy from?"

Jordan answers, "You saw him in here yesterday—he works out here."

"No, I know...before that?"

Jordan shrugs, saying, "He thinks you're out there though."

"He's a good judge of people." Mark says, "That's gonna kill me—that'll keep me up all night, wondering where I know that guy from." Mark leaves the facility.

Jordan says, "See'ya Mark..."

"Thanks for the warning," Mark jokes.

11:30 A.M.

At the Roman house, in the doorway, Roman and Maggie are waiting on Judy to go to the track. A timid, light brown-haired, slender, sixteen-year-old named Dawna Calendar is at the door. "Happy Saturday. My name is Dawna Calendar. Do you know the lifesaving power of Jehovah?"

Maggie's retort seems to overpower the girl. "What are you selling?"

Dawna answers, "Magazine subscriptions."

Maggie snarls, "This may be painstaking for you, but I already have a life—I ain't bein' rude, but we're leaving." The girl hands Maggie a magazine and abruptly leaves. Like a delivery boy, Maggie tosses it into the fireplace.

Judy is ready. Roman says, "It's about time. Let's go ladies," rushing them, "Judy, you follow us in Mrs. Roman's Range Rover; Lincoln's gonna meet us there."

At the railroad crossing, on the way to Aqueduct, a freight train is approaching in the far off distance. The caravan of cars rushes to cross. The people, especially Roman and his wife,

hardly notice an indignant man
since they are so prevalent.

Noah Muhammad capably readies
his paraphernalia. When the cars
stop, he'll go to work. The most
obvious characteristic of the
forty-five-year-old, African-
American, Muslim man is he has but
one leg. By the way, on hand made
crutches, he sings and dances a
bit.

Roman and Maggie are inside
the Jaguar, just past the tracks.
Having made the crossing, Maggie
is outwardly relieved they did not
happen upon Noah. "Thank G-o-d,
God."

"He doesn't need God—he needs
to get a life."

"Loser—money's what he
needs."

APPX: 12:15 P.M.

At Aqueduct Racetrack, in
Jamaica, New York; Roman and the
women are seating themselves at a
dining table in the upstairs
clubhouse. Roman says, "The
trainer says I should get four or
five-to-one on my horse. This
could work out perfect—I wanna hit
for better than six hundred."

Judy says to him, "A buck and
a half on his snout will get you
six bills...nine-to-two pays
eleven...that's $675."

42

Maggie, glancing the program, asks, "Oh is he in this race right now? Maids horses who've never run a race."

Judy points out to her snootily, "Never *won* a race. And it's *maidens*: babies, virgins—as in what every real man wants—virgin: bless-ed, pure, untouched, saintly."

The trumpet sounds its traditional race track reveille. The announcer pronounces over the loudspeaker, "The horses are on the track for the first race."

At an adjacent table are Swami Oscar Mahabharata, Gabe St. Patrick, and Kara Kesh. The Swami is fifty-years of age or so; he is rotund, with a dark ruddy face and a turban on his head. A Hindu, he speaks with an Indian accent to Roman. "I apologize; I don't wish to intrude..."

Lincoln arrives. He says to Roman, "You look like shit, who and what's keeping you up at night?" He sees The Swami and snides, "Now, that's a hell of a rug." For the on-the-score Lincoln, there is a strong, sexual attraction between he and Maggie. "'Mag-pie.'" Lincoln overtly fixates upon Judy's chest. "And you must be Judy—Mary, Mother of God—your kids won't die of thirst." A waiter takes the

order. Lincoln requests, "Jack
straight-up, 'Hoss.'"

Gabe says nicely to Judy, "In
God's eyes, in a true man's eyes,
the beauty of a woman is found
from within—in her heart and
soul."

The Swami continues to Roman,
"I wish to introduce myself—I am
Swami Oscar Mahabharata. Our
horses are coupled together...I
apologize...we, own the #1 horse:
the *Avatar* colt. Please call me
'O.M.', all my friends do."

Roman informs him, "But we're
not friends."

"Then let us be...we are all
as one—so to speak. 'As was in
the beginning—so too, in the end—
The Alpha and the Omega.'" He
sees in Maggie, "You are Greek are
you not? And I believe I see some
Egyptian perhaps..."

Maggie claims, "...half and
half."

"I have a friend, Helen
Theotokos; she too is uniquely
both Greek Orthodox and Egyptian—
perhaps you met in a past life."

"I don't think so—this life
ends with me."

"Well then, how does your God
manifest Himself to you? How does
He reveal Himself?"

"I'm not religious."

"Many religions...One God....
And your husband?"

"You'd have to ask him."

The Swami asks, "Mr. Roman, what is your life about?" Roman is speechless. "Everybody has a story." The Swami pauses for a response. "The race is over at the finish line—perhaps you are only at the starting gate."

The announcer says over the speaker, "The horses have reached the starting gate—they're at the post."

Roman says to Swami, "I don't mean to be rude, but the race is about to go off. You don't bet?"

"No, I...we, race for sport. Our horse runs for charity." Swami Mahabharata politely departs. "Perhaps we will be gathered together again? Good day, Mr. Roman."

Judy says, "I'm gonna bet. Who wants what?"

Maggie says, "Here, give me Twenty to win."

Roman says, "Get me One Fifty."

Lincoln says, "Five Hundred— and if he doesn't win I'm gonna personally hang'em by the neck."

Nick Zito arrives with two men. He's just come from the paddock. Zito is the horse's trainer. "Michael, I want you to meet two of my owners...Bill Condron and Joe Cornachia. They stood by me even after I became a

Christian." He addresses Roman's
table, "Hi everyone, I'm Nick
Zito, *Beersheba's* trainer...I wish
you all the best." He speaks
collectively to Roman and The
Swami, "Michael, we got you Pat
Day. Mr. Mahabharata, Mikey Smith
went to *Lots of Promise*. He tells
Roman, "They're two of the best."

The announcer speaks. "It is
now post-time!"

The action behind the
starting gate is hectic. The #1
horse is loaded in. Roman's
horse, #1A, is unruly. He unseats
the jockey.

The announcer is heard over
the air, "Number 1A, *Beersheba*,
has unseated the rider..."

Spooked, the horse rears up
on his hind legs. When he comes
thundering down, he injures his
front cannon bone. He falls to
his knees. He hobbles up, but
cannot. The emergency personnel
and van rush to the tragic scene.
The other horses are loaded in the
gate.

"Ladies and Gentleman, may I
have your attention please.... In
this race, on the advice of the
track veterinarian...#1A,
Beersheba...has been scratched.
Scratch, #1A, *Beersheba*...."

Roman's table collectively
bangs their fists. Each person

seated blurts out characteristic euphemisms.

The announcer continues, "All wagers on the Number's 1 and 1A will be refunded. The #1 will run for purse money only.... Ladies and Gentlemen, may I have your attention—will trainer Nick Zito please report to the Steward's office. The flag is up...they're off!"

Zito is distraught. "It looks bad. He might have to be put down."

Roman explodes. He uses Zito's tie for a noose. "Go to Hell! Over my dead body!"

"If you've got a better answer—you let me know. Right now, I've got to care for that suffering animal. Now, I'll see if he can be saved. Believe me, I pray to God he can."

Judy tells Roman, "That's a hard pill to swallow Michael."

Maggie tells him, "Son-of-a-bitch Michael—our whole investment."

Lincoln declares, "200K—that's a real death sentence."

"Shut up!" says Roman. He tells Judy, "You're not the one holding the needle." To Maggie, he says, "You're not the one who labored." And to Lincoln, he says, "And you weren't there when the gavel struck down." He tells

47

himself, loudly, "It's all up to me."

There is silence while Roman deliberates. Judy gambles in speaking aloud, "Dare I?" She tells the table, "A friend of mine once said: Life is like a *Racing Form*—if you read into the past, you could handicap the future...so let me chart this out." She's looking at the racing paper. "You bought him for $200,000 as a 2-year-old.... His sire is Derby winner: *Alysheba*, his grandpa: *Alydar*—the best. He runs one race at three—dead last. So then you..."

Maggie imposes, "...try and breed it—but the mangy carcass piece of horseshit can't have b-a-b-y's."

"...So you bring it back to race it—dead last again. So you..."

Lincoln inseminates, "...have it gelded."

"...so he'll stop chasing fillies and get down to business making money—so to insure your investment, you..."

Roman discloses, "...take out a million dollar policy."

"...But it's only good for a non-racing accident. Now, today..."

Roman decrees, "...Not
yesterday, not tomorrow—today,
what do I do?"

Judy interjects, "It's a sin
and a crime to have to kill'em—but
let him put him to sleep."

Maggie implants upon him, "He
can't race and can't reproduce....
It's a sin to lose that money."

Lincoln takes his shot.
"It's a crime—but the horse is
worth more dead than you are
alive."

Roman ordains, "Everybody
listen! It's my decision, my
choice, my verdict...let's see if
first he can be saved."

A child named Sammy Goode
passes by. He speaks, out of
sight of the others. "You could
just let it live."

AFTERNOON

On the return trip, Roman and
Maggie are parked at the crossing.
The locomotive lumbers by. On
this side of the tracks is a well-
kept, rinky-dink, hobo shack. Two
large hand written signs proclaim:

† GOD BLESS
† CHRIST WAS HOMELESS

Noah, a Vietnam veteran, is
more down-on-his-luck than
homeless. He wears his green army

jacket, its patch reads: James-Muhammad 4234567. He puts a buck in his pocket. Without a doubt, Noah is the happiest man on the planet.

Noah's got many plastic grocery bags with him. Toting a bag full of trash, he walks for the car at the gate. The blonde, male, teenage driver and three females recognize Noah. They back their car up, closing the gap purposely left by Roman. The maneuver makes the handicapped man's walk easier. Noah says, "Scott, Jackie, Janeen, and don't tell me...no, no, no...please don't tell me—Ginger, yeah!"

Scott gives Noah a handful of change. He says, "Give me just one today please, Noah."

Noah says in return, "For here or to go?"

Scott answers, "...to go."

"One for the road—you got it." Noah gives him a bag. "And here's one for the ladies." He rhymes this jingle: *"Roses are red and violets are blue—I'm an entertaining stranger, 'cause I might be an angel—Hebrews 13:2. Gotta' bolt...Alláh loves you."*

Noah pogos his way to Roman's car. Roman is indifferent. Although the top is down—Maggie rolls up the window. She reaches for the glove box.

Noah rhymes, "*Shahadah, Salah, Zakah, Siyam and Hajj— give me your litter, I'll give you directions, readin' Scripture is my job—but I don't do windshields.*"

Maggie cracks a beautiful smile. She identifies with the music. Noah flashes his tooth-filled grin. He subconsciously flashes back to a day in 1972....

In the Vietnam jungle, a baby-faced, eighteen-year-old Noah is seemingly sweating blood and bullets. He proceeds cautiously and timidly. He's a virgin at the trigger. He leads a few paces ahead of a gung-ho, black, Sergeant Kazef, and a six-man platoon. Sergeant Kazef orders, "Hey Mo-sori, St. Louis! The government says kill, so you kill, none of this chicken shit. Kill or be killed—eye fo'n eye—you got it black brother?"

The men behind investigate a pile of dead soldiers from both sides. A soldier calls out, "Sergeant Kazef, it's us and them."

Noah drifts off the lead a bit. Suddenly, an equally inexperienced Vietnamese soldier jumps from a tree. He knifes Noah's arm. Each man draws his weapons. They stand alone, eye-to-eye. The enemy soldier,

without provocation, looks a few
yards above his own head. Noah
looks there too. What seems to be
the blazing white *Concorde*
passenger plane blurs by. The
enemy soldier looks with shock
back at Noah. Noah too, is
amazed.

From Noah's vantage point,
the black *Stealth* bomber is above
the platoon. The platoon yells
out, "Kill!" The seven-man firing
squad blasts the Vietnamese man's
body apart. The ricochet of
friendly fire accidentally shoots
Noah in the leg.

Noah, already in tears,
clings to his Islamic medallion,
cross, and dog tags. "Forgive
them Alláh—I'm sorry Father."

Today, back at the railroad
crossing, Roman says to Noah, "I'm
sorry man, I'd like to help, but
do you know what it means if I
give you a dollar?"

Noah answers, "*Khudo min
shan'khâtri.* You love me."

"It means, I'll have a dollar
less—and that one-dollar I give to
you will forever be one dollar.
But, I can take that dollar and
turn a profit of ten. You'll only
drink it away."

"Don't drink, but I see what
you mean. It's like Christ said:
'Whoever has will get more and
whoever doesn't what he's got will

be taken away.' Same principle,
only with blessings and the Word.
Yeah, give God anything—and He'll
give you everything."

The crossing gate is lifting.
Noah hops out of the way. "Be
good, 'Brother Man'—you too,
Ma'am." He says to himself,
"*Mahab'bi`umr*—bless'em, there but
for the grace of God go I." He
sings loudly, "*Whoa mine eyes have
seen the glory of the coming of
the Lord...*"

DAY FOUR

_____

3RD DREAMS & VISIONS

SUNDAY - APRIL 16, 2000

3:00 A.M.

In Roman's bedroom, again
there is an eerie stillness.
Roman and Maggie are sound asleep.
An omnipresent light is again
present. On his stomach, Roman
rolls over. His eyes are closed
shut.

**"I am Michael...The Archangel
Michael...save a life."**

THE SPIRIT

Roman's eyes burst open.
He's shaken, dazed—he has actually
seen something in his sleep.
Roman tosses on a long,
flowing, bathrobe. His face is

54

withdrawn and unshaven. He stares
out the bedroom window. Rain is
falling. The stable is empty.
The moonlight seems to outline a
path from his window to the
rowboat. The pond twinkles with
raindrops.

DAYBREAK

In the backyard, the rain has
ceased. Roman carries a medieval
bow and quiver. Exasperated, he
does but one chin-up. Roman also
has a slingshot tucked in his
pocket; he grabs a rock, from the
pile on the ground, and loads.
His first shot misses an archery
target—his second, a tree. He
spots a squirrel. The shot he
fires in anger ricochets and
nearly misses his own eye. The
stone raps against the window of
the house. Roman painstakingly
checks to see if the glass is
broken. He locates the bird's
nest and removes it. He is
equally careful not to drop the
egg-filled basket. Unexpectedly,
a garden snake crawls up his foot.
Startled, he juggles the nest. A
single egg splashes down safely in
the birdbath. He proceeds to put
the rest of the eggs in the nearby
barbecue pit. As if in slow-
motion, he douses the nest with
gas from a small lawnmower can.

He ignites it. "'Mother Nature.'"
A bee stings Roman. He scalds his
shooting hand on the flaming nest.
He screams, "Agh! Zagzagel!
Agh!" Roman enters into the
kitchen.

Maggie, awakened by the
yelling, is confused and
clueless on how to aid to her
husband. "Where the fuck is
Elizabeth? I can't function
without my coffee...Ohh! I don't
know...here put it under the
water. Michael, you've got to get
some sleep before you kill
yourself." Roman's anger mounts.

In the backyard, with his
shooting hand bandaged, Roman
attempts to fire an arrow at a
target. The evil determination
that possesses him is frightening.
The arrow falls short, landing
feebly on the ground. A second,
aimed at a tree, sails high into
the sky.

To Roman's surprise, Angél
unloads a heavily cast *Beersheba*.
Angél lavishes the animal with
affection. "Glorious day, Mr.
Roman—look who's home! He'll
never race, but what a blessing—
he's alive!"

Roman loads the bow. He
targets the horse. Roman's evil
eye is glued to the horse's
sympathetic eye. "One for the

money...two for the show...three
to get ready...four to let go."

As if in slow-motion, the
arrow flies. Angél has his back
turned. The arrow misses him by a
foot. It strikes the colt in the
neck, killing him. Angél signs
himself in prayer. *"En el nombre
del padre, y del Hijo, y del
Espiríritu Santo."*

At the railroad crossing,
Angél's horse van speeds to make
the crossing as the gates come
down. Roman, lagging behind,
remains. He is more upbeat; an
addictive killer with a fix. Noah
approaches, rhyming, *"Shahadah,
Salah, Zakah, Sìyam and Hajj...and
they ain't Islamic lawyers..."*
He directly asks Roman, "It's your
world ain't it man?"

"And you're lucky to be in
it."

"Don't I know it—don't I know
it." Noah spots Roman's revolver
in the glove box. "This is the
Northeast, not the Middle East."
Noah continues on to say, "God
Himself, told me in prayer; from
after the sin of death, to death's
brother murder; from after the
dawn of a new day, to God's
Commandments; and from man's
birth, to the prophets; mankind,
with time, in his created oneness
with God and the angels, has used
man's own kinship with evil to

57

murder and to kill; were it for
God, life would be eternal. In
the name of Earth, religion, and
life—man has used his own beliefs
to create holy wars. God has
created life in His name—man has
taken that life in *his* own. I
will pray for peace on the weapons
of war." Noah asks, "Where do you
work?"

"In the city."

"New York City—I don't get
it—13 million *other* people
and everyone talks to themself."

Roman asks Noah, "How come
you're so high all the time?"

"Listen up, 'Brother'; this
life's too precious and short.
Ain't nothin' perfect in this
world—only His.... You're rich,
you're poor, you live and you die—
God gives us free will man; love
and worship Him and be happy
through it all. This life means
everything—then again, it means
nothing."

"What about your..."

"Handicap? Okay to say it,
it's not a swear word—one less leg
to worry 'bout—wish I had it, but
I don't...be okay, so long as I
don't put my foot in my mouth."
He enacts the idiom. "Kaboom!
See, we're all handicapped—some
you see—some you don't. I talk
about it, see'in I believe in the
battle people fight to speak out

and help others who share
handicaps. That's God's best
principle: loving others. See, in
turn, He graces me with my
shortcomings...'sides, I don't
have to be afraid and pray I don't
become paralyzed or 'capped like
'lotta folks do." He notices the
horse owner's emblem on Roman's
windshield. "It's like with the
horse races...they'll give the one
that's stronger more weight to
carry—a handicap. Only means I
got an advantage over folks who
ain't as close to God as I need to
be."

Roman shoots a look with
respect to Noah's housing
situation. Noah accommodates him.
"Homeless...another bad word? The
best place to be on Earth is happy
inside.... 'The LORD is my
shepherd; I shall not want. He
makes me to lie down in green
pastures; He leads me beside the
still waters. He restores my
soul; He leads me in the paths of
righteousness for His name's
sake...'"

Noah loves to quote
Scripture. "Psalm 23—that's my
favorite; Reverend Mark says
everybody should have a favorite
Scripture—'words to live by.'
That's a psalm of David; you
remind me a lot of him. Even King
David was homeless for a stretch;

Adam, Moses, Saiyidna'îsa, many
prophets—all homeless. Takes more
courage and strength to be
homeless than it does to have a
place...I could live in your
house, no problem—but could you
live in mine?"

He also loves to quote
Scripture—he himself has spoken;
"Besides...my roof is Alláh's
Heaven, the moon my lantern. His
stars are my lights, His sun my
fireplace, His crippled trees my
chair, the lush grass my carpeted
floor, His river my basin, my bed
is as big and round as the earth,
my bird cage is as full and large
as the sky." Noah is flying now.
"God! I love the world!" He is
brought back down to Earth. "But,
if you must know, if there is one
thing that bothers me...it's
stealing. Bad enough in your
world you can't leave or forget
something without someone taking
it...in mine, we got to keep our
stuff all over the place. If you
find something and it ain't yours—
don't take it—good chance it's
someone's like mine.... Well,
that don't matter, I'm not gonna
be 'round this place much longer."

Roman gestures as if he is
slitting his throat.

Noah lambastes him. "Hell
no, suicide's a sin. I'm going to
California to start over. My pot

of gold's out there. Lily, pretty
Caucasian girl was gonna be my
wife. We were on our way to Vegas
when I got drafted. Maybe she's
even got the bird I gave her 'fore
I left.... Don't forget, as long
as you're alive, ain't never too
late to start over." Noah reaches
for something. "Boy, I almost
forgot...something I want you to
have, in case I don't see you
again. I've been getting a
feeling past three days—I think
it's my angel Gabriel—so to my
angel be true." Noah gives him a
coin. *"Alla yib`at'lak*! I love
you, 'Brother Man.'"

Roman looks at the man's
missing leg and wonders...
"Your *lucky* silver dollar?"

Noah tells him, "Ain't no
such thing as luck—blessed. I had
it on me in 'Nam when I got my leg
shot off—I'm blessed just to be
alive!"

"I don't understand. Why do
you say you love me—you didn't get
anything from me?"

"Love's not about gettin'—
it's about giving. 'It is more
blessed to give than to receive.'
Understand? It all comes back to
'ya in the end. Besides, that's
the angel voice in my head...Acts
12:9 'So he went out and followed
him, and did not know that what
was done by the angel was real,

61

but thought he was seeing a vision.'"

Roman tells *him*, "I'm not religious."

"Angels aren't about religion. They're the sons of God, created by God to do His will—just like you and me.... Ut oh, the gates are rising...got that deep down feelin' it's gonna rain—The Almighty One is crying for a soul today." The cloudless sky refutes Noah's prediction. He hobbles away hurriedly, singing, *"Glory! Glory! Hallelujah!... Glory! Glory! Hallelujah!... Glory! Glory! Hallelujah!...His truth is marching on."*

AFTERNOON

At Aqueduct Racetrack, outside the veterinarian's office, Roman gets into his car. Irate, he grabs his car phone and calls Goldstein. "Goldstein, it was an accident—I haven't been sleeping and my hand is hurt...forty days for the claim? Why in the hell should I have to go forty days without it? Get on it first thing Monday...One Hundred and Fifty dollars for a death certificate for an animal— it's jackasses like that, that give animals dying a bad name." He slams the phone against the dashboard. He inadvertently breaks the convertible top switch.

On the return trip, Roman approaches the railroad crossing. As Noah predicted, the skies have opened, and rain starts to sprinkle then steadily pour. Noah's shack is nonexistent. Noah waits, with his life's belongings, for the train to slow. Noah says matter-of-factly, "Hey 'Brother,' never thought I'd see you again. Remember, how we were talkin' about being homeless? Even though the Lord says: 'So I say to you, ask and it will be given to you; seek and you will find; knock and it will be opened to you.' ...Once in awhile, it'd be nice if people would just offer to help—no man likes to be a beggar. But most of all—more than any other..."

"What?"

"It'd be nice to have a friend; someone to talk to. Homeless people make people, who aren't any different inside, afraid. Just like them, we get lonely. It's a great big world out there, and nobody likes being alone—everyone needs a friend."

Roman asks, "How'd you know it was gonna rain?"

Noah answers, "It's raining, and I said it—that's all you need to know."

He tells Roman, "I want to
leave you with a story. Now,
remember this: Three men were
standing alone, at a bus stop, in
the middle of nowhere, nothin'
there but the sign. It began to
rain like there was no tomorrow.
The first man put all his trust in
the things of this world. He put
on a jacket and an umbrella he
bought—and he was dry.... The
second man put all his hope in
himself. Using his own strengths,
he thought to bend the sign over
his head—now he too was dry....
The third and final man, he put
all his faith in God, he prayed,
and the rain stopped—then all were
dry." Noah looks. "Ut oh! I see
the caboose coming." The rain is
a deluge. "I love the rain; it
brings life to all the plants and
animals in the far reaches of the
kingdom.... Remember, the angel
is God's messenger of mercy,
resurrection, and promise—promise
like the rainbow. *Alla ybarik
fîk.* God bless." A small army
mattress strapped to his back,
Noah hobbles away singing,
"*America! America! God shed His
grace on thee, and crown thy good
with brotherhood, from sea to
shining sea.*"
   The gates are raised and
Roman drives forward. From
Roman's angle across the tracks,

64

the train passes in the background. Noah is gone. The sign:

† CHRIST WAS HOMELESS...also reads: NOAH WAS ALSO HERE

With the rain pouring and Roman drenched, Roman seeks refuge under a carport. An early model, white, Ford Mustang convertible is parked outside the seemingly abandoned factory. A small sign hangs above the door:

U.C.A. LIFE + GOD - MANKIND WELCOME

Roman peeks through a window. He cautiously enters. Roman is mad. "Of all the luck."
Inside the Universal Church of Angels, Life and God front office, hard rocking music plays. Reverend Mark Anthony is seated behind a desk. He's writing. His attention is drawn to a field mouse nearing the caged *Havaheart* mousetrap he's set up. He places broken, shredded wheat cereal in a pile outside the cage. Roman observes the strange behavior. Mark speaks to the rodent. "Hello little buddy." Roman knocks loudly on the door. Mark shouts, "Agh! You scared the hell outta' me. Ough!" Mark accidentally

65

jabs his right wrist with the
pencil. He removes the
protrusion.

Roman asks, "What are you
doing?"

Mark says, "Feeding my little
friend. It's great. He eats just
what I eat. Feed'em then free'em—
sounds good to me."

"It's just a dumb animal."

"Not to other animals."

"But it won't know if you
kill it."

"I'll know." Mark suggests,
"Watch one of those animal shows
on TV sometime. I love those
things. They teach you a lot
about people. Listen—if everybody
keeps killing animals, that show
will be all we got left. Let me
tell you a cool thing I once heard
this Jack Hanna guy say; he said,
animals were good for kids as
pets, because they expose the kid
to the death of a loved one at an
early age, so the kid can better
handle people passing away.

"Now that's good, huh? But
let me tell'ya one better—we also
need to start practicing on
animals the 'going to the ends of
the earth' to keep them alive way
of thinking; instead of the
'putting them out of their misery'
mentality. That'll teach us
something about life. Do you know
99 out of 100 killers kill animals

66

before they kill people? Life is
life, and killing is killing."

Mark is wound now. "I'm
sorry. I just go nuts when I
think of people killing animals.
There's something in the Bible on
animals." Mark taps a Bible on
his desk. "Exodus 20:13. I am
telling you, check it out." Mark
says obligingly, "What can I do
for you?"

Roman asks, "How did Noah
know it was going to rain?"

"Noah, from the Bible, Noah—
or Muslim Noah, from the railroad
crossing, Noah?"

Roman gestures outside.

Mark jokes, "He's got ESPN."

"That's really funny—you mean
E.S.P.?"

"No, ESPN—he checks the
weather report to see who he
should pick; either he picks the
over in the Jets game, or the
underdog in the Giants game. We
play for fun. They're our
warriors."

Roman counters, "It's not
football season. Tell me the
truth?"

Mark tackles his question.
"Truth be told—sometimes he prays,
sometimes he listens—I believe he
was probably listening."

"God?"

"God or one of His angels."

Roman is bewildered. He checks the surroundings. There are few furnishings. "I don't even know why I'm here."

"You're here to get out of the rain—though I suspect putting your top up might be a solution." Mark explains, "It's okay, I'm picking on you.... The Lord works in mysterious ways. Don't think you're here by accident—it's what I call 'perfect coincidence', 'ya know, divine intervention—destiny. There's a reason you're here. In the long run, I imagine it's the reason we're all here...to find an answer to the eternal question—the question we all want to know.... What is the meaning of life?..."

Roman reveals, "I've been having a dream. My voice wakes me in my sleep, I hear myself say... I'm Michael—the Archangel—save a life."

"Wow! You had a vision—that's the archangel Michael. He's God's personal messenger—that's God talking to you. His archangel speaks to you in a voice you can understand—your own. Wow! Good for you! Wow!" Mark, in oneness, reveals, "I dream like crazy every night—it's one of the best parts of my life. Dreams, that's what life is made of."

Roman wonders, "Will it ever end?"

"Not if you don't save a life it won't. You'll never be able to sleep, let alone rest in peace—if you don't listen to that angel. I don't know what you've done in your life, what sins you've committed...but we're all sinners—none of us is perfect—only God. Michael is calling on you for salvation, for repentance...he wants you to save a life."

"Why should I believe you?"

"Because I talk and listen to God, but like Michael, I'm just an instrument, just like this pen I write with is an instrument. The archangel Michael is just the messenger of God. You truly need to go to God—He's your Creator."

"Where do I begin?"

"First of all, you have the greatest power known to man—the greatest: you can get down on your knees in prayer, make the Sign of the Cross, and talk one-on-one with the Almighty God: The Creator of the Universe...all of this, and all of us—you and Him alone. Wow! Oh, wow!" Second: worship Him—ask Him for forgiveness—then sacrifice to change your life from evil to good. And finally: listen to His Commandments, love mankind, and save a life—do so, or you're as good as dead."

"But what can I do?"

"Think of the God-given gifts
and abilities God has blessed you
with? Surely with one of these,
think of the lives you can
save?...Everyone alive has a gift
to give mankind—their time, their
love, their self.... How 'bout
your dreams?...You've heard of
'following your dreams'?...Think
of something you've always dreamt
about that you've never done?
Something, that if you knew you
were going to die tomorrow—you'd
do it today."

Roman remarks, "I'd write
something."

"Then do it. If that's your
gift to mankind, so be it. But
listen, when the desire of your
dreams crosses with God's will,
then the divinity of God's plan,
your destiny, will be made known
to you, and your dream *will* come
true."

Roman questions, "Why's it
take so long, or why do some men
never reach their destiny?"

Mark confesses, "Well, for
me, half the time's spent doing
God's will, and the other, the
devils will: moral versus immoral,
Heaven against Earth, good versus
evil.... The nearer you are to
God—the closer you are to reaching
your destiny: because God created
it."

Roman, in confidence, asks, "Can writing a book really save a life?"

"God's honest truth, yes. Look at the Bible, it's the Book of Life, and its words have saved many a soul. I honestly believe the stroke of a pen, and the word alone, can save any person from any death. And I honestly believe, by the angelic spirit you speak of, that your book too, can mean life to one and all."

"But how?"

"The archangel knows—I don't know—I don't have to know—I don't want to know—all I need to know—is God knows."

Roman says disbelievingly, "I don't buy it—I've got to go."

"Now, that's the evil in you speaking—the man. The archangel Michael, in four words, defeated all the dark angels of sin. If in his words, God has chosen you—you better listen, or I'm telling you— you're as good as dead." Mark kindly says, "Look it, for you, like many, seeing is believing. The archangel Michael and his creator God are seen with faith. But what your soul cannot feel— I'm certain, God willing—your eyes will one day see."

"I just don't know."

"Listen, I'm like you, I'm weak. My favorite Bible quote is

71

Paul to the Corinthians: 'In weakness, God's power reaches perfection.... When I am weak, I am strong.'" Mark encourages him. "Remember, the strength of a thousand men and of a hundred horses have not one-tenth the power of the flicker of just one angel's wing." He says, "I will pray the Lord's light shines on you today. The archangel Michael is with you.... Now go, save lives, as you believe you know how. I promise your life will change forever when you become one with God.... Oh, I almost forgot, before you leave, I want to give you this...it was given to me by one of the first three disciples of this church, my friend, Ernie Goldstein."

Roman is shocked that this is the church Ernie spoke about.

Mark has no idea they're acquainted. He presents Roman with a simple, design-bordered, shoe-sized, wooden box. Mark avows, "We had a promise—a brother of ours, in his travels, would come upon a stranger—and if the Spirit so moved me, as it does with you, I was to present it to him...together, God only knows, it may save the world. When the angel of the Lord is upon you—you will know when to open it."

The pastor hands Roman a small, design-bordered rug. It is noticeably worn in one spot. Mark, entrusting, says, "I also want you to take this rug—it was given to me by Noah. He too, told me of a stranger: someone who I felt I knew—as I do you. Like he, you may use this rug to kneel on and pray. It'll also protect you from the rain."

The pastor removes a piece of paper he's hidden. He hands it to Roman. Mark instructs, "Last, I want you to put this piece of paper in your briefcase. It was sent to me in the home of my first disciple: a sacred aunt of mine. I believe your archangel would want you to have it.... It will give you a beginning—and document this promise between you and I.... God bless you on your search for the truth—I know your time is at hand."

Roman opens his briefcase. "Last question: in the end, how will I know the dream was the archangel?"

Mark confides, "Listen closely—and with faith—believe what I am about to say to you..." Mark enlightens him. "If the dream comes true...it was the archangel." Mark closes his eyes. His vision fades to black.

On the road to his house, Roman, top broken on his car, drives in the pouring rain. He holds the rug atop his head to keep him dry.

AFTERNOON

Rain pelts the house. In Roman's den, small game heads line the walls. Roman is admiring his prized weapons collection. He grabs an old-fashioned, musket-type shotgun. The huge, Sunday, paper rests on the couch. The headline reads—"BLOOD" CHRISTOPHER: FREED. Roman uses a page to clean the weapon. He sits, on the sofa, in front of the TV. Periodically, he'll look up and take notice.

On the TV, a male sportscaster is speaking. "Now, let's take a look at today's, half-time, player profile flashback."

On the taped video segment, a black, female sportscaster reports—"The projects: the heart and soul of the inner-city. These basketball courts are a battle and breeding ground for violence—gang violence: murder, killing, and death. However, in the early 70's, this playground must of appeared an oasis of hope in a desert of despair. 'Crip' they

74

called him: it was short for
'Cripple.' For nine months, in
this star player's God-gifted
life, he limped along. A stray
bullet from a gang shoot-out, that
accidentally killed his best
friend, only wounded his leg when
he jumped clear. Lucky? Lucky to
be alive. He called it; 'his
million-to-one shot that day: the
greatest shot of his career he
never took.' Today, a million-to-
one shot to make it anywhere, in
any life, in any career—he's made
it to the NBA. Tomorrow, he wants
for us all to pray for an end to
gang violence—to all violence....
That player is none other than—"
The TV screen displays the SPECIAL
BULLETIN tag.

Roman stops cleaning, and
loads his gun. He hears the rain
stop and listens to the TV
announcer. "We interrupt your
regularly scheduled program to
bring you this special report. We
take you live to Frontera,
California."

Roman motions as if he is
shooting the television. He is an
emotionally ticking time bomb.

The video plays on the TV.
The Oriental reporter is on the
scene. "This is Jen Yinyangchi
reporting live from the California
Institute for Women at Frontera.
Where, at this moment—famed,

former 'Son of Charles' disciple, Lesliannas Von Adolf, stands allegedly accused of the brutal murder of a fellow inmate's unborn child. As if by some sort of pre-destined fate, Von Adolf, by all accounts a perfectly model and rehabilitated prisoner—was sentenced to die in 1971—a time when, capital punishment was the peoples will. However, in 1972, only a short while after her imprisonment, the state overturned that ruling and Von Adolf escaped death. Today, after some thirty long years in prison—she remains alive. But, public opinion has swayed once again. The government will not rest until they also see Lesliannas Von Adolf dead. The people will be asking for the death penalty...the eternal life sentence. Reporting live—we return you to your regularly scheduled program."

The pre-empted, public service announcement plays on the TV. "The number one drug on Earth: alcohol—more than cocaine, heroin, and marijuana—*combined*. The number one addictive drug: cigarette tobacco. Now, a new drug possesses the planet—its origin—reproduction."

After a frustrated moment, Roman hits the mute button.

Judy passes the doorway. She begins to question her cousin. "Michael...Aunt Mary Frances?" Judy clumsily drops the cordless phone. It breaks a small glass elephant.

Maggie, uncontrollably furious; storms the room. She throws a home pregnancy kit at a glass armoire—shattering her reflection. She screams, "Holy Shit! Son of a fuckin' bitch... I'm pregnant!"

Roman tosses his $350 wad of cash at his wife. He screams, "That's it! That's all I got!" Figuratively, he screams, "I'm gonna kill myself!" He sees the pigeon's shadow in the window. He screams, "Die!" He jerks the trigger. As if in slow-motion, the gunshot blasts the window—rays of light, blood, and water streak through. There is a moment of utter stillness and dead silence.

In the backyard, Roman is standing outside of the window framework. He is in a deep, spiritual trance. A rainbow strokes the sky. The birdbath bowl is a red sea, delicate white feathers lay about. Maggie and Judy stand at the windowsill inside the hollowed house. Maggie lapses into a moment of compassion. "It's a dove."

Judy also, is momentarily
compassionate. "Was a dove."

Roman dips his hands in the
bowl to see if it's alive. His
face is transfigured. A trickling
tear escapes.

Judy says to him, "You're a
real doubting Thomas."

Michael, dove in his bandaged
hand, tips the birdbath. The red
water drains toward a squirrel
burrow. Dazed, he says, "I'll
walk with him to the water."
Hardly able to walk and speak. He
falls to his knees. He makes the
Sign of the Cross and prays, "God,
Oh Heavenly Father, I am sorry for
the life I have taken, forgive me.
I ask that the Holy Spirit and
your archangel please bring me to
salvation and guide my way. You
are my Father—and I am your son—I
only wish for you to be pleased
with me. My life is yours dear
God. Take me as I am..." He looks
up. "Father, with the archangel,
deliver me from temptation and
from sin. Help me to forever
change my evil ways and to
sacrifice my life for you Father,
so that I may be one with you God.
Amen."

EVENING

Michael walks, in the moonlit
path, to the wood line by the
lake. He carries with him the box
given to him by the pastor. In a
new, white handkerchief he gently
wraps the dove. He places it in
the box. He digs with his
bandaged and still-bloodied hands.
He buries the box, under soil and
rocks, beneath a tree. He prays,
"God. It is with faith, love, and
belief, in you as—The One and
Almighty God; Creator of the
Universe; Lord of Lords; God...
that I ask.... If it be your
heavenly will, please bring this
dove back to life? May your gift
of life—the life I have sinfully
taken—be the life that your grace
and promise restore.... And I
pray dear God that I may save but
one life. Amen."
With two twigs and a rusted
nail, he uses the unseen object
contained in the box to construct
a cross. When he strikes the
nail, he is overcome. Consumed by
the weight of his grief, he walks
laboriously into the lake. From
the distance, he appears to be
walking on the water toward the
rowboat.

D A Y   F I V E

LIFE

MONDAY - APRIL 17, 2000

SUNRISE

Michael's lifeless hand buoys in the shimmering water. The bandage has disappeared and the burn has healed. He lies face up in the rowboat. His eyes are sealed shut. Bearded, his long hair drapes him. A black Bible rests in the opposite hand of his dangling arm. His eyes burst open—they are full of life!

In the guest bedroom, Michael barges in looking for Judy. He checks the bathroom. Inconspicuously, a box of tampons is all that remains. He looks to the Heavens a moment; then runs out of the room.

In a taxicab, Miguel, a stoic, gruff-looking, Spanish cabby has his car plastered with

80

garish, religious goodies. Judy
sees her reflection, in the
partially open divider, against an
angel figurine. "Damn it. Mother
of all—I forgot my tampons, how
far to the bus station? Miguel,
is it?"

Miguel replies, "Not far.
You know that's a beautiful time
of the month for a woman. The
ground is made fertile for the
seed of all life."

Judy thinks, shoot, this a
remarkable comment from the looks
of Miguel. Judy demands "Go back
Pedro." He turns the taxi around.
The door on the cab reads:
MIGUEL'S TAXI—"GOD IS LIKE A TAXI
DRIVER—WITH BOTH YOU BETTER PRAY
FOR YOUR LIFE."

Miguel tells her, "Story
time.... The other day God
arrives at the airport and He
hails my cab. He told me He was
going to the United Nations to
speak about putting an end to
death. As I drove, traffic was
bad. So God switches places with
me—He said His angels would get us
there in time. So, we're speeding
down the highway and the police
stop us. The officer sees it's
God at the wheel—so he reports to
his police chief, 'This man's big,
I think we better let him go.'
Police chief asks, 'How big? Is
it the Governor?' 'Bigger' says

the cop. Police chief asks, 'Is it the President?' 'Bigger!' says the cop. Police chief says, 'Bigger than the President—is it the Pope?' 'Bigger!!' says the cop. 'How could he be bigger than the Pope?' asks the police chief. Cop says, 'I don't know, but he must be *real* big—God's driving him around.'"

In Roman's driveway, an Asian child has joined the three neighborhood children. They wait with their two mothers for the school bus. Michael runs to them from his car. He takes a knee and hugs them all. "Children, I'm sorry."

He jumps in his "Jag" and tears away before screeching to a halt. From behind the parting school bus, the cab sneaks in. Michael meets Judy. Palms clenched, he prays for the cab to wait. Michael tells her, "Judy, I'm sorry."

Judy says, "For what?"

"Everything. I want you to take my car back with you Upstate. Now!"

"Jumpin' Jehoshaphat! Why? What about my trip?"

"Forget it. Your gambling's an addiction you'll have to do without. I want you to sell it and give the money to Aunt Mary

Frances. Get her the care she needs to stay alive."

"That's all well and good Michael, but I think she'd be the first to tell you—when you die and God comes, all the money in the world won't mean a thing. She's dying. She says, money can't buy you life—only afford you death."

Michael reveals, "I've been having visions, a revelation I guess."

Judy says, "Don't tell me you saw a ghost?"

"Not a ghost—an angel."

"Jeez, Mary and Joseph, you sound like her now. No wonder she said she had faith in you Michael. Are you positive you want to do this?"

"It's my money."

"I remember she used to make me read the Bible, it's all in Matthew: 'Man cannot live by bread alone, but every word from the mouth of God.' I guess it's true."

"It's the archangel—I've got no choice. Judy, you above all should know, Matthew: 'Turn away from your sins, because the Kingdom of heaven is near!"

"Personally, Michael, I think it's hopeless...but if it's mercy you want—it's mercy you'll get."

Michael says to her, "I've got to do what I've got to do.

From here on out—I'm acting as if, no matter what I've done in my life—my eternal future, the choice between Heaven and Hell, depends on exactly what I'm doing the very second the angels come for me. And I want to make sure I'm doing something right, not something wrong."

Judy says to him, "Well that's what it says: 'You never know the day or the hour when God comes—not the Son, the angels, no one.' Aunt Mary always says, 'From the instant we're born—we're only a day closer to dying.'"

"Judy, if I don't listen to that angel and somehow save a life—either with this hand that gives, or this one that writes—I am dead."

"Hey Michael, if it helps: A little known actor I know told me a story about a big movie he and two other guys all wanted to be in. The producer told'em they all had ability, so he sent'em all to acting class. So the first guy, who had a lot of talent, he went and got better. The second guy, who had some talent, he went and learned more. My guy, who only had a little talent, he's afraid to go 'cause he knew the producer could get anybody—so he didn't do anything. Comes time to do the movie—no matter who, producer gives parts to everyone who was in the class. Movie's a big hit; first guy ends up getting best actor—second guy, best supporting actor—my guy's not even an extra."

"Judy, by the time I'm finished—I'll have given it all away. There'll be *no* money left."

Judy kisses his cheek. It dawns on her; he's giving *all* his money away.

Michael dashes for the cab.

MORNING

In Goldstein's office; Goldstein, in a camel hair coat, sits at his desk. The office looks like that of a train enthusiast. A replica of his engine-less, model train sits nearby. Papers are strewn all over. As he cleans the debris, Goldstein attempts gobbling down a bagel with honey, a salad, and a pear.

In the reception area, Michael storms through.

In Goldstein's office, Michael's jaunt is accompanied by a huge wind that swirls from the window barely ajar. Goldstein accidentally has a paperweight of a bumblebee on the intercom button—so he hears Michael say over the speaker—"Lucy, I'm sorry. Is Goldstein here yet?"

85

Lucy answers, "He's been here since yesterday—his day of rest."

Goldstein tells her, over the intercom, "That's Saturday Lucy, it's okay, the Gospel says: 'the Sabbath was made for man—not man for the Sabbath.'"

The wind picks up again. Michael enters Goldstein's office in a frenzy. Goldstein, bagel in his mouth, is ducked under the desk gathering paperwork. Michael does not see him. "Goldstein?!"

From Goldstein's point-of-view, under the desk, he sees Michael's shoes. However, Goldstein can't speak. He bangs his head.

Michael starts to exit.

Goldstein rises.

"Goldstein...Is this the day to do good, not evil? To save a life, not kill?"

"Every day, Mr. Roman, every day.... I've been waiting for you." Goldstein clumsily spills his salad oil on Michael's shoes. Michael rubs a drop from his own forehead. The wind blows again. Michael shuts the window. He does not notice the pigeon nest or raindrop trickle. Goldstein says to him, "I came in to do the insurance claim—when I remembered I forgot to close the window."

"Goldstein...Ernest...May I call you Ernie? I want you to

sell everything I own. Let's save
some lives."

        Ernie lunges to hug him. In
doing so, he momentarily knocks
himself to his knees. Ernie says
to Michael: "'The labor of the
righteous leads to life, the wages
of the wicked to sin.' You've
seen the life."

        "A proverb?"

        "Proverbs boss, nothing but
proverbs. Where do you want to
start?"

        "I've been hard, I'm sorry."

        "It's okay."

        "The business—put the word
out. But hold on—I only know what
I know, and I'm too ashamed to
beg. Then, look for a buyer for
my home. I just need a place to
write."

        "The horse claim?"

        "Cancel it. I lied. Forgive
me..."

        "Forgive and forget. But
just as easily, you need to ask
your Maker about the life you
stole and repent."

        "I did, and I am."

        "Now, your automobiles?"

        "One down...stop payment on
the other."

        "Your weapons?"

        "I don't know..."

        "Neither do I right now, but
God Himself once told me in
prayer: ever since the genesis of

creation—man's knowledge made him one with evil and the original sin of death. Were it for God, His creation would have eternal life. Man's own sin, was death's brother murder. And even so, God would have it that no other man on Earth take the life of another—lest there be the first holy war. In the name of creation, not religion, God made man in this life and the life in this man. I will pray for peace on the weapons of war." Ernie asks, "Shall I go on?"

Michael insists, "As always."

"Mrs. Roman's jewelry?"

"She can live without it."

"'How much better to get wisdom than gold! And to get understanding is to be chosen rather than silver.' ...Your savings account?"

"It's yours. Give it all to your church. I'm not sure how, but maybe the archangel Michael can save a spiritual life."

"If I may say sir, money is the root of all evil—charity is the tree of life. God bless you...Is that it?"

Michael unfurls his empty pockets like rabbit ears.

Ernie expounds, "King Solomon said it: 'The ransom of man's life is his riches, but the poor man does not hear rebuke.' Rejoice

you're free! See, the more you
have—the more you want—you never
have enough. When the end of life
comes—you don't want to go and
leave what you have behind. It's
better to give, and of yourself,
and have friends—they'll be the
only thing you have on the other
side. For tonight and eternity:
'When you lie down, you will not
be afraid; Yes, you will lie down
and your sleep will be sweet.'"

   "Thank you, Ernie. I can't
do the angel's work and
concentrate on enriching my
lifestyle—can I trust you to
steward over this?"

   "You're a shrewd man Mr.
Roman. If I may say—you've always
known me to be honest, even with
the small details—so too, will I
be with the large. Have faith,
now that you've inherited true
wealth—I won't let you down—you
have my word." Ernie implores,
"Don't let God down. *Shalóm*."

   Michael, departing, says,
"*Shalóm* and so long."

   At the Midtown District
Attorney's office, in the
reception area, a bedraggled
Michael rushes in. Lincoln's
umbrella is hanging there. The
impersonal receptionist is on the
phone. "District Attorney's
office—can you please hold?"

"Excuse me, is Abraham Lincoln Peters in?"

The receptionist answers, "Mr. Peters has a corporal case on the docket...that's at the main courthouse...next block over. The court's far behind administering justice today—they won't let you in the building—you'll have to blaze a trail if you want to catch him!"

"Thank you."

Under harshly ominous skies, just outside the DA's office, the Midtown city street is crowded. Michael, running, quickly gains speed. He sees Lincoln. Michael slows, relieved; he gently tugs his arm. "Lincoln..." The wrong man. The fearful stranger yanks back his arm. Michael says, "Sorry." The stranger returns to talking to himself.

Outside the main courthouse entrance; Lincoln, with two briefcases in hand, waits impatiently in line. In front of him, Dr. Parkinson and Mrs. Parkinson speak with their Christian attorney. Mrs. Parkinson, a middle-aged Jewish woman, is gaudily jeweled. She is boisterous and crying. "How can I live? Have peace of mind? How can my soul sleep at night knowing that monster is alive? Hatred, a

hate crime is what it is. He
deserves to die!"

A loud clap of thunder times
with Michael's trek.

The attorney speaks. "No,
Mrs. Parkinson."

Mrs. Parkinson laments, "My
son's death is senseless."

The attorney pleads, "A
victim's death is never senseless
if they know God and love life.
You're not the only ones who've
ever lost an innocent son. Mrs.
Parkinson, I know how you are both
feeling. Believe in me, have
faith and trust me, when I tell
you—there are so many unanswered
questions regarding the death
penalty: religion, fairness,
deterrence, innocence. Supreme
power comes from oneness and
truth. Imagine if you were the
only person to know the absolute
truth about UFO's. If they did
not exist, you couldn't be lied
to. And if they did exist, and
visited the planet to destroy it—
you would know how to be prepared.
And if they came in peace, you
would be their guide. On any
subject, there are many questions,
possibilities, and lies, for all
who do not know—but only one
answer, possibility, and truth,
for those who do. Without the
death penalty as law, you know the
one powerful truth—you'll never be

lied to on if it works. But with
the death penalty as law, how many
lies can be told?" He concludes:
'For if a law had been given that
could bring life, then
righteousness would in reality
come from the law.' We'll go for
25-to-life, or life without parole
as a plea. The truth is, he
lives, but he's a killer. You
live and you are not—then we can
all go on with our life."

Lincoln asserts, "That's
horseshit asshole." A bolt of
lightning and immediate clap of
thunder set off Lincoln's internal
alarm. "My umbrella!"

The rain begins. Michael has
reached the base of the steps.
Lincoln calls out, "Michael!"

Michael and he meet halfway
up the steps. They huddle beneath
a vendor-cart umbrella. "Lincoln,
I'm sorry. You've heard about
Lesliannas Von Adolf?"

"Who can forget?" He tells
the vendor, "Gimme'a fried egg
muffin."

Michael appeals, "I want you
to defend her." Lincoln thinks,
Yeah right. Michael briskly takes
hold of him. Michael demands, "I
want you to give her, her life
back."

"For God's sake Michael, she
should be executed. She's the one

who makes people today fear for their lives."

Michael says, "All fear leads to anger, anger to hatred, hatred to murder. We're afraid of each other because we keep killing each other." He decrees, "Now, why don't you be the first to put an end to it?"

"Forget now, I remember what she did before. Who can forgive her for that?"

"I can, for one."

"And who might you be?"

"Somebody, who if he's wronged, would like to be forgiven rather then lose my life out of fear, hatred, and revenge."

"Who died and made you boss?"

Michael professes, "I did."

Lincoln asks, "Why her? Why this?"

Michael admits, "I saw her parole hearing on TV once and never have I seen a human being more deserving of freedom than her. She'd make a better neighbor than 99 percent of us—not to mention safer—I *know* she's against the death penalty. How can I trust the killers out there who have no problem putting a person to death? If ever there was a case of someone being rehabilitated—it's her."

Lincoln states, "We don't rehabilitate, stupid—maybe one in

a million—we punish. I'll grant
you, our justice system is what
needs rehabilitating—and it's only
getting worse and worse, and we're
executing people, more and more,
younger and younger, for less and
less severe crimes—but it's the
best and only system we got. What
body of government do you know is
any better, 'Mr. Authority?'"

Michael responds, "When your
car breaks down, who better to
bring it to: the people who own
the repair shop, or the man who
built it?"

Lincoln snipes, "You're
outta' your freakin' mind. You're
willing to go to the ends of the
earth on this—aren't you?"

"I've sold everything I own."

"Say what?"

"I want to write a story
about what's happening to me. I
hope it may even save Von Adolf."

"Now, I know you're outta'
your skull. And you think this
can make a difference?"

"Words have freed and saved
people before. The time is now.
'If you're not for me, you're
against me.'"

Lincoln gets that cash
register look. The vendor hands
Lincoln his food. The faulty
ketchup top squirts Michael's
heart. "Sorry." says Lincoln. He

says, "Michael, you're my best
friend; like a brother almost...
there's not another lawyer in the
country who'd give you the time of
day on this, or go to battle for
you on it. But, being time is
money and your time is now; and
since you seem to have so much of
the almighty dollar to spend—I'll
do it...the whole shooting match:
lock, stock and barrel—for the
standard legal fee, a third...a
third of a million dollars:
$333,000."

"It's done." They shake on
it.

Lincoln asks, "Michael,
escape from you dream world and
tell me—do you really think
somebody like her, a person, can
change their life for the better
like that?"

Michael answers, "In your
wildest dreams—did you ever think
you would see me as I am? She's
been there thirty years—I've been
here less than three minutes—so
believe it. I'm pleading with you
Lincoln, no matter how they do it
out there: gas, injection,
electric chair—please save this
one life."

"A new Michael Angelo—this
has divorce written all over it.
How's 'Magpie' swallowing the
news?"

"Oh my God!"

95

In the abortion clinic procedure room, Maggie is harnessed in the apparatus. Dr. Bob "Bubba" Beals is in his early thirties; he has brown hair and appears the all-American father—wholesome as white bread. He counsels Maggie in preparation. Maggie bemoans, "Shit. I forgot my music tape in the car."

Jairus, a nurse, passes by. Dr. Bob asks, "Jairus, would you grab the lady's music cassette from her car?"

Maggie tells her, "The red Rover." Maggie asks him, "Dr. Beals, how far along am I?"

He says personably, "Bob, 'Bubba' to some." He says to her, "You wouldn't know it to look at you, but seven to eight weeks."

She asks, "That's the cutoff point isn't it?"

Dr. Bob answers, "We could've used the FDA approved Methotrexate, similar to RU 486, in conjunction with Cyotec or Misopostal to induce a miscarriage..."

Maggie says, "RU 486, that's...that abortion pill would've done the trick after my birth control misfire." She asks him, "They're like the same, right?"

Dr. Bob answers her, "It would make life easier." He tells

96

her, "Notwithstanding, and more importantly, you the patient must've agreed to undergo a surgical abortion if that treatment was medically incomplete." He asks, "Why?"

She tells him, "This early, I've heard that it's alive and kicking, and that it has all its once-in-a-lifetime characteristics." In seeking confirmation, she asks inquisitively, "And, is it true that the brainwaves have begun? And, if it were to exist, when those brainwaves stop, it will never exist again and is considered dead?"

Inside a taxicab, Michael is frantic.

Back at the procedure room, Dr. Beals replies to Maggie's inquisition. "The cessation of brainwaves would signify the death in a life-form, yes."

Personally concerned about the terms of the abortive procedure, she asks, "Could that be a problem?"

Dr. Beals replies, "No, piece of cake. You've got another thirty-two or thirty-three weeks. The law is progressing right to the point of birth. The normal pregnancy lasts forty weeks; ironically, numbers-wise, the same forty days it rained on Noah; the same forty years Moses wandered the desert; and the same forty days, 'you know who,' was tempted.... I wonder if God planned it that way?"

Jairus returns. She reports, "Dr. Bubba, it's stormin' like there's no tomorrow out there."

However, she's returned too late with the cassette tape. The doctor inserts his own angelic sounding tape into the stereo. The green indicator light looms boldly.

Maggie asks Dr. Beals, "You're not into G-o-d are you?"

Dr. Beals replies, "God? I go to a service, but my religion teaches things like medically-assisted suicides, and mercy killing, and the death penalty, are all okay—so this shouldn't be too sinful. Beside, I only believe what I agree with. And who else is going to pay my family's bills?"

Maggie wonders, "Doctor, is it gonna be painful?"

"No. It should be dead in a couple of minutes." Like vultures, he and an assistant circle around her.

With Michael riding inside, the yellow cab flies through a yellow traffic light.

The assistant says comfortingly, "It's okay, you're

not alone, statistically roughly one in every three and a quarter babies gets aborted."

The doctor informs her, "I'll be performing the most common procedure—the suction curettage method." He and the assistant ready their masks. The latex gloves make a suction sound as their applied.

Maggie says, "I've heard that's where you insert a sword-type-of, sharp-edged plastic tube and cut the thing to pieces?"

The doctor responds, "To put it quite simply—the contents of the uterus are removed by suction, by a machine that operates under the same principle as a vacuum cleaner." On the machine, the red power light glares.

Maggie asks, "Does that get it all?"

He retorts, "It is particularly common that you'll need a repeat D and C to remove some placental fragments. Then, for up to a couple of weeks, spotting and cramping may occur when tissue is being expelled." He utters, "I sense this may be a difficult experience for you. Our intent is to provide the service as efficiently and economically as possible. *All in all, the procedure has been medically proven extremely safe...many, many times safer than childbirth.*" Lightning strikes with a thunderous boom! White smoke billows out from the ventilator delaying his preparation. "Nurse, the transformer's out again. Get maintenance to check it will you?" He informs Maggie, "They'll use the emergency pro-generator.... What did I say, pro—progenitor... propane generator, while the transformer is being fixed. The emergency power should kick-in any minute."

A wet hand flings open the clinic's front door. Raincoat sopping wet, a *Right to Life* pamphlet distributor attempts to drop off a stack. The "*Right to Lifer*" propagates, "Life, life— life, liberty, and the pursuit of happiness."

He is actually kicked in the butt by a young, all-American-looking nurse. "Get your freedom of speech ass outta' here 'Jefferson.'"

In the doctor's office, Bubba Beals proclaims, "Power's up and..."

Michael, soaked, rushes past the entanglement at the clinic front door. He swiftly gains entrance to his wife. At the procedure room door, amid the regenerated white lamps and smoke,

100

Michael emerges with Maggie. She is dumbfounded. She carps, "For Christ's sakes, what in the hell are you doing?"

"I'm sorry Maggie, but this just may be the death of me."

At the reception area, in the front of clinic, Maggie readies herself for the storm outside. Jairus Martin-King, the nurse, is a fifty or sixty-year-old black woman with gray hair. She is at the reception desk with the all-American-looking nurse. Michael and Maggie only catch a glimpse of a fishbowl positioned on a mirrored stand; it and an aquarium against the wall, are each full of jelly beans.

Maggie asks, "What's up with all the jelly beans anyway?"

Jairus responds, "Been here as long as me, 1973."

Her clinic cohort says, perplexingly, to all of them, "They keep trying to get fish, but they keep dying; must be something in the water."

Jairus whispers to the Roman's, "Keep a secret? Bosses think it's a major Easter thing with the jelly bean factory cross the sound." Jairus shares with them her version of show and tell. She cups in her dark palm, a single red bean; "But you see this jelly bean...figure this is one

youngin' who's life ended in a
clinic just like this."

She points to the fishbowl
full of red and blue beans,
perhaps 170 in total. She
contemplates retrospectively,
"And in that year [1973] when Roe
versus Wade made this all legal-
like, in the time it takes to
watch a picture show, *that* many
child'n never once let out a peep
or even got to cry."

She motions to the reds and
blues in the aquarium tank,
perhaps 4,000-4,400. "Today, on
the twenty-seventh birth...
anniversary, you might say—by the
end of the day, one day—*that* many
will be gone forever...more than
double that ever-increasing, sky-
high rate."

She points to the back wall
of black bean-filled tanks. They
are stacked like staircases of
offertory candles, forty in all.
"But oh dear child, by the time we
all have our next birthday, and we
all turn one year older, it's sad
to think, but *that* many babies
won't ever make it out of their
mama's alive...times 10!...40
million babies!..." Nearby, a
woman's family is playing. From a
table of toys, Jairus picks off a
puzzle of the United States. "In
the U.S. alone!" The puzzle
pieces collapse. "In the world,

it's over 200 million lives this year; the number of people in the whole country."

In her hand, she reveals one white, baby blue, and pink bean. "And *this...this* is the number now saved each time that transformer give out."

A robust doctor plucks the beans from the palm of her hand. "Don't mind if I do."

Maggie asks Jairus, "Then lady, why do you w-o-r-k, work here?"

Jairus replies, "Better legal-like, than done at home—safe than sorry." A woman is leaving. Jairus says to her, "Good bye, Miss Norma." Miss Norma departs alone, like a wounded pup she is disconsolate, her face bears her shame.

Michael tells Jairus, "You could not do it at all."

Jairus becomes abruptly angry. "You got to go. Go, go, go—get on 'outta here."

Michael walks Maggie out like a child into the rain; the coat held shielding her face like a captured criminal.

Maggie says to Michael, "I thought you were pro-choice?"

"I am."

D A Y   S I X

WORKS

TUESDAY - APRIL 18, 2000

DAWN

BORN AGAIN

　　At the backyard pond, Michael
floats in the rowboat a few yards
from shore. His briefcase is in
his lap, Bible by his side. He
writes in a loose-leaf binder,
sketching an unseen figure along
with the book text.
　　Maggie, half-asleep;
approaches in a black robe and
pink, white, and baby blue
undergarment. The pond repulses
her. She demands of him, "Talk to
me. After that scene yesterday,
you've got a lot of explaining to
do."

Michael remarks, "This is a great book." He mandates, "You should read this second Gospel... *this story is definitely too good not to be true.*"

"When Hell freezes over. For Christ sake, what's up with you Michael Angelo?"

He informs her, "So far I've been in contact with Lincoln, Goldstein, and Judy is helping to save Aunt Mary. Part of the plan is for you to become a parent and keep this baby alive."

"Are you nuts? You know I'm pro-choice."

Michael insinuates, "Pro-choice, or do you mean pro-death?" He observes, "That doctor was evil. By the power of the archangel Michael, I've been chosen to save a life. If you were against death, you would be for life. My father once wrote, 'once a team fights among themselves, they're bound to lose!'"

He states, "If your goal is to make your own choice—no matter what the law—then make it. No one will convict you for doing the right and loving thing, and giving a child life. Even the archangel believes you should be truly pro-choice...God's given us all free will; the will to choose for ourselves, but you need to make

105

the right choice, His choice, and choose life."

"Is this what those others told you? None of them are your wife."

He replies, "If I had a brother, my mother, my wife—" He says, "Whoever does the will of the archangel—that's who I'm beholden to."

"I can't believe what I'm hearing."

He speaks to her parabolically, "Maggie, a human life is like a flower. Can a flower grow from anything but a seed? If we destroy all the seeds, then there will be no flowers—all the flowers left standing will soon perish—then there will be none, period. If we so easily destroy a seed, how much easier to destroy a flower that is withering away, or one that is fully grown?" ...He adds, "With a ray of light, a seed grows. And just as the tears from above fall on the many weeds in the garden—isn't the lone flower the chosen one?" ...He answers himself saying, "Can we even imagine how to instruct both the flowers and the weeds to multiply? How do they know?" ...He says, "I ask you, who are we to cut any life short?"

"I just don't understand. I just don't understand you at all."

He says, "Since it's our nature that each and everyone of us believes in something—who are we not to believe there must be a Creator? What life would exist if there wasn't one?" He tells her, "There are only two ways of being: man-made or Creator-made. Can we, let's say, grow or create a human from the ground up? Where? We know the where. We know this earth was made for man.... The when? When from the dawn of creation, until the end of time—all has begun and ended with life...therefore, only life may be the reason why. Life is the reason why we were created—and only God knows how."

"Is my baby supposed to be some shining example of the powers that be—and not the fact that you and I did the dirty deed?"

He says, "You've heard the expression, 'the older the wiser'? Is there any older than the Creator? Can a son ever be older than the father? Can a newborn ever tell the mother how to give birth; or a dead man ever tell a living one about life? How then, can we tell our Creator when we should live or die?"

Maggie, while growing
incensed, is brought to a profound
silence.

He muses, "Think hard—in all
our intelligence, can a man create
a bird or tree, a flower or a
seed? No. And no man could've
created me."

"Professor Michael now is
it?"

He says, "Maggie, be calm,
don't be afraid. God's archangel
knows what to do."

"I'm the woman. You're the
man. Now it's up to me to get me
out of this. Who do you think you
are telling me I don't really have
the power to make my own choice?"

He tells her, "You're not
alone. The archangel has given me
no choice with my life either....
A 'Son of Charles' disciple whose
name I'd only heard once before is
costing me a fortune to show her
mercy. Is that unborn baby she's
accused of killing any less
meaningful than the child you
carry?"

"She's gonna fry. Why
bother?"

Prophetically, he says,
"Nobody believes in what I'm
doing, but that's okay, I don't
expect anyone to have as much
faith in me as I have in
myself..."

Maggie gives hard thought to
the power and profundity of the
phrase.

He says, "That's why I've
sent Ernie Goldstein out to spend
it on anyone who'll listen."

"What! The money! Not the
money! How can you do this to me—
I loved you.... Was it; was it
Lincoln that bastard? Did he
trick that thief Goldstein into
doing this? 'Cause if he
did.... Was it Goldstein? Did he
brainwash you? 'Cause if he did,
I'll kill that fat Jew.... I put
on my strip show for your
birthday. Then you think I'm
gonna let you fuck me over? Well
let me tell you, you foolish
freak—even in a settlement a girl
gets half. You tell your
Goldstein you have a choice...if
he doesn't cut me a check and give
me a piece—I'll serve this baby up
on a dish."

Michael shouts, "God no!
You'll make this house a tomb."
He assents, "Take it—the house is
yours...just keep that child
alive. I just need to be alone to
do my writing. All my money may
only save three lives, but more
than one million readers could
read this." He asks her, "What
time is it? I've been here since
three."

Maggie answers, "Almost seven." She says condescendingly, "Don't drown in your righteousness."

"It's the only way to go."

TRIALS & TRIBULATIONS

ALMOST 9:00 A.M. PACIFIC STANDARD TIME

At the California Institute for Women at Frontera, Lesliannas Von Adolf is alone in her cell. Von Adolf is fifty-years of age. She has a fair complexion. She is attractive with a natural grace. Her bleak dungeon of a home is full of her life's belongings. The only colorful object is a scenic, grade school, shoe box, display project of a nature setting. It is home for an absent fly. She slowly peels the foil lid off a tiny, condiment-sized *Smucker's* apple jam and sets it in the box. Lesliannas mutters, "Here's an apple Raphie, once a year during Holy Week...please be with me."

The cell door clangs open. The correction officer beckons, "Release 619-low."

Lesliannas moves gingerly. She is injured. In the prison

attorney/client meeting room, a posted guard watches the door. Lesliannas shuffles in fully shackled. "Mr. Peters, I'm Lesliannas Von Adolf. How do you do? I was hoping your file would be able to cut through the bars."

Lincoln sits, smugly smoking a cigarette. He has a newspaper, thin paper file, and a yellow legal pad. "Let's rock 'n' roll 'Lester.' I've got some serious dough-re-me wait'n for me when your shit hits the pan."

"I beg your pardon; may I ask you, would you be so kind as to extinguish your cigarette Mr. Peters? I would greatly appreciate it."

"Every con I know smokes more chimneys than 'Santee Claus.'"

"Not I, Mr. Peters; I am blessed to be alive. I would like to keep it that way—thank you."

"It's evident to me 'Sis,' that the reason you've agreed to let me represent you is because of the publicity I bring to this case." He whips out the tabloid paper and proudly shows her the front page's bold headline: PERSECUTOR PULLS SWITCH—DEFENDS DISCIPLE VON ADOLF.

Lesliannas expresses to him, "No disrespect, Mr. Peters, but I am not the one who sent for you, nor am I cognizant of who did. I

have yet to discern if you are;
the devil, or a blessing in
disguise."

Lincoln tells her, "You'd
have a snowball's chance in Hell
without my help."

Lesliannas acknowledges,
"While I am not helpless Mr.
Peters, I cannot tell a lie, your
stature in society I hope will
benefit my mission."

"Okay, 'bird lady,' if it's
not your acquittal or your flight
to freedom someday on parole—then
what say you, pray tell?"

Lesliannas replies, "I must
admit, while I am innocent and
would welcome the truth to come to
light—my eventual freedom on
parole may be eternally hopeless.
There is not much more I can do
this side of Heaven to improve my
chances of that happening. Praise
the Lord, the truths' in my heart—
have already set me free." She
invokes, "Infinitely more
important, I pray my purpose and
redemption may, by the grace of
God, bring me closer to Him as I
hopelessly face the remainder of
my life in prison. And that my
imprisonment, may be a once-in-a-
lifetime opportunity to make good
from evil."

Lesliannas declares, "Mr.
Peters, my sole objective is to be
a true-life testament, and show by

112

example, that a repentant, rehabilitated, resurrected ward of the state—a person—may by their actions, and not words, prove that punishment may be levied and sins forgiven. And in the end, justice can be served and lives not yet lost may be saved." She petitions, "To that end, I pray daily we as a people abolish one of the most supreme human injustices of all-time: punishment by death—the death penalty."

"Them's powerful words. My client strongly suggested I witness your next parole hearing on the tube—that is, if you get one."

"God willing," hopes Lesliannas.

Lincoln glances over a flimsy, single sheet of paper. He says, "This goddamn, virtually spotless, incarceration report of your imprisonment doesn't tell me shit." He looks over a slightly thicker stapled packet. He reads aloud, "Prison job—you're a pencil pusher."

Lesliannas says concurringly, "I'm a secretary."

He continues, "Hatched in California in 1949—artistic, creative..."

"I was blessed."

He peruses the report, saying, "This is all bullshit."

He comments, "Parents divorced..."

"My dad left." She recalls to herself, "I was seeking someone to love."

He notes, "And you wanted to be a..."

"School teacher."

He says indifferently, "Fascinating. It says you wanted to quote, unquote, 'help the world.' ...For cry'n out loud..."

"I did..." She pauses to rethink. "I do."

Lincoln hits it. "Bull's-eye. This is the background bad boy I was looking for. Flashback, to the hippie sixties: while the normal parents of today were free lovin', partying, and rock'n and rollin'—your teenage self is sexually boffin' your brains out, blowin' your mind on hundreds of acid trips, and fillin' your head with devil music played over and over again. It's during this one-year exodus when you chose to take up and disciple with that madman cult leader, the demon of my generation, that homicidal maniac: 'The Son of Charles.'"

Lesliannas responds, "I must confess, I was taken in: the brainwashing, all that talk about 'oneness and power of love...' He is the devil incarnate; the symbolic, demon-possessed, dark, fallen angel; the creator of sin

114

and lies. All the fake crucifixions, 'I would die for you, would you die for me?'" She quotes: "John 8:44 'You are of your father the devil. He was a murderer from the beginning, and does not stand in truth, because there is no truth in him. For he is a liar and the father of it'" Lesliannas says disgracefully, of her own self-examination, "God was I deceived."

Lincoln says condescendingly, "And with all your intelligence, you thought that murderous maniac was some sort of Messiah?"

She admonishes, "He was as John warned in his first epistle: 'Little children, it is the last hour; and as you have heard that the Antichrist is coming, even now many antichrists have come, by which we know that it is the last hour.'" She counsels, "Do you know Mr. Peters, how many untold ways the devil can deceive and tempt you? Three times he tempted the Lord with everything—all He had to do was go against The Father; hunger for the truth and I will feed you; fall, and the angels will lift you; follow me, I will give you the world. He could trick you so many ways. He and the Lord could appear virtually identical, even resemble one another and you wouldn't know it.

The only difference—the only way
to ever tell them apart...the
original sin was death; worship
the devil, and you kill; worship
God, and you save lives."

"And so it was, in the summer
of '69, under the maniac's satanic
spell—that you did just that, you
went out and murdered. And now
you would have us believe you have
rightfully paid your debt to
society? Cut me some slack from
the noose around my neck
'Lester.'"

She says remorsefully, "I
take responsibility for what I
did. The older I get the harder
it is...I took away all that
life..." Lesliannas concedes, "I
was nineteen years growing Mr.
Peters, twenty when I committed my
crime and my god-awful sin. I've
spent near to the last thirty
growing up. I don't look forward
to spending the next forty, in
here, growing old."

"Not unless you can free the
world from the death penalty?"

"I believe in God."

In the report of her history,
Lincoln unearths a flagrant
coincidence Lesliannas has
frustratingly lived with for
thirty years. "You were busted in
'69?"

"Correct."

Lincoln intervenes, "Hold the phone—the Governor's on the line." He recounts, "This is truly amazing. The record states, the people sentenced you to death—that's on March 29, 1971. While you're on death row awaiting execution—you stated, and I quote, 'I was more than willing to go the gas chamber. I didn't fear it. The death penalty at the time justified my not dealing with what I had done. It was the *eye for an eye*, they're gonna kill me, I don't have to deal with it,' end of quote. So you're facing death in the eye.... But the next year, 1972, California overturns the death penalty—so you get to live.... But the ironic part is—if the death penalty was illegal just the one year earlier, when you were convicted—you would've gotten the mandatory life sentence..."

In a state of shock, he rolls his last cigarette onto the table. Lesliannas knows....

"Amazing grace, Mr. Peters. Amazing grace, how sweet the sound that saved a wretch like me."

Lincoln concludes, "...you would have gotten the mandatory 25-to-life. In 1994, *you would've been automatically released.*"

"I once was lost, but now am found—was blind, but now I see."

Abraham Lincoln Peters
ignites the flame on *his* last
cigarette.

THE JUDEO-CHRISTIAN BOOK

ALMOST NOON - EASTERN STANDARD
TIME

    Outside of the U.C.A. Life +
God Church, Reverend Mark Anthony
pulls up in his Mustang
convertible. He vaults out over
the passenger door. A female,
volunteer gardener is but one
amongst a handful of the
volunteers landscaping the lush
garden growing around Reverend
Mark Anthony's mission. She is
about to snip a flower. Reverend
Mark hollers out, "No don't!
Don't kill them!"
    "Sorry," she says
unwittingly.
    "It's okay." He says,
"Here," handing her a pot. "Put
the roots and dirt in some pots
and we'll bring them in later.
They're alive with spirit. St.
Augustine, another bad boy who
went to God to get good, once
said, 'Every visible thing in this
world is under the charge of an
angel.' Now I'm no Einstein, but
those flowers don't look invisible

118

to me. You know, even Einstein
said, 'Either you believe
everything is a miracle or nothing
is.' Imagine the work God must've
put into making these. Who could
make anything on Earth more
beautiful?" He becomes markedly
less serious. "Listen, keep your
eyes open, a girl I once knew told
me they buried valuable coins in a
coffee can around here. So, the
next day, she told me she found
her little brother digging in the
ground—I'm so dumb, I said,
'What's your brother—a dinosaur?'"

Outside of the church
doorway, Reverend Mark bumps into
a healthy, white bearded, hip,
forty-two-year-old helper with a
bandana on his head. The helper
says, "Hey Mark. Long time no
see. Do you still think your time
has passed? Will your dreams ever
catch up to time?"

"Have faith my man. Listen,
they said this project would never
get off the ground, but your
dreams are numbered by the things
you've done. Remember, the magic
word is *ask*—that's what my father
would say." Reverend Mark places
the helper's hand against the
structure. "Touch it. This
building is no *Fig Newton* of your
imagination. If God can bless
you—He can bless me."

A cynical construction worker exits. He asks Mark, "What makes you think God's the boss?"

Reverend Mark says, "Look up." He raises the question, "Do you see the man upstairs?"

The bewildered worker asks ethereally, "God? No...Why?" In an earthly sense he asks, "Is there someone in the window?"

Reverend Mark is thinking, You see—God *is* who He *is*.

Inside the church, the wooden skeleton of an elaborate stage, sparse decorations, and furnishings, a large number of chairs, benches, and bleachers start to bring the former warehouse's main floor to life. A uniformed team of construction workers labors diligently. On stage, Reverend Mark is on his knees doing carpentry. Goldstein assists by handing him nails.

A worker tells Reverend Mark, "It's 12:00, we're gonna break."

Reverend Mark says, "Okay. Great work, thanks." He tells Ernie, "Let me have a nail please, Mr. Goldstein?"

Ernie inquires of Reverend Mark, "How many people do you think will show up for the first official service tonight?" Ernie hands him the nail.

"Thanks." Reverend Mark answers, "Hopefully at least

twenty-six, if all goes according to plan and you and each of the first twelve disciples brings just one person. Remember, Mr. Goldstein, if every person who believed in God would bring just one other person to church—then everyone would come to know God and the whole world would be saved."

Ernie reminds his friend, Reverend Mark, "Did you remember to invite the Bishop?"

Reverend Mark answers, "Yeah. I told him an angel of God told me one of the goals of this church should be to unite Christians and Catholics. The fundamental Christian biblical teachings, and their personal relationships with the Lord, teamed with the established, organized, mass-appeal of that first church built on the rock: One body, one blood, together in Christ—a match made in Heaven."

Ernie asks his friend, "Will there be any other Jewish folks there?"

He answers, "I hope so."

A spiritually unacquainted construction worker offers a comment. "I thought Jews and Christians hated each other?"

Reverend Mark relays to him, "No—Christ hates no one."

Ernie tells the worker, "Do you know what the word Christ means?"

Reverend Mark enlists Helen Theotokos, a twenty-one-year-old, Greek woman with an olive complexion into the discussion. An original disciple, she helps decorate. The threesome directs their verbiage at the worker. Reverend Mark says, "Helen, Christ in Greek is what?"

She answers, "Messiah."

Reverend Mark tells the worker, "Right. Christ is the Messiah. The Lord came when He did to bring the Jewish and Christian people, all the people, together. There was a reason God did what He did; a reason why Christ, His Christian Son was sacrificed."

Ernie reproves, "And Jewish Son...Jewish first."

Reverend Mark says to Ernie, "Sorry, you're right, forgive me. There's a reason why Christ, His Judeo-Christian Son died for us...hate is not it...Helen?"

Helen remarks, "Jewish and Christian hatred—no way. In the Bible, Luke writing for Christ explains: 'Judge not and you shall not be judged. Condemn not, and you shall not be condemned. Forgive and you will be forgiven.'"

"Right," says the Reverend. He sets up Ernie, saying, "Back in Mark's Gospel, Isaiah said..."

Ernie follows through, saying: "'Behold, I send my messenger before your face, who will prepare your way before you.'"

"Right," says the Reverend again.

Helen, again, remarks, "And in those Greek Scriptures, Luke went on to record for Christ: 'The Son of Man must be delivered into the hands of sinful men, and be crucified, and the third day rise again.'"

Reverend Mark, with a sincere warmth, plainly demonstrates for the worker the message of love he conveys. He sets up Ernie, again, by saying, "I love the Lord and the Lord was Jewish. So, I love Mr. Goldstein."

Ernie follows through again, by saying, "And I love you too."

"Quick! Why?"

"Because you love me."

Reverend Mark tells the worker, "See. Mr. Goldstein, by loving him, is bound to love me; and I'm bound to love him."

Helen asks her friend, "Reverend Mark, there'll be other religions there too, won't there?"

He answers, "I hope so, Miss Helen. Life knows no religion."

The worker has seemingly lost interest. He departs. Helen too departs, returning to work. She mutters to herself this Orthodox mantra, "Christ is risen. Truly He is risen."

The pastor and Ernie are mildly disgruntled that the worker has walked off. Ernie entertains second thoughts about the probable attendance. "I hope so too," he says despairingly.

Reverend Mark says encouragingly, "Every synagogue, every temple, every church started with one brick, one board, one stone. Mr. Goldstein: 'The stone that the builders rejected has become the cornerstone.'" Reverend Mark nails the final nail in the gargantuan cross set upon the stage. Ernie has a troubled look. Reverend Mark holds out his empty hands for a magic trick. He sets up Ernie, a third and final time, saying, "Mr. Goldstein, what do you see?"

Ernie follows through a third and final time, saying, "Nothing."

"And that is how many disciples we stated with; therefore, we have nothing to lose." Reverend Mark, sensing an underlying concern, magically pulls a penny from Ernie's ear. "Now, a penny for your thoughts?"

"Mark Anthony I trust you,
but in my opinion I question if
putting the $13,650 into first
building a church is the right
thing to do? Perhaps it might be
better served elsewhere?"

"Mr. Goldstein, God has been
known to fortunately bless His
followers, I'm confident He, the
archangel, and all the angels are
with us." Reverend Mark encases
the coin in a ceremonial
container. "This is the first
cent of that $13,650 donation."
He buries it, in the ground
beneath the stage, like an ice
fisherman. "You can't take it
with you."

Ernie asks, "Reverend Mark
Anthony, what is the first
preaching going to be on?"

"Life! I'm thinking of this
poem I'm working on. Reverend
Mark extricates, from his back
pocket, a poem he's scribbled:

> "Eternal
> life isn't
> just about
> your soul—it's
> about your
> state of mind.
> Without belief
> in God the
> Father, and
> God the Son—
> man fears

death. He
wishes life in
the material
world would
never end.
God forbid, if
he were
terminally-ill
and could know
and see the
end in sight.
To try and
understand the
meaning of
life, when
life is all he
knows—the
finality to
see life end.
       Eternal
life is as
much for the
living as for
the dead;
Earth and
Heaven in an
infinite
straight line,
when the human
mind cannot
differ between
where one
begins and the
other one
ends.
       How can a
man possibly

know if and
when he is
dead? Eternal
life begins as
soon as the
living believe
there is a God
in a place
called Heaven—
not when he
thinks he's
dead and
transforms
into a soul,
in this life,
he cannot see.
Eternal life
is never
knowing when
and if you
die—it's not
only about
your soul—it's
about your
state of
mind."

Ernie comments, "That's
great," he asks, "But Reverend
Mark, have you also considered
what to say to the people, who in
their mind, their religion won't
allow them to join together to
accept God's universal plan or
accept your Christ as a real
person?"

Reverend Mark replies, "I thought about that." He concedes, "For those who can't accept Christ as a real man—I'll tell them to think of Him as God appearing in the body of a human, like a Spirit. Like, He came in the disguise of a human being. Then, if they don't believe in Christ, just believe in His teaching. He only taught two things you know.... One: love God. And two: love thy neighbor. If you love someone, you forgive them. To love is to forgive.... And since every human being on the planet is alive—then love life. If you love them, let them live. That's it: love and life."

"Anyone could say that—I could've told you that."

"I know. God is not far from us—He is in each and every heart. That's why God also, was able to have His Son appear in the body of a man."

"I pray all this works."

"Mr. Goldstein, who was history's greatest underdog?"

"David."

"The greatest knowledge a man can have is to know God and know himself. Well, I know I am a lot like David—so if David can do it, with the power of God—I can do it."

"I hope so."

The spiritually unfamiliar construction worker, whom the trio engaged, returns with a newfound compassion for the church's program. He attempts a respectful gesture of generosity; he offers the pastor two dollars. "This must've fell out of your pocket."

Reverend Mark's onto him. "God bless you, but that's okay. The next time you pass a homeless person give it to them and know God has truly blessed you. I'll never forget this."

Ernie submits, "That reminds me, what do we do about further offerings?"

Reverend Mark discloses, "Thank God, an angel brought me this idea since I hate money and it only manages to bring out the evil in me; not to mention, I've got to feel guilty about spending it." He reasons, "Since the Bible says it's cool to donate ten percent of what you make to the church, and now we're a church. We'll keep ten percent for personal overhead and put the rest back into the congregation—and to helping the most important people in this or any other church..."

Ernie resolves, "The ones who aren't here."

"Exactly." Reverend Mark concludes, "Remember, all the money in the world never leaves

the world—it only changes hands
for awhile. So it seems stupid to
live or die over it. We'll do the
best we can until we're dead. The
less we keep, the less we'll be
tempted. The more we get, the
more we can give away."

SOS - SUICIDE OR SELF-DESTRUCTION

6:00 P.M.

    Inside the religious art
shop, a few shoppers straggle
about. Mary Frances is behind the
register reading the Bible. She
closes the book and finishes from
memory: "'This will prove that
your are the sons of your heavenly
Father, for His Son rises on the
bad and on the good, He rains on
the just and the unjust.'" She
reads a wall plaque; "IT TAKES
BOTH THE SUN AND THE RAIN TO MAKE
A RAINBOW."
    The doors' angel, wind,
chimes signal the entrance of the
concerned procession of her three
best friends. Sister Zoe Namath
is thirty-one years of age. She
is a petite and very pretty French
woman. She is the good daughter
Mary Frances never had. Zoe is
carrying a foil-covered dinner
plate. Reverend Billy Shoe is

130

forty-five or fifty-years-old. He is a southern Pentecostal preacher. Rabbi Eli is in his mid-sixties. He brings up the rear. He tells her, "Mary Frances we heard. Sister Zoe brought you supper."

Mary Frances gasps, "Oh! You scared the life out of me! For the love of God! Sister, thank you for dinner. Bless you, one and all."

Reverend Billy Shoe asks, "Mary Frances, do the doctors know why?"

Mary Frances replies, "Why what? All I can do now is determine *who* I am. No one knows where, when, or how we will die—and only God knows why."

Sister Zoe Namath says to her, "Mary Frances, we heard it was cancer of the breast. I know abortion leads to breast cancer, but what grave sin did you commit?"

Mary Frances replies, "Sister Zoe, you know no man, including Adam, has been free from sin.... I admit, I feel like a dog who gets punished days after the owner discovers they've done a no-no in the house; the doggie doesn't remember what he or she did—they just remember being punished. After all, we're only human—and I

131

understand—being human is
punishment enough."

Rabbi Eli says to her
disparagingly, "Cancer is God's
disease, God's plague—He's
punishing you. Pray and ask
for forgiveness Mary Frances, have
faith. There's a lesson to be
learned here."

Mary Frances says to him,
"Rabbi Eli, my childhood friend—
you know, the lesson to be learned
here is: Be it illness descended
from God or the devil, and if from
God, to punish the guilty or draw
the innocent nearer to thee—why is
not the question." She instructs
him, "Understand not the wisdom of
which and why God does what He
does, the answer is: how to live
with it; to live with the undying
faith that the Lord is our Savior.
The answer is not to curse God or
reason that God has wronged me—to
not lose hope as people do—to not
abandon God. Man cannot escape
from his Creator, as Adam learned
after the original sin. Godless,
I am on my own—and man on his own,
is a defenseless animal in Satan's
snare. Man cries out in pain for
the trapper to free him from the
trap—but Satan captured you for a
reason—so Satan releases you to
slaughter, suicide, and death. In
painful times like these, the Lord
and the angels offer the earthly

and eternal freedom of salvation."
Mary Frances flinches. Her chest
in pain, she no longer conceals
the anguish.

The door chimes are ringing.
She sees a priest enter. He is
fifty-five-years-old, balding,
with rectangular rimmed glasses.
He never looks directly at anyone.
He is unbelievably intense and
focused—in a world all his own.

Reverend Billy Shoe says to
Mary Frances, "I declare, you must
be in bad pain?"

Mary Frances says to him
arbitrarily, "Am I in *bad* pain, or
great pain?" She tells him, "What
is so bad about pain? You know;
if a person's introduction to
angels is when an angel ministers
to us in times of spiritual,
mental, or physical pain—then pain
is a great way to welcome angels
into your life."

Sister Zoe Namath tells her,
"I'm sorry you're in such pain."

Mary Frances says to her,
"Sister Namath, don't be. Pain,
like the angels, guides me to God.
Ask yourself—why is it that once a
person has a bad, let's say, life-
threatening experience, they often
become good? Or, for some, born
again? Stop and think about
it.... If your Creator knows you
better then you know yourself, and
He does: every hair on your head.

133

And God knows that you are being bad and heading down a deadly, self-destructive path—why not stop you with a life-changing pain or problem that will re-direct you on a path to Him? God does this not for His sake, but for your own good."

Rabbi Eli says patronizingly, "Pain, punishment, penance—are you at peace, Mary Frances?"

Mary Frances says to him, "Only the dying will tell you in their final breath, but believe it or not—a person is most at peace in their life when they are near death." She clarifies, "The pain in a person's life may be God's way of preparing them for Heaven. Since there is only perfection in Heaven, sacrificing with the pain and suffering on Earth may give a person a better understanding of what Heaven is. Imagine...being that close to Heaven may change your life forever. It's like this: man is an animal. As man, the animal, we are not intelligent or enlightened enough to understand God. God teaches man, the animal, like man teaches an animal. If you let an animal be punished when it goes near the fireplace, it learns the pain of being in the living room. But outside the house, it comes to know the peace of being in the garden.... Remember, God never gives you more than you can endure. The peaceful and divinely angelic release from the pain of this life will allow you to die with dignity. It will be a tribute to your faith, trust, and belief in God and His perfect home: Heaven. What a glorious way to die.... The one who has greater reward: is not the rich man who inherits a million dollars—but the poor man who lives through the pain of poverty."

Reverend Billy Shoe tells her, "That is rich." He asks, "But aren't you the least bit afraid of dying Mary Frances?"

She relays to him, "Every time you leave—you go. Reverend, Hell I'm afraid of—not Heaven." She elaborates, "If this earth was all that there was, put it this way... all I know about this earth: is that it began when I was born and will end when I die. All I don't know about this earth: is that there was a history before my birth and there will be a future after my death...I'm not leaving the earth, God willing, I'm going to Heaven." She explains, "As I am still alive, dying has enlightened me. Knowing what I know, I'd welcome death the next minute—or go years looking forward

to the minute I do die." Aunt
Mary flinches in pain again.

Sister Zoe Namath is
heartbroken to see her plight.
"Oh, Mary Frances, I love your
poetic nature; but Mary Frances, I
don't understand *why* God allows
such pain and suffering?"

Mary Frances consoles her,
"Sister Zoe..."

Rabbi Eli tells Sister
Namath, "How would you make heads
from tails? How would you know
reward without punishment? How
would you tell the good without
the bad?"

The Sister needs comforting.
Mary Frances obliges. "Zoe..."

Reverend Billy Shoe
contemplates. He says to the
Sister, "'Lordy,' 'Lordy' that is
life's great mystery." Mary
Frances says to her, "Zoe, I love
a good mystery in my life—I look
forward to when I'm dead and
buried and the secret mysteries of
this life are revealed to me.
Child trust me; God is God; and
God only knows..." She tells them,
"Pain and suffering are facts of
life. The truth is; God does not
reveal all the facts to man for a
reason. Facts you would not
believe or comprehend if you saw
them with your own eyes..." Mary
arranges five angel statues. She
says to the triumvirate, "Lookie

here...there are five angel statues: One, two, three, four, five angel statues. That is a fact. A fact you believe because you know the truth for yourself—you see for yourself."

She hides two of the angels beneath the counter. She demonstrates: "Now, the fact remains, there are still five angel statues—but now you see only three. The truth has not changed—only now, because I have not revealed all the angels to you, you're left to trust me—you need to take my word for it. *That is why God does not reveal all the mysteries of life—God teaches you to trust in Him—and you need to take His Word for it.*"

The three remaining statues, on the counter, are of the "see, speak, and hear no evil" design.

Sister Zoe Namath says to her supplicatingly, "You trust the Father that much?"

"I trust Him with my life."

There is silence as the group contemplates the wisdom. Mary Frances turns to place a figurine on the top shelf. She is drawn to view the priest. He is intently staring to the rear of the store. He mesmerizes Mary.

Judy enters from the side door in the rear. A statue falls from the shelf. It nearly hits

Mary Frances in the head. It
shatters at her feet. Judy yells
at her, "For God's sake!" Mary
Frances is altogether unfazed.
She grits her teeth and flinches
in pain.

Rabbi Eli tells her, "Mary
Frances, you're lucky you didn't
get struck or knocked out."

Judy tells the friends,
"She's been having accidents like
there's no tomorrow."

Mary Frances informs them,
"Rabbi, you should know there is
no such thing as luck. That was
an angel, or my guardian angel,
protecting me. The advantage to
being terminally-ill is that you
are freed to better see God at
work. Daily, I'm entertained,
educated, and enlightened by
angels—visible and invisible. The
louder death knocks—the greater
total of God's angels at the
door."

Judy, in playful
respectfulness, greets the
threesome, "What's up,
'Muscatels?'"

"Howdy, Judy," says Reverend
Billy Shoe.

"Hi, Judy," says Sister
Namath warmly.

Eli nods a sneering, but
sincere hello.

Judy says to the friends,
"She been telling you that the

138

angels are keeping her alive, protecting her from death." She says condescendingly, "Right, Aunt Mary? The angels are in charge, so you don't even bunk your toe against a rock."

Aunt Mary Frances says, "I've been right so far. I've been alive sixty-nine years; and in one second, I'll be dead. If angels keep me alive that time on Earth— How blessed will I be when it's time for Heaven? And if I'm wrong, I'll never know it until my guardian angel tells me in Heaven— and I can live with that."

Judy says, "Yeah. And then she won't have to hear me say, I told you so." The trio and Aunt Mary Frances are amused by Judy. Judy is entertained at herself.

Aunt Mary Frances asks, "Judy, my love, how was your trip?"

Judy answers, "I'm a $600 part owner of the casino, but I'll win and get even at church." Aunt Mary Frances and friends look inquisitively. Has Judy repented? They're fond of Judy, but know better. "Bingo," Judy explains.

Aunt Mary Frances is disappointed. She scolds her niece. "Oh Judy, for the love of God."

Judy says, "I know, I-21, B-12, Bingo! Matt: chap. 21, V-12:

"'He overturned the tables of the money changers...my house shall be called a house of prayer.'" She blurts out, "By the way—I saw Michael."

Aunt Mary Frances calls out, "Dear God! Michael? The Michael? You saw..."

Judy interjects, "Ah see, you're losin' it. 'Michael, Long Island, cold as iced tea Michael.' Michael Roman, your long lost black sheep nephew. He gives us both his love." She mumbles, "I'm driving it."

"What?" asks Aunt Mary Frances.

Judy replies, "Nothing. I think he's seen the light: angels, God, the works..." Aunt Mary Frances, in joyous praise, waves her angelic antennae arms in the air! Judy says, "I know, I know: 'angels in heaven always look upon the face of my heavenly Father.'"

Rabbi Eli mutually responds, "*Shvakh Got.*"

Reverend Billy Shoe also responds, "No one looks for light in the day—in darkness is when we search for the light."

Sister Zoe Namath, as well, responds, "What is a miracle to man..." She and Aunt Mary Frances joyfully complete the response, "...is a habit for God."

140

Mary Frances continues to
say, "God lives...for even in
darkness we cast a shadow." She
says, "Judy love, it's that famous
Matthew parable I hoped you'd one
day yourself learn."
Judy says, "I know, my lucky
number: 11-18."
Aunt Mary Frances cites, "18-
11."
Judy quotes: "'For the Son of
Man has come to save what was
lost.'" She says, "My dad used to
tell me a version." She recites,
"In the back of dark theater, two
women are watching a movie and one
of them drops her box of candy—but
she goes up near the screen to
find it. When she gets back to
her seat, the friend says, 'Why
did you look for it up front, you
lost it back here?' And the woman
says, 'I know, but that's where
the light is.'"
The trio laughs, especially
Aunt Mary Frances, who's never
heard that story/joke before. She
looks to see if the priest could
hear, but he's fixated staring at
the wall. She says laughingly,
"Oh Judy, you kill me." Her
inadvertent language halts the
laughter.
Judy goes 180 degrees,
asking, "To know we're gonna die—
do we wish we'd never been born at

all, or would we be better off
dead?"

Rabbi Eli replies, "My eye
shall never see the day I am
better off dead. On that heavenly
day, my soul is all that shall
see."

Reverend Billy Shoe also
replies, "Ya'll know you have to
die, to have had a life."

Sister Zoe Namath, as well,
replies, "It's better to have
lived and lost, than never to have
lived at all."

Aunt Mary Frances
illustrates, "Judy...life is a
Christmas gift from God and your
birth certificate is the receipt.
If you can hand God the receipt,
only then can you return the
gift." She says pragmatically,
"And if you can ask that question—
I am alive with life, and there is
no reason on Earth to answer it."

Judy is perplexed at her
aunt's statement. Judy is
frustrated that Aunt Mary Frances
is not getting a subliminal hint.
Playing Aunt Mary's subconscious,
Judy diverts Mary Frances'
attention to a plaque on the wall.
Judy reads it aloud, attempting
some reverse psychology on her
aunt. "LIFE IS AS LONG AS TODAY—
SO MAKE THE MOST OUT OF IT—LIVE
YOUR LIFE LIKE THERE IS NO
TOMORROW." She implants this

142

warning, "Whatever you do Aunt
Mary Frances, over Hell or high
water, don't think about doctor-
assisted suicide."

Aunt Mary Frances is
appalled. "Suicide? Physician-
assisted suicide?" She says
rationally, "We're all terminally-
ill. You could die in a day, a
week, or sixty-nine years....
Some people don't *start* living
until they *start* dying." She
catechizes, "Suicide is a sin,"
saying wisely, "*And we are all
terminally-ill.*"

SERVICE - PART I
"Entertain"

EVENING

Inside the U.C.A. Life + God
Church, the stage is black but for
a couple of pilot lights.
Reverend Mark's voice is
heard from out of the shadows.
"Life. Of all the creations in
this existence, of all the blades
of grass, or all the stars that
shine—none outnumbers the grains
of sand, from with God's breath,
He made His greatest gift—the life
of just one man."
A single spotlight beams on
Reverend Mark standing center

stage. His voice echoes as he speaks. "Mankind welcome...to the Universal Church of Angels, Life and God."

Like the melodramatic production number at the start of a basketball game—the musical crescendo begins. The lights go dim. Around the auditorium, angel-shaped lights fly; dry ice clouds the stage. From offstage, at a new position at the rear, Mark Anthony intros the originally written theme song. "I am the Reverend Mark Anthony...and I ask you all a question..." The accompanying band and small chorus join in. The rappin' rock and roll song is off! Reverend Mark sings out:

> "[REFRAIN] Do you...
> Agh!
> See...Agh!
> Life...Agh! In God?"

The atmosphere is powerfully energetic. The dozen original disciples, and dozen guests, stout-heartedly sing in response:

> "I do!"
> [END OF REFRAIN]

Reverend Mark sings the countdown:

"1...2...3...4...5...6..."

An elevated platform explodes with dry ice and sparks. Reverend Mark vaults down onto the main stage. The neon sign ignites:

U.C.A. LIFE + GOD

Reverend Mark sings:

> *"God made all of creation from the earth to the Heavens, on the seventh day He rested, do you think He was pleased with it?"*

And the people sang:

> *"I do!"*

> *"Then I ask you all a question...*
> *[REFRAIN AND REPEAT]*
> *Take a breath..."*

Six female dancers choreograph their ballet movements with a hard-rocking Reverend Mark:

> *"God made a man named Adam but he was lone-ly, with a rib He created woman, do you think He was pleased with Eve?...*

[REFRAIN AND REPEAT]
And a one, and a two,
and a one-two..."

A rainbow of laser lights
colors the stage. Glitter streams
from Reverend Mark's hand. Birds,
in the colors of the rainbow, are
released. They fly out the
overhead windows.

"God told a man named
Noah the earth would
be a sea, with a rainbow
He made a promise,
do you think He was
pleased to keep?
[REFRAIN AND REPEAT]
10,9,8...7,6,5...4,3,2,1
..."

With the microphone as his
staff, an electric lift raises a
portion of the stage. A large fan
gusts wind. Reverend Mark's
elaborate wardrobe billows as he
strips down to another layer.

"God sent a holy Moses
to the top of the
mountain, He delivered
10 Commandments,
do you think He was
pleased with them?
[REFRAIN AND REPEAT]
One..."

146

The large cross is lowered
from the ceiling to its permanent
resting-place. It will forever
remain a fixture of this church.

"God gave His only Son;
His name was Jes-us,
He died for all of our
sins, do you think God
was pleased with
Him?..."

"We do!"

Reverend Mark shouts—"Then I
welcome you...to the U.C.A. Life
n' God!" And they all sang:

"Amen!"

Reverend Mark Anthony stands;
stretched out, in a crucified pose
before the mammoth cross; a
glowing tribute to his idol: The
Christ.

D A Y   S E V E N

WORKS II

BORN AGAIN 1

WEDNESDAY - APRIL 19, 2000

MORNING

A park adjoins an
unidentified building; trees and
flowers are abound. The manicured
dirt walkways are aligned with
cot-sized benches; some are
experimentally solar panel
equipped, others have retractable
blankets. A huge sandbox,
cleverly concealed pooper-
scoopers, underground receptacles
and natural tabernacles; await the
two hundred people and their
accompanying pets. The homeless
in the crowd blend in naturally.
The puritan-looking, partisan
rally looks to the podium for:
Chief "Spirit of Life."

The ruggedly handsome, middle-aged, Native American Chief wears a combination of his ancestors clothing and a business suit. "I am Chief Spirit of Life, a Native American. As tribal leader of my nation and CEO of the casino; it is with honor, love and reverence we institute this program to restore the traditions and ancestry of our forefathers, and the divine plan of the Father of Creation, by maintaining the sacred values of both life and Grandmother Earth. Welcome, to the groundbreaking of the first: ADOPTION REGENERATION CENTER OF THE EARTH AND ADAM & EVE CHILD LIFE PRESERVE...the 'ARC in the Park.'"

The people applaud and chant, "Long live life...long live life...long live life..." At the podium, J. Bartholomew Gautama IV, a forty-five-year-old, pale-skinned, brown-haired, classy and powerful, Buddhist businessman claps and chants along.

The Chief counsels, "The parents plan for the neighborhood is that we don't fall prey to the sinful scavenger Satan who roams Mother Earth feeding on souls. I quote from Moses' fifth book: 'I call heaven and earth as witnesses today against you, that I have set before you life and death,

149

blessing and cursing; therefore choose life, that both you and your descendants may live...'"

The people clamor, "Pro—choose life...pro—choose life ...pro—choose life..."

The Chief entreats, "Those who neglect to consider the adoption option, especially the one percent yearly who think their unwanted pregnancies due to rape, incest, or birth defects are necessary—I speak to you this infinite wisdom." He charges, "Truth, no lie, the only two factors which influence the physical, mental and moral growth of a child—are genes and environment. Genes and parental environment are the determining factors in the evolution of all children. And no matter which one is unhealthy or unproductive—God, God the Great and Holy Mystery, can remedy them both. Truth, no lie, there is never, *never* a reason on Mother Earth to have an abortion. Heed the lesson in nature: the mother, she is constantly in danger. To destroy newborn life is unnatural. Look at the sage, or the fish; the aged die, so the young may live. That is the nature of life." He explains, "It is my inherent understanding that the person who will not, so much as, step on an

150

ant—will kill anything. But, the
man or woman who can kill even the
egg of another—can kill anything.
After all, there is nothing, no
nothing, more meaningful than a
life." He concludes, "And after
we kill each other, there will be
nothing left for us to kill.... I
cry, long live..."

In the Roman's bedroom;
Maggie is alone in the black,
satin-sheeted bed wearing a black,
silk negligee. She rises.

At the rally; Cally Pope is
the almost twenty-year-old,
perfectly pretty, blonde
Californian speaking at the dais.
"...mother and housewife, bringing
up a little boy and girl, and a
pet dog. I wonder how, when the
time comes to teach them about the
birds and the bees; I'll explain
the fact of life that not even the
animals kill their own unborn.
Gifted as man is to be the most
intelligent of all creatures, we
are also the stupidest. We kill
not only our four-legged friends,
but we kill each other—how foolish
to the survival of our own
species. Man, in breaking the
laws of nature, is the only animal
that kills out of hatred—not like
the wildlife who do so for natural
survival. In my home, man and
beast are as one, and the spirit
of death has no resting-place..."

The rainbow-clothed people applaud whenever possible. Now is possible.

Pope says, "When you discuss your parenthood choice with the man you've offered up your body to God with—if you hear him say, 'Have the baby'; he is held close to God. If he says, 'Abort, don't have the baby'; then he is evil. He dances with the devil—that's that. And if your man abandons you—God, your first Father—is there to stand by you. This is why women are the only persons who can have a baby—with God being the only true Father—you are never alone. God is not a woman, but He is in her. He expects you to give..."

In the bedroom, Maggie dresses in a hip, entirely black outfit including mink coat. She slips on her gloves, boots, and black shades.

At the rally, Cally is saying, "...a fact of faith, adoption is like an Easter egg hunt. If everyone who had an Easter egg would let it hatch—then everyone on the hunt would have a little chick. The Easter bunny has a way of naturally balancing these things out. I have compassion for people who cannot have children, but don't let science be your guide—let your

152

guardian angel be. What is not
meant to be—so be it, God needs
people who will adopt. It gives
the abortion-minded an easier
adoption option." She
illustrates, "Put it this way:
some baskets have no Easter eggs,
while other baskets are filled
with fake straw; artificial
baskets get filled with plastic
eggs. Trust me, *there are enough*
unwanted, natural, Easter eggs
being hatched. If the Easter
bunny wanted to leave an Easter
egg in everybody's basket—he
would. He's the Easter bunny..."

An Islamic, African-American
man, in his thirties, named
Mlaykiki Hâyat-Alláh yells out,
"What about race?"

She cracks, "How much
livelier the Easter parade, when
the white and colored eggs are
mixed together."

The people love this analogy.
They cheer and throw flowers at
the podium.

Cally tells them, "'Show me a
miracle, then I'll believe.' How
many times have I heard this?
There is no greater miracle than
the miracle of birth or life: not
Old Testament, not New—whether of
this earth or not of this
earth.... Generations have gone
lifetimes looking to see a
miracle—when always just a

heartbeat away, right before our very eyes, the miracle of birth happens every day!"

The crowd cries, "Ask me, says the baby! Ask me, says the baby!"

"Long before the Lord and all the disciples and prophets—there was the beginning. And in God's perfect creation, He made Adam, the one man, alone. And His Adam longed only for what he had not. So God, in all His glory, made woman; not as He made man, to not only be man's wife; it was in the body and soul of woman, that God made Eve—with the power and choice to create another life..."

The people's applause grows...

"...God gave the world to Adam—but He gave mankind to Eve!"

...the applause crescendos.

"Can't you see a woman with child is the most blessed of God's creations—within her: the Son of Man. I tell you openly, selfishness is a sin to sacrifice. It is selfish not to opt for adoption. In the end, selfishness is the lone reason a woman has an abortion; her life is more meaningful than the next life. To sacrifice lives to abortion is a sin. To God, the redeemer of sin, the living sacrifice is..."

The people chorus, "Life!"
It's as if the sound waves
resonate to Michael's hearing. At
the backyard lake, Michael is in
the rowboat. Briefcase on his
lap, he writes diligently in a
charcoal black, loose-leaf binder.

At the front of the property,
Maggie boards her truck in the
driveway. She checks her watch.
It's as if a voice from the rally
carries to Maggie's brain. "...as
we know it, would cease to exist
if a woman sold her soul."

At the rally, the voice
originates from a working class
mom. The woman is in her early
forties. She is pretty, with a
dignified elegance and warm-faced
motherly appeal. She is in an
impassioned debate with a
counterpart. The shameful woman
she speaks with is unkempt and
overweight in her tight slacks.
She's a TV talk show-type. She's
saying, "Hell, I would never in a
million years give a live human
being away. I'd be too ashamed.
People, what would they think?
I'd rather just keep killing the
eggs."

The working class mom
replies, "People? Who are you
kidding? Who cares what society
thinks? Let God, not your
conscience, be your guide. He'll
forgive you for past abortions,

155

but if you walk away from here
today believing like you do—Heaven
help you."

Maggie is driving the Rover.
Her profile, in the auto window,
appears behind the reflections of
the roadside buildings she passes:
a hospital, a church, *Toys R' Us*,
a school and playground, a *Chuck
E' Cheeses* restaurant, and a
cemetery.

Michael is at the lake. The
sunlight breaks on him. He speaks
in prayer, "God, knowing you as I
do. I can't picture what dying is
even like—*everyone else dies*.
With you, I've been there and
back. I can't imagine what life
would be like without you." From
afar, he seems to vanish as he
lies back in the boat.

At the rally, Mlaykiki is
having a tenuous discussion.
"...friends Izzy, Zeke and I, were
just speaking about the prophetic
books of the Bible and now this."
He discerns, "When the things I
see and hear in prayer come true—
then I read them in the Bible—how
can I not believe in God?" He
explains, "Every story told in the
Bible is an example or prediction
of stories today—people don't know
that, only everything is
multiplied—most of all: death,
murder and killing...suicide, the

death penalty, and now abortion—
just like Izzy and Zeke said....
You should see these two: Izzy's
skinny-as-a-rail, and Zeke's big
as a mountain."

The man, with whom Mlaykiki
speaks, is best described as a
beefy jerk in his late twenties.
He has a comedic mind of his own.
The beefy jerk declaims, "Sounds
like cartoons, but don't be dumb
you idiot—abortion ain't killing.
Nobody punishes you when you do
it, so it's okay." He claims,
"Ain't nothin' that ain't here
ever more important than me or
anybody else who is." He depicts,
"Abortion's only like returning a
Christmas present you don't want."

Mlaykiki argues, "When
aborting the life, do the mother
and father think so little of
themselves to not believe their
child might be the next genius,
world leader or star? Regardless
of your religious beliefs—how do
you think God may be sending the
next prophet: The Brahman, the
Buddha, Confucius, Moses, my
Muhammad, me or you? *Where would
the world be if when God sent a
prophet or savior, we had it
aborted?*"

The beefy jerk exclaims, "Hey
'Bub,' I got my rights, I'm a
voter, I'm protesting, so keep
your opinions to yourself and mind

your own beeswax!" He shoves
Mlaykiki and Mlaykiki shoves him
back. They get into a heated
match.

On the road by the railroad,
a snail is racing on a railroad
rail. The wind blows his shell to
safety. Maggie barrels through
the red crossing signal—narrowly
missing the engine car. The snail
moves on.

At the rally, a thirty-nine-
year-old man, with tightly cropped
hair and standing shorter than
average in height, speaks with a
distinctive voice.
"...Assemblyman Cain Pettograsso.
That dispute over protest was just
as I have with my political
colleagues daily. Who is right?
Who is wrong? Who is weak? Who
is strong? I am a Christian, and
to be the best of all, I must be
servant to all."

The people cheer. Cain's
baby is hoisted onto the lectern.
His wife, and his five, ten, and
fifteen-year-old kids look on.
"Children, let the Commandments be
your Constitution: God first,
family second, country third."

The people wave their
banners. The signs read:

•PEOPLE WHO PREACH ABORTION SHOULD
BE THANKFUL THEY HAD PARENTS WHO
DIDN'T

•YOUR CHOICE...WILL BE YOUR CHILDS LAST
•YOU SAY—"ABORTION," YOUR UNBORN CHILD SAYS—"MOM"

"Religion, speech, press, assembly, and petition: the first Amendment of the Bill of Rights; the Constitution of the United States of America, guarantees the freedom of worship and religious practice...the right to speak without prior restraint and the right to publish and disseminate information..."

Local Christian church members distribute flyers with a poetic verse written on them.

The assemblyman continues, "The right of the people to congregate for discussion of public questions...and a request to a public official that seeks to correct a wrong or to influence public policy." The assemblyman accordingly asks, "Question: Adoption or abortion?"

The people carol, "Opt for adoption!" They chant, "Opt for adoption! Opt for adoption..."

The assemblyman attests, "If you protest against the abortion-minded and the government in the ways of the past—you will be defeated, put out. Their hatred and anger are like fuel for a torch and fire. The two will burn

159

and fight each other to death."
He says, "If you wish to freely
protest—do so. Here's how the
Lord works, in *not-so mysterious
ways*, and it calls for the one
person: each and every one of
you." He endorses, "In absolute
silence, sit in or outside a
clinic. Cross yourself: in the
name of The Father, The Son and
The Holy Ghost...and pray. Pray.
Pray for the archangel St. Michael
so that the mother is not
possessed by the spirit that is
death but guided by the Spirit
that is life. The devil fears
God. With a peaceful, personal
prayer of protest—the heavenly
hosts and Holy Spirit attack with
the good guilt of godliness from
within and the evil spirits
retreat." He forewarns, "But
beware and be strong, on the other
hand, Satan works his magic and
his evil anger is exorcised out—
and he won't soon disappear—for
the abortion-minded too, fear
God." He contends, "If the evil
one wins the battle, pray for St.
Michael in the war for the soul of
the child—that it be laid to rest
in the hand of God."

     The first half of the people
clamor, "If abortion is right?..."
The second half of the people cry
out, "...Who's left?"

Cain refers to the
Declaration of Independence to
illustrate his next point.
"Declare your independence this
day from death, and declare your
dependency on life. For in the
declaration of our forefathers,
men of religious righteousness:
George Washington, Thomas
Jefferson, and the greatest of the
great, Abraham Lincoln—all swore
to these words and phrases, each
before the word government appears
a single solitary time." He
reads, "And I quote, 'When in the
course of human events...people
among the powers of the earth...to
which the laws of nature and of
God entitle...mankind declare
truths that are created by their
Creator...with rights that are
life...'"
        The people applaud.
        "Next sentence, 'that to
secure these rights...whenever any
form of government becomes
destructive of these ends, it is
the Right of the People to alter
or to abolish it...'"
        The people retain their
applause.
        "You've heard of—'winning the
battle and losing the war'; battle
the government against the war on
abortion. But more significantly,
wage war on the killing spirit
within each and every one of you.

161

The government may do what they
do, but no one can preside over
the God-given right of free will
that rule and govern over you..."

The people applause reaches
its crowning point.

"God loves the sinner—He
hates the sin. God loves
democracy—He hates the death."

Inside the Rover, Maggie's
hand steers the wheel. Her foot
rams the pedal. Her eyes blaze
with intensity.

The assemblyman visualizes,
by saying, "At times, it's like
viewing a monster movie. The
government is the monster's body.
It is supported by the peoples two
legs, but once the head gets
cutoff—the separate body takes on
a life if its own. Each leg needs
to stand for what is right, rather
than stamp out all that we have
left. The severed head voices,
but the body has a mind of its
own."

He vies, "Roe versus Wade;
adoption versus abortion; the
Commandments versus the
Constitution; God versus
government; life versus death; do
not fight fire with fire. Fire
does not extinguish a flame—water
does. Fight fire with water;
water stops the fire from
burning."

The people applaud.

The Chief whispers to Cain, "It's seven before nine, better move it, they are rapidly approaching."

The assemblyman provokingly punctuates by saying, "In closing, I ask the people recite the great Commandments in, and of, our protest poem, *The Adoption Equation.*"

The people chorus, "One, love thy God—Two, love thy neighbor—Half mom, half dad—Three, makes a baby."

They rhyme the carol:

> *"One, love thy God—Two,*
> *love thy neighbor—*
> *Half mom, half dad—*
> *Three, makes a baby...*
> *One, love thy God—Two,*
> *love thy neighbor—*
> *Half mom, half dad—*
> *Three, makes a baby."*

With everyone at the podium singing along, Maggie zooms up in her truck. She marches, behind the handful of white-clad abortion clinic employees, onto the rally scene.

Assemblyman Cain Pettograsso sanctions, "Thank you Michael Angelo Roman for your $50,000-plus contribution—praise you—wherever you are."

The Chief whoops, "Sorry.
We're closed!"

Maggie is infuriated. The
people celebrate. The dignitaries
cut the red ribbon with a
tomahawk. Neon green confetti is
tossed. A monumental amount of
pink, baby blue and white balloons
are released.

TRIALS & TRIBULATIONS 1

MORNING - P.S.T.

That morning, at California
Superior Court, the courtroom is
packed with an array of religious
leaders; included are a Mother
Theresa-looking nun, a Muslim
leader, and a Catholic Cardinal.
Also in attendance are some
bikers, and Mr. and Mrs. Parkinson
and their attorney. Present as
well are the Weissman's; who are
three generations of Hasidic
Hebrew lawyers each wearing a
yellow necktie; and a general
cross-section of society. Seated
prominently behind the prosecution
is the victim: Hillary Paul. She
possesses red-streaked, black
hair; and tattoos. She is
alluring in a demonic way. She's
short, and wears a denim biker
skirt to match. A large section

of perimeter seating is reserved
for press coverage, but no TV.

The judge enters. The
bailiff announces, "All rise. The
Superior Court of the State of
California is now in session. The
honorable Pietro Caesaro DePilate
presiding."

On the bench is Pietro
Caesaro DePilate. The Italian,
sixty-year-old, has solid gray
hair with prominent black
eyebrows. He is distinguished in
appearance. He speaks with an
Italian accent. Judge DePilate
tells those in the courtroom, "You
may be seated." He tells the
opposing attorneys, "In the case
of the people and Ms. Hillary Paul
versus the defendant, Lesliannas
Von Adolf—the prosecution may
open."

The prosecution is headed by
Thurgood Stone, a cocky, light-
complexioned, black attorney in
his early thirties. "Thurgood U.
Stone for the people Your Honor,
with Urim Af-Thummim, co-counsel."
His co-counsel is an Egyptian man
in his late twenties.

Stone states, "The people
will subsist, depend, on the cold
hard facts. We need call one, and
only one, witness." He explains,
"The surviving victim's
corroboration, or agreement, with
the five pieces of evidence,

should speak for itself." He
says, "In the death of the
deceased, dead, victim—the unborn
child, who cries from the grave—
the people will be seeking the
retaliatory, just, execution-
style, penalty of death."

The judge asks, "Does the
defense wish to make a statement?"

"Your Honor, Abraham Lincoln
Peters for the defense. I'm
joined by my able-bodied
assistant, Ms. Harriet S. Camael."
Camael is the tight-hairdo,
workman-like, female seated
adjacent to him. Lincoln tells
judge and jury, "If it pleases the
court—the defense will
systematically compare,
numerically, the sworn affidavits
of my client with that of Hillary
Paul's sworn deposition: A checks
and balances process to determine
who is bearing false witness
against whom. It is our
contention; the murder against the
unborn must have been self-
inflicted."

Hillary Paul takes the stand.
Lincoln eyes her wantonly. Seated
at the defense table; Lesliannas
Von Adolf, in a pale yellow prison
dress, pays little attention. She
begins pencil sketching on a
yellow, legal pad. The back of
her right hand flows smoothly.
She is still partially shackled.

166

Two, posted, prison guards hover by her.

The bailiff, Bible in hand, asks Hillary Paul, "Do you swear to tell the truth, the whole truth and nothing but the truth?"

She replies, "Yeah, I do."

The bailiff says to her, "State your complete name and date of birth for the record."

She replies, "Hillary Marta Paul, February 29, 1972."

Stone throws his first question at her, "Miss Paul, would you perpetrate, commit, this crime against another inmate: an abortion?"

She replies, "No. In prison, an abortion like this is a crime; out there in the real world is where it's legal."

Stone gathers the first item off the evidence table. "I present evidentiary exhibit A: Miss Paul's bloodied, standard-issue prison uniform. It is tattooed with the scars of life, and finger printed with that of the deadly—the accused." He displays the second item: "Exhibit B..."

The spectators cannot see the weapon, only the witness, and the jury. Stone asks her, "Miss Paul, is this the murder weapon?"

Hillary answers, "Yeah. That's what she almost killed me with—shoved it right up me."

Stone shows the witness— "Exhibit C..." He asks her, "Can you identify this?"

Paul answers, "Yeah, that's the empty container of jam she smeared on my cell wall. There's the red apple on it." On the shiny silver seal, a red apple indicates the flavor.

Stone presents—"The final two items...the bloody writing implement, pencil, with the prints of both women—it belongs to the defendant—and, her personal Bible." He asks, "Miss Paul, do you recognize these items marked D and E?"

Hillary replies, "That's the pencil her and me fought with... and that Bible she always writes in...*Miss Born Again*, I wouldn't touch that." At the defense table, Lesliannas' hand sketches her drawing on the legal pad.

Stone tells the court, "I relinquish, give over, the questions to co-counsel." Stone relinquishes the questioning to his partner.

Counselor Af-Thummim formally introduces himself to the witness. He cants, "I, as an expert on human nature, ask you Miss Paul—I know women don't like to talk about it, it's difficult I understand, but to gain sympathy for your eventual freedom—would you do this to yourself?"

She replies, "Not for my freedom or like my life was more important if that's what you people think. For now this killin' got me out, but I got to live with it. What if it starts hauntin' me later like a ghost? Will I ever be free? Sometimes livin' with guilt is worse than dying without it."

He says, "Last question: What was our final belief on what might happen, if you, a victim, did not actively pursue the death penalty—and the accused was found guilty and years later released on parole?"

She answers, "I think they'd probably be happier if you didn't try for the death penalty to kill them back. I mean, I would, I'd probably buy you a drink. But, I can't take that chance; it's best if I, we, just kill her now."

Af-Thummim tells the court, "That is all." He tells Lincoln, "Your witness..."

Lincoln nonchalantly approaches with Hillary Paul's statement in hand. He digs her and is almost playful. "Hello, Hillary. I'm going to make this short and sweet like you. I'll

169

read my client's version of the
events, that we've numbered, and
you recount yours. We'll do a
little paint-by-numbers to see if
we can get a better picture." He
gives the judge a copy. "Your
Honor, I enter in Exhibit F: the
famed fondue fork..." The
courtroom mutters in astonishment.
A couple of people giggle.
Lincoln is amused with himself.
"Inside joke." He straightens up.
"I'll begin."

He reads, "Miss Von Adolf
claims, Number One: 'I walked by
her [Paul's] cell to wish her best
on her parole hearing Monday
morning.' Number Two: 'I also
said a prayer because she [Paul]
was blessed with child.' ...And
you said?"

Hillary Paul, reading over
her statement, responds, "One:
'She come by my cell, I suspect to
say good luck the next day.' Two:
'...and 'cause I think she was
jealous she had no rug rats.'"

Lincoln tells her, "Good.
Okay, okay..." Lincoln takes the
metal hanger, from the enclosed
plastic, and begins to stow it in
his coat.

He reads, "Three: 'concealed
beneath her [Von Adolf's] bed she
removed a hanger'" He uses the
hanger for a prop joke. "My spare

set of car keys—I've been looking all over for these."

This time more laugh, a few are outwardly shocked. Thurgood Stone leaps, yelling, "I obje—" Urim yanks him in. Stone, having been assessed of his rival's maneuver, says, "—retract, withdraw, never mind."

Lincoln says to her, "Your Number Three..."

Hillary Paul reads, "Three: 'From under her [Von Adolf's] dress she whips out a hanger.'"

Lincoln now uses the hanger as an antenna that rotates above his head. He jests, "Go ahead, Number Four and Number Five—but watch, I'm picking up a signal, I'm getting some interference, there's a discrepancy here."

Hillary Paul reads, "Four: 'She [Von Adolf] jams it up me, trying to kill me and it...' Five: '...and I miscarried my insides.'"

Lincoln reads from the text, "Four: '...and sadly destroys her [Paul's] own body and that unborn new life...I feel sorry,' Five: 'I feel sorry, and I know God will forgive anyone who ever did something like that.'"

Hillary has momentarily lost place in her statement. She is not unsettled; but she stutters, "Six...six, six: 'but that's the

171

way women her [Von Adolf's] age used to do it."

Lincoln reads Von Adolf's Number Six—"'I hope that's not what women choose to do legally in the world today.' Seventh..."

Among the courtroom observers, a nun crosses herself and says, "Heavens forbid, God I hope not."

Lincoln continues with Von Adolf's Seventh: "'There was blood all downside her [Paul's] dress.'" Lincoln unfurls, from the bag, the dress in question. The bloodstain almost resembles a fetus.

Hillary Paul reads, "My Number Seven: 'there was blood gushin' out like a fountain.'"

Among the spectators, a woman weeps, "God, I can't watch."

A Muslim leader tells her, "The truth hurts, but the truth—"

A Catholic Cardinal tells them, "He died for us."

Lincoln reads, "Eight: 'I reached out to physically and spiritually take hold of her [Paul], saying, please believe in the Gospel.'"

Hillary Paul screams, "Don't believe that!" She reads, "Number Eight is: 'We fought with the pencil, and I jabbed her [Von Adolf's] side.'"

Lincoln reads, "'The Holy Spirit overcame me—with my pencil, I noted a Scripture left for the disciples according to John...'" Lincoln opens the pencil and uses the eraser to thumb the Bible. He tucks the pencil in his ear. He continues reading: "'If you forgive the sins of any, they are forgiven them; if you retain the sins of any, they are retained....' Duly noted here..."

He asks Hillary, "The infamous Number Nine: Miss Paul?"

Paul reads, "'I gave her [Von Adolf] the red jam she forgot at dinner and she [Von Adolf] wrote some satanic cult thing on the wall. At the time I couldn't remember it, but it got smeared. That's how we'd know it was her [Von Adolf], in case she [Von Adolf] lied.'"

Lincoln tells Hillary, "She swears you must've wrote on the wall."

Paul tells Lincoln, "Then see, we were right, she lied."

Lincoln reads, "Her Number Ten was: 'I told her [Paul] it was Palm Sunday; I would pray to Christ on the cross for forgiveness and repentance, and to Raphael for healing.' Eleven: 'I went crying to my friend the guard.' Twelve: 'Then I took my pencil, and Bible, and went to

pray in my little sanctuary.'
Finish yours, Miss Paul..."

Hillary Paul reads, "'Then I
screamed to the "C.O."; and
Twelve: 'the rest is history.'"

Lincoln says, "That concludes
the statements." He asks the
witness, "Last question: Hillary,
why do you think Lesliannas Von
Adolf did this after all this
time?"

Hillary Paul responds,
"Killers kill. People who don't—
don't. There's only two kinds of
people: those who've already
killed and those who haven't yet."

Lincoln presents her the
hanger and a leer. "Here, hang
around after." He tells the
judge, "Your Honor, go ahead and
reserve the right to recall." He
mumbles, "I just like looking at
her."

Judge DePilate says, "Very
well. We'll reconvene this
afternoon with closing arguments.
Court adjourned."

Appearing suddenly, at the
defense table, is an elderly, very
elderly janitor. He's equipped
with flaming orange hair and a
spotless white outfit. He totes a
three-foot long, bright orange
flashlight and a mini-oxygen tank.
The janitor tells Lincoln, "Goin'
home, just remembered found this
here when I came on this morning."

He gives Lincoln a large, white envelope.

Lincoln takes no notice of the envelope and gives it to Ms. Camael. She reads the cover to herself. Lincoln sarcastically says to him, "Hey, 'Old Man.' How's business at the morgue?" Lincoln asks Camael, "Who's it from?"

Camael answers, "Just says: FOR DEFENSE—IN CASE OF LIFE OR DEATH."

Lincoln asks her, "Postmarked?"

She says, "Sabbathiel, Somewhere..."

Lincoln tells her, "I ain't tryin' to win—let it fly."

SOS - SUICIDE OR SELF-DESTRUCTION
1

APPX: 10:45 - E.S.T.

In the religious art shop, music plays from a portable radio, shaped like a ladybug, next to the cash register. A genuine ladybug creeps along the open page of David's Psalm 23. Mary Frances readies to dine on her lunch; canned salmon, a small jar of applesauce, pita bread, and water sustain her. She is seated at the

register reciting grace aloud.
"In the name of The Father, The
Son and The Holy Ghost.... Psalm
23: 'You spread the table before
me in the sight of my foes; You
anoint my head with oil; my cup
overflows. Only goodness and
kindness follow me all the days of
my life; And I shall dwell in the
house of the LORD for years to
come.'"

A Caucasian, poor woman in
her early forties approaches with
a bag of merchandise. Mary
Frances inserts a picture Bible in
the bag. She quickly hits the
'no-sale' button. The register
drawer slings open and shut. The
poor woman relays her gratitude
for the charity. Mary Frances is
understanding and compassionate.

Judy enters from the back
room toting a fast food lunch.
Mary Frances partakes in a forkful
of fish. The poor woman leaves.
Judy yells, "Mary Frances!" Aunt
Mary Frances jumps. She chokes on
the fish. She battles the twinge
of pain in her chest. Judy is
semi-frozen in her own tracks.
She yells out, to her aunt, "The
water!"

Aunt Mary Frances is
unflappable. Instinctively, she
splashes her fingers in the glass,
crosses her forehead, and mightily
expels a gulp of air. A dime

dislodges from her throat. It rings the fish can. Judy nears. A thankful Aunt Mary Frances crosses herself again. She says to Judy, "Oh, you scared me to death!"

Judy tells her, "That's what you get for eating fish." She demeaningly says, "For Christ's sake, what's the matter with you? How's that woman going to learn a lesson on the value of money?"

"That woman is my best, most loyal customer. She comes here; well, religiously, every Wednesday. She's afraid to go to mass, so this is her church. She's illiterate, can't read or write—all she wants on Earth is to understand the Word of God." Aunt Mary Frances advises her niece, "If there is a lesson to be learned—it's that church is free. If you're *forced* to pay—stay away. I tell her, as a Roman Catholic—I've yet to see someone evicted from church for not feeding the basket." She explains, "God does not want your money. He wants your sacrifice, your time, your life. If you spend your time making money—then sacrifice *it*. If not, then give your time and your life—because God's sacrifice gives you the time of your life. God bless you, Judy, if you ever cast that humble child away."

Judy is somewhat remorseful. Aunt
Mary Frances flips a bookmark from
the Bible. She hands the Bible to
Judy. Aunt Mary Frances asks her,
"Judy, please read this Scripture
aloud—"

Judy reads: "'When the Son of
Man comes in His glory, escorted
by all the angels of heaven, He
will sit upon His royal
throne...'" The door chimes ring;
Sister Zoe, Reverend Billy, and
Rabbi Eli orderly parade in. A
gust of wind captures the closing
door, and the priest blows in. A
yellow pad in his hand, intently,
he positions himself staring out
the window. Judy loses her spot
in the text. She again reads:
"'...The King will say to those on
His right: "Come. You have my
Father's blessing! Inherit the
kingdom prepared for you from the
Creation of the world: For I was
hungry and you gave Me food; I was
thirsty and you gave Me drink. I
was a stranger and you welcomed
me, naked and you clothed Me. I
was ill and you comforted Me, in
prison and you came to visit Me."
Then the just will ask Him: "Lord,
when did we see You hungry and
feed You, or thirsty and give You
drink? When did we welcome You
away from home or clothe You in
your nakedness? When did we visit
You when You were ill or in

prison?"'" Judy looks at Aunt
Mary Frances and finishes from
memory—"In whatever you do to the
least of my children—that you do
unto me."

Rabbi Eli tells Aunt Mary
Frances, "We came to take you to
lunch."

Reverend Billy says, "Let's
all break some bread."

Sister Zoe says, "Come on
Judy, you too."

Judy responds by holding up
her bag and burger. She jokingly
taunts the trio by taking a
monstrous bite out of a bacon
double cheeseburger.

Aunt Mary Frances scolds,
"Judy!" She says to her friends,
"Bless your hearts, thank you, but
I've work to do."

Judy, with a polite mouthful,
says, "Um! Meat."

Rabbi Eli tells her, "Meat to
you—life to some."

Judy asks, "Vegetarians?"

Reverend Billy answers, "One
and all. We don't need it to
survive, and we won't die if we
don't eat it."

Judy asks, "Sister Zoe?"

Sister Zoe sheepishly says,
"I'd rather pet a squirrel than
eat a cow—just as I'd rather have
a pig for a pet than I would for
dinner." Aunt Mary Frances and
friends applaud the

characteristically meek and soft-spoken Sister Zoe.

Judy returns to her meal.

The others open up a spiritual and intellectual discussion. Rabbi Eli has honed himself on the Holy Book—high and mighty, he quotes: "'Now a word was secretly brought to me, and my ear received a whisper of it. In disquieting thoughts from the visions of the night, when deep sleep falls on men.' 4:12." He haughtily says, "Mary Frances, like a dream, a vision, a life that flashes before your eyes, you watch, but devoid of wisdom you do not see. This image shines not from you, but at you. The spirit is in the story; Scripture stories once seen and told—when written last a lifetime, and a lifetime of generations. See for yourself, not the vision, but the proverbial *writing on the wall.* Read for yourself the meaning, which is written in the Book—the Book of Life. 'Now acquaint yourself with Him, and be at peace; Thereby good will come to you. Receive, please, instruction from His mouth, and lay up His words in your heart.' 22:21." He asks her, "Have you looked to the Hebrew Book? To the historic, poetic, literary masterpiece—the Old Testament Book of Job?"

Mary Frances confirms for the scholar she has studied Sacred Scripture; submissive, she quotes: "'What strength that I have that I should endure, and what is my limit that I should be patient?' Eli, Job is my biblical mentor." She subscribes, "For Job had no story on which to draw faith and human experience. His life was truly between God his Creator and himself: One-on-one, God one with mankind and God one with man. The Lord Himself spoke to Job. My story is a ladybug on the back of a hippopotamus in contrast to Job's. I pray I could be that holy, that faithful, to be personally spoken to by God. Then, above all, be made to make such a miraculous recovery." She informs them: "'Why are not times set by the Almighty, and why do His friends not see His days?' Friends, Job is my soul inspiration."

Reverend Billy works with the Word, well-versed, he quotes: "Job 8: 'Look for a moment at ancient wisdom; consider the truths our fathers learned. Our life is short, we know nothing at all; we pass like shadows across the earth.'" He wryly says, "Mary Frances, Job was right with goodness and faith; but he questioned God to learn and

understand why bad things happen
to good people. If Job were
wrong, he would have gained no
such knowledge when bad fell on
him. He wouldn't have known the
difference. The wrong people
think they've got life's right
answers, wrong for them seems
right. Job 25: 'Can anyone be
righteous or pure in God's sight?'
Job was right to ask—a man among
men. He was never in *denial* over
the condition he was in."

Mary Frances quotes: "Job: 'I
know well that it is so; but how
can a man be justified before God?
Should one wish to contend with
Him, he could not answer Him once
in a thousand times.'" She
willfully says, "Billy, I will not
deny it—once is enough. God bless
Job. Job's actions got him a
personal lesson from God that
saved Job's life—and enlightened
all of mankind." She instructs
them in the ways of the Word:
"Job: 'I will teach you the manner
of God's doings and the way of the
Almighty I will not conceal.'
Friends, now, 'The King of Kings,'
Christ on the cross, in His
sacrificial pain and suffering,
personally took my life with Him.
So now, I don't have to save my
own. God's love for us; that is
what saved Job."

Sister Zoe turgidly says, "Mary Frances, if our lives are healed mercifully by divine intervention, by our love, through prayer, or our labor for the Lord, then it is God who saves us; but if we are freed from our misery by any other method known to man, then it is from the devil." She too, has been taught the Book. She tutorially quotes: "Job, chapter 20, verses 4 and 5: 'Do you not know this from olden time, since man was placed upon the earth, that the triumph of the wicked is short, and the joy of the impious for a moment.' I believe that is the spirit of Job." Even Sister Zoe's confidence has her lecturing Mary Frances.

Mary Frances' steadfastness and intellect are superior. Mary Frances says, "I, I believe, with power of prayer to guide me—the timeless story of Job may not lie in what is written about sacrificial pain. Conspicuous to me in its absence—is what is not mentioned one solitary time in the Book of Job: suicide." She unalterably says, "Pain is a fact of life—suicide is the end of life. Parents tell their children, 'the facts of life.' The fact of life is—since a mother-less Adam originally sinned, pain is present before the human existence of every life begins. The word is—labor; a mother in labor, doing God's work giving birth—a sacrificial pain, a labor of love. A mother cries out in pain before every male or female child cries for the first time. Even after conception, a mother's pain relays to the unborn child the fact." In subservience, she says, "Hail, Mother Mary who bore the pain of birth for God's only Son. Christ, as the Son of Man, labored His life with the sacrificial pain of all mankind, with His never-ending love, only to die and rise, free and forgive; every man, woman, and child on Earth for the original sin that leads all our lives to death." She concludes, "The act of belief, faith, and love by Job—never to have attempted suicide—is the gift of Job's life. Death is the devil's answer to the question of why there is pain and suffering. Furthermore, suicide is the worship of that evil answer...God made life to last—that is why He created it in the first place." She incontrovertibly says, "True story...Job lived because he did not commit suicide."

Judy is done eating. She is frustrated at her aunt's piety. She fires a barbed question at her. "Aunt Mary Frances—why is it of all the religious, biblical, holy people you speak of: Adam; Noah; Abraham; Moses; Job; Mary and Joseph; Matthew; 'The King of King's,' God the Father and God the Son—why is it so life-threatening that you believe, and I know you believe, don't lie, that an angel chose you now to be the saintly spokesperson on the sin of suicide—say it, 'Hail Mary, Full of Grace, The Lord is with Thee'"?

Rabbi Eli asks, "Yes? What miraculous act that will change the course of human history?"

Reverend Billy also asks, "Yeah? What could God have in store for you? The fact is you are dying as we speak."

Sister Zoe as well, asks, "*Oúi*? What dream come true?"

Mary Frances answers them, "I do not know. But I know He knows! The fact is: I'm alive, so God wants me alive." She purports, "Maybe by the fact, my personal relationship with His Son will be enough in His eyes. Maybe by the fact, I'm allowed to just die in my sleep, wake up in Heaven, and my life was my dream. Maybe by the fact, all I ever do on Earth is say to Him, 'Thank you God, we're even...this life will never end in suicide.'"

185

Judy finalizes the discussion with her aunt on her own terms. Judy says, "So sacrificial pain gives glory to God and gains oneness with Him?"

Aunt Mary Frances coins, "If you win the jackpot—do you beg for food? But, if you're dying of hunger—don't you search high and low for the breadwinner?"

Judy derives, "You gain from the pain."

Aunt Mary Frances says to her, "That's a winner."

The priest—staring out the window—seems to vanish from Aunt Mary's Frances' sight. Her pain beckons. Unnoticeable to all but Mary Frances, she dismisses the oddity. The tension and strife have taken their toll: Mary Frances, especially, who weakest, has been strongest. A twinge of pain attacks her.

The friends march for the exit. Rabbi Eli says, "We had better go to lunch."

Reverend Billy tells her, "Mary Fran, you keep the faith now 'ya hear?"

Sister Zoe says to her, "We'll see you this evening."

Judy says to them, "Later.... Hey you guys—*get a Job*." Everyone's laughter subsides. A Muslim man and a Buddhist man are the only

186

customers remaining in the store.
In pain, Mary Frances goes back to
work. Judy confronts her. She
asks, "What on Earth are you
doing?"

Aunt Mary Frances says,
"God's given me work to do."

"You're dying. If you're
gonna keep working—you might as
well end it now. It'll all work
out in the end—right?!"

"Judy love, do you believe in
God as the Creator?"

"Naturally."

"Then you must know this rule
of nature: If you quit on anything
today—you'll quit on life in the
end...I did not come forty years
to quit now. If I am to die, time
needs to take its natural course.
Who knows what or who God has in
store for me? I have a lot of
unfinished business. This is the
holiest week of the year. Last
Sunday was Palm Sunday, tomorrow's
Pesach and Holy Thursday, then
Good Friday, Holy Saturday, Easter
Sunday, coming up is *I'da el Adha*
for the Muslim faithful; God
bless, they love Gabriel angels."

Judy says, "We're Catholic.
Who cares about those other
religions?"

"Christ does for one.
Secondly, I do. There are many
religions Judy, but only one true
God." Aunt Mary Frances speaks

about the customers; "For that
Buddhist man celebrating Wesak—the
first noble truth in his belief is
that—suffering is universal. What
denomination is pain? What
religion is suffering? For that
Muslim man, angels saved Isaac's
life. What religion is the angel
Gabriel? It's my job and I'll be
damned, if I don't show that man a
symbolic angel that may deliver to
the Islamic people God's message
to stop terrorist killing." She
says to Judy, "If by fate, I may
see everyone I know these final
days—any murderous end to my
natural existence will rob me of
these upcoming valuable moments in
my life; the final words, the
apologies, the 'I love you's'—it
would truly be for me, a fate
worse than death. Let it go. God
knows what He's doing."

"You let it go! I'm afraid
you don't know what you're doing—
that maybe you got old-timers or
the cancer has spread to your
head."

"Maybe. But Judy, cancer can
never spread to my soul or kill my
will."

Judy unveils a plain, white
business envelope. "In this
envelope is a very large check. I
think your nephew's taken the
Bible stuff literally: 'If you
wish to be perfect, go, sell what

you have and give to the poor, and you will have treasure in heaven...'"

Aunt Mary Frances says, "But it's not about the money and what it can do—it's the love. I love Michael."

"I told him that. I think he thinks the Bible's a how-to book, like a history lesson where he can guarantee his future if he studies the past."

"He's right in a way. God bless him. Here's a saying I heard: *The historical truth of the Bible is the Word we discover while scientists shovel.*" She says, "The history lesson is: Footprints never last very long, but Christ walked the earth. That is the everlasting truth."

Judy tells her, "The bottom line is: Michael insists you get the money—he put me in charge and made me swear to use my judgment—it's my call."

Aunt Mary Frances says to her, "You and he can trust me. I'll give it to charity."

"No! He wants you to use it to personally save a life."

"God bless him. Then I'll give ten percent to church and keep the rest to improve the store and help spread the Word."

"What are they: your bookie? Over Hell or high water am I gonna let you do that. Bottom line is, I see four options: One—you can continue this hold out for a miracle, but you're bluffing yourself. Two—you can try to sell the store and take the money and pay for surgery and chemotherapy, or get some hospice care—but I know you won't do that. Three—we can take the money and you can live it up, before you die, in 'Sin City,' that one, big day. You can lug out some of the Elvi', and we'll go see Elvis—one of him is probably performing at a dozen Vegas hotels tonight.... Fourthly—once we're there, you can go out in style, you can be one of the pioneers for doctor-assisted suicide—before it has the chance to become really popular. You can be the first on the block."

Aunt Mary Frances, almost succumbing to the notion, sadly says, "You mean last."

Judy tells her, "You better hurry. Society, the government, insurance companies, doctors, families—it's bound to become a way of life."

"It sounds like the way of death." Aunt Mary Frances says, "You make me feel like there is a price on my life. REWARD—WANTED DEAD NOT ALIVE. Life is priceless. The economic welfare of a person's family is of

190

absolute zero consequence to God. God provides. Their spiritual understanding of the God of Love and the knowledge of right and wrong are what counts." She adds, "And even if I become what society thinks is unproductive, some economic burden or loss, some financial write-off for the government or medical profession—a God-given life cannot be bought without selling its soul.... Money, it's all about money." She reminds her niece, "Matthew, Judy..." She shows Judy the Good Book, but Judy knows the point.

Judy says, "I know: 'No one can serve two masters. He will either hate one and love the other or be devoted to one and despise the other...' You cannot serve God and money."

"Money, money, money—if you want to leave something behind— live your life to God's end, then those whom you love with time left on Earth, don't have to wait so long to see you again."

Judy deduces, "What? The older *you* live to be—the older I am—then there's less time until I die and see *you* in Heaven..."

"Exactly right."

"If that's true, a person could just kill themselves and see a loved one in Heaven the next day."

"Not in Heaven they won't."
Aunt Mary Frances says to her,
"Listen, did you hear yourself?
That's how a demonic angel starts
to work playing tricks on you. If
you are for suicide—there is an
amount of evil that leads to that.
They say, 'be careful what you ask
for—you just may get it yourself
one day.'"

"[You mean...] You asked for
it."

"You said it."

Judy says, "I'm no jump off a
bridge Judy. Trust me; I'm not
the type to put myself on ice."
She tells her aunt, "Bottom line,
I swear, I don't care about the
money. For some on Earth, it
makes the world go round—I just
want you to know about the right
to die." She changes pace,
jokingly saying; "Even though
suicide may technically be a
crime—how do police think they can
come between you and something
like that? What are they gonna
do, put your coffin in a jail cell
then throw the book at you?
'We'll give you the death penalty
next time you try to kill
yourself.'"

Aunt Mary Frances, in
concordance, says, "God and
government are not a match made in
Heaven. God loves you. Suicide
is a crime against God.... But,

there is hope if this physician-
assisted suicide does not spread
legally. No *one* body is perfect—
not mine or theirs. But as the
Gospel says: 'Seek first His
kinship over you, the way of
holiness, and all these things
will be given you besides, Enough
then of worrying about tomorrow.
Let tomorrow take care of itself.
Today has troubles enough of its
own.'" She amends, "The law and
politics by vote, I feel I cannot
change; so I don't vote. But the
ruler that governs my body—hears
my prayer—His vote is the one that
counts. 'Ask, and you will
receive. Seek, and you will find.
Knock and it will be opened to
you.' Too many of us try to live
by our rules—democratic as they
may be—but it's God's rules that
truly set us free. Love God
first. Love each other second.
Matthew 7:12 'Treat others the way
you would have them treat you;
This sums up the law and the
prophets.'"

Judy deciphers, "The golden
rule. That's great. But keep in
mind what happens as you lose your
mind—and you can't make a
competent judgment—and I become
your guardian. I'll have to do
what I think."

Aunt Mary Frances informs
her, "That's why it's crucial

euthanasia is illegal. If the government encourages me to kill myself, or let a sinful physician murder me—then it automatically affords someone acting as a surrogate the legal opportunity to murder an ill victim, one who society believes can't think for himself. That will offer the government, the people, and the so-called guardian, a reason to kill a human being." She emphatically says, "Man sinfully thinking he can play God—the devil will love that!"

Judy tells her, "For Christ's sake, you're lucky to have family like me that would inflict God's mercy on you. That's why it's called mercy-killing you know."

"Judy: 'Blest are they who show mercy...' The Beatitudes? Mercy is mercy. Killing is killing. I hope and pray Judy, whom I love and forgive; that the angels, like Gabriel, show you only God is truly merciful. You'd be defying God's supreme will and doing the angel of death a service, no matter how you select to humanely justify it, and no matter how the devil tricks you into believing killing spares someone's life. It's like the deer hunters who proudly hang dead deer in the trees in your neighborhood, and then try and

194

sell you on the notion that they must hunt and kill the deer for the deer to survive. They're lying to themselves. A deer, instead of *perhaps* dying of hunger, has a better chance of living if a hunter kills it. God bless them."

"We'll see when your life's a nightmare—a living Hell."

"Judy, realistically, even if you don't believe in a life after death—people who take their own life when their life is a 'living Hell'—why should they think anything will be different?" She says conversely, "Just as we whose life is 'Heaven on Earth'—if we persevere through the trials of life—why then would our eternal life be anything but heavenly?"

Judy is confounded. "How in Hell do I know?"

Aunt Mary Frances says to her: "Judy, what's the Gospel say? 'That is how it will be at the end of the world.'"

Judy finishes the verse: "'...The angels will go out and separate the wicked from the righteous.'"

Aunt Mary Frances says to her, "Judy, for the life of me, why tell people to commit suicide? We could all die tomorrow in an accident or disaster. Don't take the power God's given you from His

hands. If the day after you
wanted to kill yourself—you were
struck by lightning—you would go
right to Heaven. But by one day,
one fateful day—killing yourself,
you go straight to Hell." She
insightfully says, "If you want to
learn about life—live it. Don't
wait for the movie—read the Book."

She hands Judy a Bible. Aunt
Mary Frances points to a verse
that Judy recites: "'Enter through
the narrow gate; for the gate is
wide and the road broad that leads
to destruction, and those who
enter through it are many. How
narrow the gate and constricted
the road that leads to life, and
those who find it are few.'" She
sarcastically says to her aunt, "I
think I got it." But she doesn't
really.

Aunt Mary Frances speaks to
her a parable. "Eternity in
Heaven is like a party. If a
person wants to be the life of the
party—then go when you have
received an invitation. Don't
arrive uninvited at the front gate
and risk being trumpeted out by
the host and told to leave, never
to return. Everyone, of every
religious faith, will have an
invitation Heaven-sent; and the
party never ends!"

Judy says, "But suicide
invites you to be a party to

murder—and that promises to be a hell of a party?"

Aunt Mary Frances poetically says, "It is to walk this earth in the way of the Lord that unlocks this life's key to happiness unending; it is to thank God Almighty upon getting there, for the key, that opens for eternity the gates of Heaven."

BORN AGAIN 2

NEARING 11:00 A.M.

Inside Roman's den, the weapons have all vanished. Michael's Olympic medal is also gone. The trophy animal heads are all shrouded. At the base of the cardboard-filled broken window; Michael, Bible in hand, is deep in prayer on Noah's rug. Maggie returns from the abortion rally. She is livid. She *Frisbee's* a plate, narrowly missing Michael's head. It knocks out the revamped window. She stalks after her husband. "You son of a fuckin' bitch! Talk about grounds for divorce."

Michael shouts, "Holy cow!" He says, "Come and talk to me."

Maggie tells him, "Security, sex, solitude—these are the

reasons woman and man should m-a-r-y. Don't you know being married's like having a j-o-b, job? You get safe and easy sex, and no one has to be afraid of being alone. I didn't leave California so you could knock me up then fall in l-o-v-e, love, with angels and G-o, God. No wonder half of all couples get divorced."

Michael uses his hands to convey to her a concept. "Maggie, marriage is like a triangle, life like a pyramid—like a Christmas tree with an angel on top. The closer we get to God—the closer we get to each other." He counsels her, "People should marry because they want to have a child and not be as foolish as parents who have a child to save a marriage. Children will learn love more from the way the parents treat each other—than they do from the way the parents treat the child." He contends, "Divorce me—but in the eyes of the archangel, you will never be separated from the life inside of you."

"Too bad—because this baby's as dead as dirt." She tells him, "You'll need more than just you to stop this abortion. These clinics are like drive thru's—you think you see a church on every corner—look close. There'll be more

198

suicide houses than fire hydrants—
more clinics than churches. I
need this abortion. Half the
women I know have already had at
least one, so it's really a method
of birth control. And just
because most feel guilty after
because it was a mistake, doesn't
mean I won't try to have k-i-d's
in the future, but for now I can't
handle the responsibility. What
if I wanted to go to school or get
a j-o-b, job? Besides, I can't
afford it if my husband gives all
his G-o-d, goddamned money away.
Fuck, I don't know if I even have
a husband. How'm I supposed to
bring up a k-i-d alone? I got no
time. What guy will want me? My
body, Christ, what about my body?
Why bring a child into this shitty
world? I can think of a million
reasons why I should have an
abortion. Give me one good reason
why I shouldn't?"

Michael counters,
"God...love...life...m—"

"I got news for you—money
makes the world go round and you
can put a price on l-i-f. You
giving all your money away—is that
what you call love? You left me
no choice."

Michael Angelo Roman reads
his first Scripture passage: "'You
need only one thing. Go, sell all
you have, and give the money to

the poor, and you will have riches
in heaven; then come, follow me.'
Mark, chapter 10, verse 21."

Maggie is teeming with
sarcasm. "Right."

Michael tells her, "You'll
not only sell out your own child's
life, but you wouldn't give me the
coat off your back if I begged
you." Michael picks up the coat
she's draped over the furnishing.

Maggie snaps, "What? How
dare you? I'll kill you!"

He tells her, "I'm returning
the coat. It's a sin that I paid
to have that animal slaughtered.
How many hungry mouths could I
feed? How many innocent animals
needed to die? It's a mortal sin
to kill any living creature—food,
clothing, or otherwise. There is
life in the eyes of every animal;
and where there is life—there is
God.... To kill a life is to kill
God."

Maggie throws a tantrum. "I
want it back! I want it! I want
it! I want it! Give it to me!
I'd rather see it turn to shreds
than belong to someone else! Give
it to me! You think you can save
your own ass?"

"Man cannot save himself—only
God's angels can."

"You're telling me
sacrificing your money, your

house, and your wife is worth it in the end?"

"What comes around goes around."

They exit down the hallway. Maggie follows Michael in fear. Michael cradles the fur. Maggie points out the Bible Michael left on the furniture. "That book is costing you your life."

Michael profoundly remarks, "In the game of life, it's when a player sacrifices himself for the good of the team—that the team wins the game."

Maggie is enraged. "Michael!" She slaps him. He merely turns his cheek. She slaps him twice more. In her own inimitable (lack of) style—she spits in his face. Michael trudges to the backyard. From within the home, Maggie throws the prayer rug out the window. The rug lands directly beneath the outside pane. She yells, "Do what I tell you."

"What more do you want from me?"

"Get your holier than thou self out of here. There's no room for you here. Get out!"

Michael lays the coat in the barbecue pit over the nest's charred remains. He says to himself, "David, Mark, Paul...

sacrifice what you own in the Old—
sacrifice who you are in the New."
He douses the coat with lighter
fluid.

Maggie stomps out the door.
She chucks handfuls of dirt at
Michael. Short on ammo, she
flings her cigarette at him; it
missiles by, landing in the pit.
"I hope you burn!" She unleashes
a stone, striking him. The coat
ignites. The explosion
temporarily blinds Michael. He
clutches his face. Maggie runs
inside. Michael remains calm.
Sparks shoot toward the basement
window. From inside the doorway,
Maggie heaves his Bible into the
mire at his feet. "Pray some more
see what you get!" She slams the
door shut.

Michael crumbles to his
knees. He patiently unfurls his
hands. He gropes for and picks up
the Bible. He outstretches his
arms. He tests his restored
eyesight by reading his
wristwatch. "Faith...10:52." He
throws his watch into the woods.
"Archangel, help them to see the
life." Demoralized, he shrinks
far off past the driveway and down
the road.

SERVICE - PART II
"Educate"

APPX: 7:00 P.M.

Inside the U.C.A. Life + God, without missing a beat, Reverend Mark Anthony approaches the microphone like a comedian opening a monologue; the now forty-eight strong, including a Catholic Bishop, applaud. Reverend Mark Anthony is intent and energetic. "Thank you.... How's everybody doin'? Agh, never mind, I don't care. I love when people do that, 'Hi, how are you?' "Nothing. What's new with you?" 'I'm good.' Nobody listens, nobody cares...."

He remarks, "I see in the news we're sending another person to death. Death row, this is a joke right? This is where they take you from the regular part of prison and put you in a special row of cells—to remind you you're going to be killed—yeah, this is something I'm likely to forget. I've got so much on my mind I can barely remember today is Tuesday."

A heckler howls out, "It's Wednesday."

"See what I mean?" ...Reverend Mark Anthony comedically proceeds, "When you're about to die, you'd think they'd

give you a break. Instead, they
punish you more; this is like
torture, you could be on death row
for years. But it's okay when
they give you the 'good news, bad
news.'

'Alright, so it's worse than
where you've been; but it's not as
bad as where you're going.' It's
like taking a cow from the farm to
the slaughterhouse and stopping by
McDonalds for a hamburger on the
way....

"There's one I don't get—the
last meal. They give you the best
plate of food you've had in years—
then they kill you." He thinks,
Where's the logic? "I guess if
they're willing to waste you—
wasting food is no big deal.
Nice, they'll save their best food
for you, but they won't save
you.... It's true; they feed you
crappy food for a year, then tell
you if you want to eat better you
need to die. 'Shoot for the death
penalty, it's your only guarantee
of getting at least one good
meal.'...

"You know, they give you that
great last meal, again, just to
torture you. It's to remind you
to be thankful that years of
prison food hasn't killed
you.... Still, I don't get it.
If they want you to kill you so
bad, why do they even bother

feeding you? What are you, a cow?...

"Then, they get you all cleaned and dressed up. You get your once a week, whether you need it or not, shower; then a shave, and a brand new prison uniform— only one without a number. I guess it's tough figuring you into the prison count after your number's finally come up....

"And then they give you that God-forsaken, butcher-job haircut that looks like a lawnmower, without one of the blades working, went over your head. Me, I'd die right there. 'Convict dies in chair! Yeah, because of embarrassment. Claims would rather die than live with haircut like that!'...

"That night, they post a suicide watch over you—because of the haircut. No! Because they don't want you to kill yourself before they can. I can hear the warden now; 'Die on your own—over your dead body! We're killing you whether you like it or not!'...

"At dawn, they come to wake you and take you away. Me, I'd do like when I was kid—I'd fake like I was sleeping. You just have to concentrate on keeping your eyes closed and not blinking. Just be real careful when you do that little peek to see if they're gone. That'ta kill 'ya if you get caught....

"Then from death row, you take that last walk. I love the way they always put you in a ton of shackles and handcuffs—that's in case you try to escape back into regular prison....

"Finally, and I mean finally, they lock you in that room they're gonna murder you in; where they invite people to sit on the other side of a glass wall and witness. I wonder, are the witnesses there to make sure you die—or to witness that they're trying to kill you? I guess it must be the second—I mean, I think you'd know if you were dead.

"They invite your family. This has gotta' be a tough ticket to sell. Do you think they'd be disappointed if this wasn't a sellout? Families go generations just dying to see a loved one executed don't they?...You know there's also a reporter from the paper there. But oddly enough, it's never the person who does the obituaries....

"Finally, you get your last words—like they're gonna give you a second chance. If it were me, mine would be, 'No fair! Do over!' It worked when we were kids....

"Then the priest gives you the last rights." He grabs a band player. "I'd say, 'Get over here! You're coming with me! I'm not goin' alone!' No. Truthfully I'd say, 'Father pray for me. God, please take my soul, and if it be your will, let me live...because, I wouldn't want to be caught dead in that haircut!'"...

Reverend Mark Anthony opens up a newspaper's obituary section and reads verbatim.

"Here's my obituary: Mr. Me and You, of the world, died suddenly, instead of 25-to-life; although, he probably would've gotten cancer anyway from all the cigarette smoke where he lived in prison. Born, though he may have been born again at a moment's notice—he only

got to die
once.... He
worked in the
laundry and
made license
plates, for
a dollar a
day, which
ironically,
went to paying
for other
prisoner's
cigarettes,
which again,
would probably
have killed
him anyway....
He was a
member of the
sick ward—
because of the
cigarette
smoke—solitary
confinement,
and the chain
gang.... His
interests
included:
reading the
one magazine
over and over,
and watching
the TV show.
Not to
mention,
reading the
Bible every

day. He also
enjoyed
lifting the
weight of the
world off his
shoulders
during his one
hour of
recreation
every
month....
Survivors
include: John
the Baptist—Oh
no, he also
got the death
penalty in
prison. He's
survived by
everybody who
loved him and
everybody else
who hated him
enough to
convict him to
death....
Relatives and
friends were
invited to
witness the
execution.
'We're killing
your loved
one—and we
think it'd
mean a lot to
him if you

were there.'
Thanks state,
good timing,
it's never too
late to show
you care....
Calling hours
are between
when and when—
but don't
expect an open
casket—because
of a bad
haircut.
Funeral
services will
be brief.
Hurry up and
bury me—to
think I'd have
to go through
life with that
lawnmower
cut....
Contributions
in my memory
may be made to
the prison
barbershop for
that butcher
job do. Sure
it'll cost you
your life, but
look at the
good news—you
get a free
haircut."

Outside of the U.C.A. Life +
God, an unidentified person is
approaching the building.

Inside the church, Reverend
Mark Anthony remarks, "How they
kill you is also a joke. In the
Bible days, they would first put
people to death by stoning them.
When I was a kid in the 70's, we
used to play by throwing rocks at
each other; so I guess killing's
not much fun anymore if you can't
tell it's punishment.... Then
came crucifixion; but after the
Lord was crucified, there was a
letdown. I guess you find a way
to kill God—you've sort of
mastered the death penalty....

"Centuries later came the
'Old West,' although, the way they
were always hanging people—nobody
ever got very old.... At first
they had trouble, well, 'getting
the hang of it.' They'd tie the
rope around they guy's neck, but
he'd hang onto it, like the rope
in gym class. After they caught
on, they'd tie your hands behind
your back—but then guys would use
their feet to straddle the
platform. But the people doing
the killing were dumb back then,
instead of just making a bigger
space to fall through, they'd tie
your feet. Once they figured the
key was to tie the neck—and the

feet—some dumb guy suggested, 'Why
not just hang'em by the feet?'
But eventually they got tired of
watching some guy hanging upside-
down for hours."...

The heckler hollers, "So then
what'd they do?"

"They shot him," jokes
Reverend Mark Anthony....

He marches on..."Now that's
when they came up with the idea
for the firing squad. Here's what
I don't get; they want to shoot
you to death, but they stand like
a half-mile away. How in the hell
can they see you from way back
there? The object is to hit the
guy, right? If they miss your
heart, that's gotta' hurt like
Hell. On top of that, they put
you in dreary gray prison clothes
and stand you in front of a big,
gray, cement wall where you blend
right in. Why don't they just
paint a big, red, bull's-eye on
your chest? Then it would really
be like target practice. Seems
stupid to me, but better yet, if
they're trying to hit the guy—why
don't they just get real close and
put the gun right in your chest?
...Then again, these are the same
people who give you that last
cigarette, even if you don't
smoke—I'm tellin'ya, that'd kill
me right there.... The reason
they do that though is to tell

when you're dead. Blood's hard to
see from far away—but that smoke
blows right out the holes....

"Eventually, that's how they
came up with the electric chair.
Did you know it was a dentist who
invented the electric chair? I
guess he got tired of hearing
people complain about toothaches.
At first, it was sure-fire—your
toothache always went away....
But then, the chair used to
backfire and smoke and flames
would come out of the guy. See,
this wasn't any good because they
didn't want you to be in pain—they
just wanted to kill you. Then, to
add insult to injury, they'd do an
autopsy on the guy—funny, but I
got a good feeling he's dead.
And, I gotta' stinkin' suspicion
of why he died.... But, the funny
thing was, they found out the
prisoners weren't dying of
electrocution at all—they were
dying of smoke inhalation—so that
was no good.... If you're gonna
spend a couple of million to
electrocute someone—you better
make sure they're blue in face
with lightning in their veins.
Breathing in smoke, how much evil
excitement can that bring? To
stop breathing's too natural a
cause of death....

"But that's when they got
the idea for the gas chamber.

'Hey, if breathing could actually kill you!' I guess they'd never lived in LA.... See, they figured you could only hold your breath for so long. They hoped sooner or later you'd yell something stupid, like 'help' or 'save me,' and they'd get you. Even though one guy took like eighteen minutes to die once. 'He's gotta' lot of nerve trying to live by not breathing. What's he think he is—some kind'a fish?'...

"This was all getting pretty ugly to look at, so they came up with the idea to use a mask. See, I like when they put the mask on the person who's pulling the switch or dropping the pill. I always thought this was so the people who voted to have a person killed wouldn't see who lived next to them or wouldn't know who to blame when something went wrong; that or the executioner is too afraid to be seen, *not* brave enough not to kill, just too afraid to be seen. But really, it's so the prisoner won't know who did it. See why this doesn't make sense? The state did. They said, 'This is dumb. Why don't we just put the mask on the guy who's dying? See? Then we can kill two birds with one stone. See, then he can't see us and he can't see what we're doing to him.' Yeah, put a mask on him; you can run, but you can't hide....

"Now the death penalty is so popular, no one has to hide. Even the people who are supposed to save us are getting into the act; they need to get doctors to give those lethal injections that kill. If I'm lying strapped there, seems a little late at that point to call a doctor.... I like that little traffic light, on this and the injection machine that lets you know when you're going; green, yellow, red—that'd drive me crazy. Don't they know it goes against all teaching? In driver-ed you're taught *not* to hit the gas when you see the yellow light.... See, I guess that shot in the arm is supposed to slowly send that poison right to your heart. Again, I don't understand why they don't just stick the needle into your heart? Oh yeah, because that'll hurt too much.... I'd like to see someone roll over and let'em stick them in their ass-assassinate—so they'd really know how you felt.... It seems to me, they're trying to make dying as painless and fun as possible. Oh yeah, dying's a lot of fun—that's why nobody ever comes back to do it again. Funny, maybe it's just me, I've never died, but I get a funny feeling that at some point—

215

being killed has gotta' hurt. Let me ask somebody that's been sentenced to death before..." He cups his ear to the sky; "'Yeah, it hurts—it's a pain in the ass.'...

"Do you know now doctors are giving these death penalty injections during house calls? Yeah, there's a special name for it...Oh yeah, it's called, *assisted-suicide*. It's like the guy in the woods who gets bit in the butt by a poisonous snake; so he sends his friend to the doctor, and the doctor says, 'the only way to save him, is to suck out the poison.' So the friend runs back and the guy says, 'What'd the doctor say?' And the friend says, 'You're gonna die!'...

"Do you know it's illegal to attempt suicide, but it's legal if you go through with it? That's like jumping off the Empire State Building and the cop says, 'You better hope you die on the way down, 'cause if you fall too fast— I'll give you a ticket for speeding.... Listen up! If you're alive when you land—we're giving you a ticket for attempting suicide, but if you're lucky enough to die—we'll only give you one for trespassing.' ...I've been suicidal for years, that's why I get a kick out of the other poor

souls who try killing themselves
like fifty times. Me, I'd
probably try to kill myself all
over again if I was that
unsuccessful at something. Seems
to me, if you're so unsuccessful
at trying to die—you'd be a lot
more successful if you just tried
to live....

"Oh, by the way, with regards
to the death penalty—if you're
asking yourself, 'Who are <u>they</u>?'
The '<u>they</u>' I keep talking about.
'<u>They this</u>' and '<u>they that</u>'....
If I am you, and you are <u>they—they</u>
is <u>we</u> and <u>we</u> are <u>they</u>....

"I truly pray to God, we get
rid of the death penalty; I truly
do. Because that bad hair day
will kill'ya every time!"

The congregation appreciates
Reverend Mark Anthony's relentless
humor. Goldstein, standing by,
retreats to a private area.

Outside of the U.C.A. Life +
God, an unidentified silhouette
eavesdrops with his or her ear to
the building.

Inside the church, Reverend
Mark Anthony remarks, "You know,
all the world is made up of only
three different lives: <u>baby</u>, <u>me</u>,
and <u>we</u>. There are no exceptions;
this is our existence. Everyone
was once a <u>baby</u>. I will always be
<u>me</u>. And I will always be a part
of <u>we</u>. These three, we all have

in common. And there are only
three ways to end those lives:
abortion murders the next
generation; suicide murders me;
and the death penalty murders my
fellow man. And of the three, the
one we have in common—is murder.
Outside of nature, this is the
only way to end life: abortion,
suicide, the death penalty—
murder.... Now, that's when life
ends. But when does life begin?
Let's perform an abortion and see.
Mr. Goldstein, if you please..."
The church is in obvious shock at
the proposal. But shock gives way
to hilarity, when Ernie escorts in
a chicken on a leash—with the
chicken leading! Reverend Mark
Anthony jokes, "Who's leading who?
Looks like the chicken's walking
Ernie. Mr. Goldstein, I see you
got your chicken to go."...

Ernie says, "Now you know why
the chicken crossed the road."

Reverend Mark Anthony
answers, "Yeah, 'cause Ernie
Goldstein had it on a leash."
...Ernie walks the chicken to
Reverend Mark Anthony's feet.

The Reverend says, "I'm
afraid to hold it. I don't want
to hurt it." He picks it up.
"How do you tell a chicken you're
chicken? It'll think I'm crazy."
He tells the cackling creature, "I
won't hurt you."

He addresses the audience again. "Now look at me! How am I doin'? I'm trying to lead people to God and I'm asking chickens how do I tell them I'm chicken without them thinking I'm crazy.... Now it's wondering, 'What chickens? Do you see chickens? I'm one chicken.'" He says to himself, "I need my head examined. Oh great, now I'm talking to myself."...

The nature of his speech changes. "The question is: Which came first, the chicken or the egg?" He displays an egg. "Is it possible the chicken? Is it possible the egg? I'd say the chicken, but isn't the truth: we really don't know? Then let's stick with the truth and something we do know..."

Reverend Mark Anthony steps down to confront a family of four in the front row. He demonstrates: "This is a man; he has life. This is a woman; she has life. If I kill either one—I kill a life..." Reverend Mark Anthony holds their baby. "This is a baby boy, I think, yeah blue; he has life. This is a baby girl; she has life. If I kill either one—I kill a life."

He discontinues with the family foursome and steps back up on stage. "This is a chicken; it comes from an egg. This is an egg; it comes from a chicken. There is life in this chicken; it comes from the egg. The life *is* in the egg; the egg *is* life. If, *at anytime*, you kill the egg—you kill the life..." He purposely breaks the egg in hand. "There is your answer on abortion." He towels his hand dry and lets the message sink in.

Ernie is surprised to see his disheveled boss, Michael, enter. Michael heads directly to the office. It's his first time at a church service since his horrific baptism a half-century ago. Reverend Mark Anthony watches very closely. He prompts Ernie to follow Michael.

Reverend Mark Anthony continues speaking. "The death penalty, suicide, abortion, the one thing they have in common is—murder; which leads to the fourth and foremost reason we murder. The only reason on Earth anybody murders, for anything, or anyone in any way, at any time—the only reason we murder—is hate. We kill, because we want to kill. The good news is: at least we can't murder anybody who's already died...thank God!"

In the pastor's office, Ernie is shaking Michael's hand in a warm embrace. Reverend Mark Anthony enters his office. They all sit. Reverend Mark Anthony says, "Mr. Goldstein, mark this day when you and twelve, when we started with thirteen—" The Reverend asks, "You two know each other?"

Ernie answers, "You might say that."

Michael says to Reverend Mark Anthony, "I'm sorry about the way I acted before."

"Forget it; all's forgiven."

Ernie asks Michael, "Don't you like what has been done here?"

Michael answers, "I do."

Reverend Mark Anthony tells him, "We have Mr. Ernie Goldstein to thank in part."

Michael says, "He's served to make my life meaningful." Ernie wishes to express it was Michael's financial contribution, but Michael shakes his head at Ernie hoping to maintain his anonymity.

Ernie inquires, "Reverend Mark Anthony, churches and synagogues were destroyed in biblical times as they are today, you don't think this church will be burned or some war in the

221

streets will threaten to destroy it do you?"

Reverend Mark Anthony tells him, "I hope not. There is only one God, and as long as the Son of God remains at the center of this church—not even the evil hand of man shall bring the walls of this house down. Do you know, for the thirty-three years the Lord walked the earth, there was no war on Earth? What two things does that tell you?"

Michael pauses in reply to the rhetorical question; "War is hell." Ernie gives a perplexed look and a shoulder shrug. He cannot discern the second appropriate answer.

Reverend Mark Anthony says to them, "When Christ came, all that had ever happened—will be all that ever happens; wars, disasters, disease, starvation—these may never change—but *we* must be changed when the Lord comes again at our death to take us all one by one." From his desk, Mark holds a rock and a disarmed warhead in his hands to demonstrate his point. He focuses his speech on Michael, not knowing of Roman's former passion for weaponry. He holds out, for Michael, the rock. "See this? In war, the cavemen used rocks then spears. In medieval times, we used spears then hatchets. The Indians used tomahawks and arrows; and the cowboys used guns and rifles; in the revolution, rifles and cannons; in the world wars, cannons and bombs; in the millennium, nuclear bombs and chemical warfare." Demonstrating for Michael, he holds out the warhead. "A human hand used a rock to kill the first man. This contaminated warhead in human hands can kill millions—then the last man. The weapons change..." He empties his hands. "But the human hand remains the same."

Michael inferably counters, "So guns don't kill, people kill?"

Ernie fused the two. Having read into it, he says, "Both guns and people kill."

Reverend Mark Anthony lays Ernie out, saying, "Ernie's right. I've yet to see somebody shoot a person to death by *throwing* a bullet at them."

Ernie is besieged with the answer to the question posed earlier. "I know it! There are wars, and there are holy wars, but without God present in our lives there will be no peace on Earth."

Reverend Mark Anthony tells him, "That's it. God's honest truth, with God in our lives there is no hatred." He radically tells them, "Listen, God asks that we no

longer war in His holy name.
There is no right in killing one
another. We are all one—the
family of God. One life lost is
one life too many. To war in the
name of your religious beliefs is
to kill. God does not want you to
take or lose a life, like the
earth, a life He worked so hard to
create. God did not create
religion—He created man. Man and
Earth are His greatest creations.
He created them both to last an
eternity." He advises, "If you
holy war because you hate life—you
honor the devil's name.... If you
believe in a religious holy war to
make greater your domain or your
descendents, or to enforce your
doctrines—that is unspeakable to
God. This earth and we His
people—are God's domain." He
unceasingly bombards them with
rhetoric. "When has getting
yourself killed ever made your
earthly life longer? Isn't there
enough death in nature alone?
Death comes to us all soon
enough." He warrants, "On this
planet, the killing of each other
and of ourselves in the name of
war, the war of human weaknesses
and the holy wars of religions—
must end." He fundamentally
concludes, "And if, 'fighting for
a life' means to kill one another—
evil is winning the war on life.

224

To 'fight for a life' means to save a life. *There are no holy wars.*"

Ernie implores, "May we pray on the weapons of war?"

The men bow their heads as Reverend Mark Anthony recites the prayer he's written. "God Himself told me in prayer:

> "From after
> the genesis of
> creation, from
> man's original
> sin of death,
> to death's
> brother
> murder, from
> the
> Commandments
> to the
> prophets; man
> has been both
> one with good
> and evil. For
> it is God's
> doing, that
> the sons of
> light and life
> wage war on
> the sons of
> darkness and
> death. And
> that God, the
> sole Creator of
> Life, and He
> alone, be it in

the Man or the
Spirit, is the
one and only God
and all life
belongs to Him.
Only the Son of
Man, in worship
to the Father
and love for one
another, has
been victorious
in the war
between life and
death on Earth,
and has God
would have it,
with the angels
in eternity. In
the name of God,
not man, not
Earth, not
religion; the
Lord would have
it that no man
take the life of
another. In the
name of the God
of Life—I will
pray for peace
on the weapons
of war."

The triumvirate bows their
heads in the blessing for world
peace. Reverend Mark Anthony
informally asks Michael, "So how's
life?"

Michael tells him, "I'm dying to save the life of a woman facing the death penalty in California. I know she must know God, but I pray the people don't kill her."

Reverend Mark Anthony encourages him, "Pray. God hears your prayer and God's will be done." He instructs, "Christ too, once faced the death penalty simply because the people thought they knew God better than God knew Himself. The people didn't believe God, the maker of Adam, the maker of man, could appear to be a man Himself."

Ernie ingrains, "I believe God is in the soul—the soul is in the man."

Reverend Mark Anthony says consentingly, "True, so I tell people: what did the Lord do that proved He wasn't God? Nothing. He was perfect. All He did was miracles and rise from the dead. He never made a mistake, never once committed a single sin. If He weren't the Son of God, would the truth in His Word have spread to 2 billion people 2,000 years later? No one before Him was truthful enough to live up to proclaim he was the Son of God, and everyone after that has lied to himself and died a failure."

Ernie subscribes, "The questions I asked myself were

these: *Why* would He say He was the Son of God if He were not? Did He ever once not give all power and glory to God? Did He ever once sin against those who believed in Him? All He did was tell the truth and people didn't believe Him. Think, Why else would He say He was God's Son—to get Himself killed?"

Reverend Mark Anthony acknowledges, "God loves you Ernie. You should be a Rabbi." He queries Michael, "How's the writing going?"

Michael replies, "I've got writers block. I don't know how the story ends."

Reverend Mark empathetically says, "God knows, I've played on that block before." He relays, "Just keep following the Word of God. *He* knows the story. Keep your spirit up—the archangel will show you the ending." The Reverend stops in his tracks. "Oh my God! Wow! This is so strange. Mr. Goldstein, show him that thing Noah showed me. Watch..."

Ernie uses his hands for the childlike demonstration. He intertwines his fingers and fists together at the knuckles. He says, "Think of the block like a building, a building on the way to an entire *city of angels*...

Here's the earth—
there's a tower—
open the doors—
then save the people."

Michael says, "I don't think I get it."

Reverend Mark Anthony says, "I know. Neither do we; it's unexplainable. That's why it's so strange. It's just something I remembered..."

Michael shares with Reverend Mark Anthony, "I'm also afraid my aunt may soon be leaving this life. I may never see her again. I know she knows God, but..."

The Reverend shares with him, "Then hang on. Believe in the God who sent His Son to die for your aunt—your aunt does." He tells him, "Christ came and personally told us the truth about the meaning of life; and how to never die, but live and live again. He showed us in a way we could actually see and hear—like that of a human being. Your aunt knows that."

Ernie upholds, "Mr. Roman, the Reverend will tell you how, when he comes to my synagogue to visit, there are those of my friends who hate me because I'm learning about Christianity." He resolves, "Which to me, is only believing that the same God my

Hebrew brothers and sisters believe in came to Earth as a man teaching love. And to prove that by dying, going to Heaven, and returning again, that indeed there is a Heaven. And the lesson for any man—is by believing in that self-same God of Love—we may see Him, and all who believe in His love, when our days on this earth end. So hold on."

Reverend Mark Anthony proffers, "What I like to remind the people is that love is the oxygen Earth needs to survive. I think people believe there will be some catastrophic ending—when the planet and life as we know it ceases to exist. What they don't realize; is that God won't be the one doing it. If anyone destroys this world God created—it will be man. God has done enough creating to last a lifetime." He says circumspectively, "The end will be just as the beginning: the devil and the evil who kill, against God and the good who live. And the one man who remains at the end—will also die." Prophetically, he tells them, "Mr. Roman, Mr. Goldstein, *mark my words*—Earth and man's eternal existence depends on only two things: love and hate. *If you love life enough to save it—the world will survive. If you hate life enough to kill it—the earth will die."*

Ernie says to Michael, "But like anything: no one ever made a million dollars without making a dollar first. No one ever climbed a mountain without taking the first step. A billion people aren't born until one is born first. The life we must first save is our own."

Michael tells him, "I'm trying to save a life, but now even my wife wants an abortion."

Ernie is mortified. "Dear God! There's a million ways to kill and die at the end of life, but now she's unearthed the one way to kill life at the start!"

Reverend Mark Anthony says to Michael, "See, Mr. Roman, your wife is lying to herself. The truth is, any woman who thinks of taking her child's life—"

Ernie intercedes, "—or man— even though it's really the woman's choice..."

Reverend Mark Anthony acknowledges, "Right...but any woman who thinks of taking her child's life—ultimately does so to save her own...whatever she says, she does so to save her own life." The Reverend explains to Michael, "See, at the beginning of life is God the Father and Creator. He created life and is The Truth.

And everything that is not God is not true and is a lie. And the devil is the father of lies. The devil is the dark angel; the pride of humanity that has people believing they know life and truth, but the people are lying to themselves. Since man always dies in the end—the devil lied." His reasoning precedes his revelation. "If women brought no more babies into the world, the entire planet would be empty in a hundred years. The world was made for people." He tells him, "The killing of Christ was the only way to forever save a life." He concludes, *"Women die and women give birth—that's how people remain on Earth."*

Ernie expounds, "People think dying is the end. When in reality, it's just the beginning of a new life. Death gives meaning to life."

Reverend Mark Anthony philosophizes, "People will never start living until they overcome the fear of dying. People fear what they don't know—and death is the great unknown. All we truly know is that everyone else dies. It is unthinkable, impossible, unimaginable for the living to know what being dead for eternity truly is. Death cannot be understood in this life, only the

232

next. Have you ever seen a one-sided coin? Can a person stand on the sun and the moon at the same time? No. No one knows for certain what Heaven is. I like to say, Heaven is only what this life is not." The Reverend encourages, "And there is nothing to fear knowing Christ will one day come to lead us all one by one." He confides, "Now twice I've had angels lead me close—and being near-death is the greatest experience in life. Because let me tell'ya—where we are going, God is there."

Ernie says to them, "The lesson in life for me—is not only when the end is near, but how it will happen. I hope I die the second greatest way; that is, to die performing the blessed gift each of us is born with: like the scribe when they're writing or the Reverend when he's preaching."

"Like the athlete when they're playing, or the rabbi when he's teaching," harmonizes Reverend Mark Anthony.

"Amen," says Ernie.

Reverend Mark Anthony hypothesizes, "The Lord is alive every minute of the day—because people pass away every second."

Michael says, "The Lord is alive every minute—because people pass away every second.... That's

along the lines of my, 'the world
ends when we die theory,' so I
need to act like God every single
day." He speculates, "To me,
that's why the Bible teaches the
end is near. It's only the day we
die away. From my view, we all
have one day to change our world
from evil to good. Am I right?
What worker, whose day ends at
five, lets their work remain
undone until after that hour? Or
what person, who goes to bed at
midnight, starts getting ready for
sleep at noon? The time is now."

Ernie retrieves the Torah and
a Bible from the pastor's
collection of the holy books of
the world's religions. With the
Torah in hand, he agreeably says
to Michael, "Those are words to
live by." Similarly, he says,
"If our life were a Broadway play,
our time on Earth is the
intermission." With the Bible in
hand, he equates, "In the Book of
Life, the words never die.
Because, once the message gets to
you—it becomes a part of your life
forever taken with you—and thus,
the words have come alive."

Michael says, "So Earth is a
proving ground with life or death
consequences?"

Reverend Mark Anthony
instructs, "Yes, it's like a
field. Life is a countdown:

10...9...8...7...6...and in the
end, there are only two plays that
determine if you are a winner, or
a loser: In the one second you
have left on Earth, God will call
on you—and you get one, and only
one, play. And the one play you
make—is it: winner or loser."
He contends, "To win in the final
second: In your mind, your words
and actions are good. In your
body, you are working or playing
with your God-given strengths.
And your soul, your soul is full
of your blessing. These will mark
a victory for life." He contends,
"To lose in the final second: Your
words and actions are bad. You
are working or playing with your
weaknesses, and your soul is full
of your curse. These will mark a
defeat in death. God calls with
one second to go. In the last
split second, you'll be gone from
the field of Earth forever. The
game of life ends—when the clock
expires: 5...4...3...2...1."

    Michael has exited in a
determined flurry. A coach's pre-
game speech for the record books
has lit his fire. Reverend Mark
Anthony, watching very closely,
gives a distinct look for Ernie to
follow Michael.

LATE AFTERNOON - P.S.T.

In California Superior Court,
the courtroom remains full of
spectators. Judge DePilate goes
over his notes. Ms. Camael
confers with the Weissman's before
approaching the defense table. A
man with a rainbow Afro displays a
JOHN 3:16 sign. He is rudely
ushered out. Lesliannas watches
closely, quoting to herself: "'For
God so loved the world that He
gave His only begotten Son, that
whoever believes in Him should not
perish but have everlasting
life.'"

Lincoln says, astonishingly
to his client, "Damn, the word got
out on this one." He comments,
"For Heaven's sake, don't these
sick people have anything better
to do with their lives than watch
other people die? I wonder what
the people who see and hear the
news think? What do parents tell
their kids?" He asks, "Camael,
what's the status of Roman's
money? Did you call that chick
fillet secretary of his, or that
round mound of bread he calls an
accountant?"

Ms. Camael answers, "They're
working on it, as soon as there's

236

a verdict." She points out the Weissman's to Lincoln, and asks, "See the three, yellow ties?"

Lincoln says blatantly, "Yeah: 'Re,' 'Peat,' and 'Offend-her.'"

Ms. Camael says, "Laugh now Abraham, they're the real deal Lincoln." She informs him, "Weissman, Weissman and son. The top law firm in the west. They're prepared to offer you $500,000 a year, up front, for your services—if you can win her an acquittal."

Lincoln dishearteningly says, "Fuckin' A. For God's sakes, how in creation am I gonna do that? I can't reintroduce the evidence; besides, I've already iced that."

Ms. Camael banefully says, "Yeah, for 'Eve of Destruction' over there." She's clearly referring to Hillary; who she jealously, longingly leers at.

Lincoln, less baneful, says, "Cool it. If everybody were like you Harriet, there'd be no more people. Shouldn't you be off having kids somewhere?"

Ms. Camael proposes, "Motion for the mistrial."

Lincoln bursts out, "No! That'll be the death of me." He is the epitome of pridefulness. "No, I'll look like a jackass. I've got my reputation to think about. The 'Wiseguys' over there

will think I couldn't try a field
goal. Plus, who knows where 'Joe
Born Again's' mind is at?" With
regards to Hillary, he concedes,
"I'll have to recall her; maybe
she'll bury herself alive. After
all this, I don't think I can tell
fact from fiction, truth from
lie." Under his breath, he says
of his defendant Lesliannas Von
Adolf, "Little do you know the
heavy price that's been paid for
your life." He loudly tells her,
with dismay, "Sister, you're off
the meat hook." From the defense
table, he recalls Hillary Paul.
Lesliannas positions her left hand
and draws.

Judge DePilate tells Paul,
"Please be advised, you are still
under oath."

Lincoln's frustrated at
playing defense. His stance
weakens. He says to her, "To the
best of your recollection, would
you repeat the testimony you gave
earlier today; from the point
Number 8: where Miss Von Adolf
talks about the pencil, the jam,
it being Palm Sunday, and her
praying to Christ on the cross."

His tone sets Paul back on
her heels. Paul testifies, "She
said it was Sunday. We got in the
fight. And I jabbed a cross on
her palm, and her side, so we knew
it was her. That's when she wrote

down the same thing, I've seen in her Bible a hundred times, on the wall with the red jam. Then I screamed to the 'C.O.' And that's all she wrote."

Lincoln asks, "But you couldn't recall what that was?"

Paul says, "Yeah, I do...I remember..." She gestures with her finger, hand, and wrist; "It was X, like in times, two thousand thirteen."

"Does that mean anything to you?"

"Knowin' her, I figure it probably means times she's thought about doin' this."

"Hopeless." Lincoln says to himself. He belligerently asks, "Miss Paul, you're not too thrilled with my client are you?"

Paul says venomously, "'Miss Goodie Two Shoes?' Who's she kid'n? 'Miss Little Angel,' all white'n all. 'Miss Teacher' wants to save the world or somethin', drawing with some special angel pencil. She's a liar and a chicken shit. A *Barbie Doll* tells more truth than her. I'd slap her silly if I could. Show us that white pad of paper she's been drawin' on—I'd love to see that. Let's all see how she can save her life now."

Lincoln mercifully completes his recall of Paul. "No more questions."

Hillary Paul steps down. Lincoln returns to the defense table. He asks Camael about the mindset of the jury. "What are we looking at with them?"

Ms. Camael says, "Evidence?"

Lincoln presumes, "No chance in Hell." He asks, "Conscience?"

Ms. Camael replies, "Maybe?"

Lincoln implies, "So it's up in the air."

Ms. Camael asks, "Spirit?"

Lincoln responds, "Heaven only knows." He says, "We'll have to win it off the close, on a wing and a prayer..." He is in disbelief over his word usage. "Oh God, listen to me. God, ugh, what's come over me?"

Judge DePilate asks the prosecution for their closing argument. Thurgood Stone states, "The people have seen the truth. Seeing is believing. The prosecution rests Your Honor."

The judge, in turn, asks the defense for their closing argument.

There is a sense of anticipation—a wave of silence. The electricity in the air becomes grounded. The defense is prepared. The lights in the courtroom go dim. Lincoln melodramatically speaks toward the witness chair. "The envelope please.... People...witness...for the defense—I hearken to the stand: The Defender of Life...The Prince of Israel—" A hand presents him with the aforementioned white envelope. At the witness box, Ms. Camael holds a full-length white cloth that conceals the stand. Lincoln resounds, "—The Viceroy of Heaven...Michael! Michael: who fought with Satan over the body of Moses. Michael: the guardian angel of Jacob, son of Isaac, who, an only son, was at the point of dying in sacrifice by the will of his own father—when it was Michael who stayed the hand of Abraham! To the rescue...the one and only...Archangel!"

As the linen drops, the word ARCHANGEL is boldly projected onto the screen. The courtroom lights brighten again. Lesliannas beams a smile. Some of the religious faithful applaud. The opposition laments. The projected image of the word is replaced by a canvas. It serves to bring the written word to life. There, on the witness box, the word A-R-C-H-A-N-G-E-L rests like a painting on an easel. Lincoln will refer to it systematically during his presentation. Lincoln reads from

241

a dictionary to open his
discourse.

He says, "Let me spell it out
for you...A: A—stands for
<u>acquittal</u>. In Webster's
Dictionary: not guilty."

Lincoln stands center stage.
The courtroom is his theater.
"Once upon a time, there was a log
cabin lawyer who read his own way
to being the greatest president in
the history of the free world.
Maybe by the fact I stand here at
this very moment having been named
after him, is some sort of divine
pre-destiny. But when Abraham
Lincoln autographed this
document—" He holds a copy of the
Constitution. "There must have
been some force of nature that
makes it this day, [19 April,
2000], easier to A: acquit—find
not guilty—if the prosecution and
the government elect for a life
sentence instead of corporal or
bodily punishment. Because of the
phrase, 'innocent until proven
guilty,' and the two words:
<u>reasonable doubt</u>, the prosecution
will have a more difficult time
getting a conviction if they try
to put a defendant to death. I'm
giving you a handicap—it's to the
people's advantage to go for life.
Perhaps that fateful July 4, 1776,
the force of nature Abraham
Lincoln encountered was one of

what he called, 'the better angels of our nature.'"

Lincoln chooses the second letter of the word. "R: R stands for <u>rehabilitation</u>—rehabilitation versus punishment.

"The penal system doesn't work because at its core it only punishes—it rarely rehabilitates. If execution is a punishment—how is that rehabilitation? And if the highest penalty doesn't work, how can the least? If the core of an apple is rotten, then the entire apple is bad. *You can't rehabilitate the dead....*

"Point two: No one who commits a crime thinks about the punishment—if they were more worried about getting caught then doing it—they wouldn't do it. To stop crime you need to re-create what once was a criminal mind....

"Point three: Here's a lesson in rehabilitation we can all learn from Lesliannas Von Adolf, the teacher. Today didn't just happen overnight; every overnight has had a lifetime of days before it. It's taken Lesliannas Von Adolf fifty years to reach this minute. Her first twenty years were spent learning how to be bad; her last thirty, learning how to be good. The lesson to be learned: if she were released tomorrow, there is less of a chance of this ex-convict killing again—then your twenty or thirty-year-old neighbor killing for a first time—*especially* if *that* neighbor believes in the death penalty....

"Point four: Give a person something to live for. A life sentence breathes hope and expectation. Rehabilitation *can* work for a criminal and society alike. But the death sentence breeds despair and desperation; the person has nothing to live for....

"Point five: A convict writer sent me this poem, it reads:

> *If you want to*
> *see a criminal*
> *disciplined*
> *for the rest*
> *of their life—*
> *know every*
> *man, no matter*
> *how tough on*
> *the outside,*
> *who lives in*
> *prison with no*
> *hope of*
> *escaping*
> *alive—always*
> *cries at least*
> *once on the*
> *inside.*
> *Capital*
> *punishment is*
> *a law of anger*

and hatred—to
be just and
fair, you need
to see a man
rehabilitated.
You people who
think prison
is easy, I
swear to you
have never
been. I
invite you to
jail for just
one day, and
see if you
don't cry,
'I'd rather be
dead.'"

Lincoln chooses the third letter of the word. "C: C stands for <u>crime</u>—crime and violence."

He refers to a statistical sheet. "Statistics show these states lead the execution hit parade: Louisiana, Missouri, Florida, Virginia, and the big daddy of them all, Texas. Texas leads the league in executions. Yet, since Texas re-instituted the death penalty in the bicentennial year, 1976; their violent crime rate has risen over fifty percent. Violence breeds violence. So if you're ever driving on I85 or 10, and you forget to pay a toll, don't run out of gas or let your car battery go dead—someone you know may not make it home alive....

"Violence breeds violence. Perfect example: In the course of world history, at public executions; nine out of ten times violence breaks out. And when we televise an execution in the near future, it will become evident— violence breeds violence."

Lincoln opens a black case and places select items in the hands of those at the defense table. In Lesliannas' right hand, she holds a rock and a spike, in her left, a rope. Ms. Camael holds a gun in her right palm, and a leather mask tied with an electrical outlet and cord in her left. Lincoln holds a syringe in his right hand, and a gas pellet in his left. "Look in our hands, see how the death penalty alone has given birth to newborn ways to kill ourselves. I ask you, what do these weapons of death have in common? The answer: the killing hand that lies beneath them....

Violence breeds violence. *The more violent we become—the more violent we become."*

Lincoln chooses the following letter of the word. "H: H stands for <u>hypocritical</u>. By definition: pretending to be what one is not.

"Who respects a hypocrite? The government of the people is trying to be just. Criminals who kill are unjust. If you kill a killer, you're trying to beat a criminal at their own game—they're criminals—murder is their number one weapon. If killing becomes the government's number one weapon in the war on crime—then we don't even need a government—we'll all just be murderers. This is what weakens the power and strength of the government." To demonstrate, he separates his crossed arms and positions them parallel to each other like a referee signifying a touchdown. "If all the wooden beams in a house point in the same direction, the house falls.

"If the law says killing is wrong, aren't we wrong when we kill? Actions speak louder than words. When you sentence a person to die, believe it or not, you tell the criminal mind it's okay to murder. You lose any right to seek true justice, because now you are no better. A criminal kills a person; we the people say it's wrong, so like hypocrites we decide to kill the criminal.... Parents please don't set a bad example or try this at home: A kid steals a candy bar—so to punish the kid—do you steal something of his? A kid shoots an elephant.

247

In teaching the kid it's not right
to kill elephants—you don't go out
and shoot one yourself. 'Hey
Johnny, here's what that killing
you did looks like, don't do it';
boom! Then you shoot Johnny....
People...the government, we the
people, me, you—if you're for the
death penalty—you're a hypocrite."
He reads from the dictionary. "In
the dictionary: hypocrite—not
truthful, not to be trusted—a
liar. *But I suspect if you're a
killer—lying's not such a crime."*

Lincoln chooses the
succeeding letter of the word.
"A: <u>Accused</u> innocence.

"In this century alone, fifty
people on death row have been able
to prove their innocence. Twenty-
three people, who have been
executed, have either been later
proven innocent—or from the great
beyond, a shadow of a reasonable
doubt has been cast. How would
you like to be one of the twenty-
three?

"If you execute the wrong
person, that means the real killer
is still out there. And the one
person, who'd like most to see him
captured, is dead. Everybody
rests easier, and the real killer
becomes more murderous because he
knows he got away with one.

"You need only make one—one
mistake—condemn just one innocent

human being to death, kill one innocent person and capital punishment is wrong. The greatest injustice known to man is the death of an innocent person. And isn't that the reason you want a death penalty to begin with—to fight injustice? If you don't kill, you'll never kill an innocent person. How many times do you need to die to know you never come back from the dead? 'Sorry—we the people killed your mother or father, sister or brother, but they didn't do it. Oops! Here's a few bucks—have a nice life!'"

The courtroom bristles with reactions. Thurgood Stone indicts, "I object to the use of humor to make us laugh."

The judge declares, "Overruled."

Lincoln chooses the following letter of the word. "N: N stands for <u>non-deterrent</u>. By definition: does not stop or prevent.

"Even the pro-death penalty people agree corporal punishment is not a deterrent. Think about it, people who kill give no value for human life—their own or anybody else's—if they did, they wouldn't kill in the first place. How do they know they won't be killed in self-defense or by the cops? What do they care if

society threatens to kill them? I
know for fact, no one I've ever
tried for murder stopped to think
about the death penalty before
terminating someone. No one who
commits a crime hopes to get
caught. Everyone tries to get
away with it. If you're more
worried about getting caught—then
doing it—you don't do it. Point
is—*no punishment deters a murderer
because the criminal mind doesn't
think a crime is a crime until you
get caught.* The District of
Columbia has no death penalty—you
don't see anybody moving to
Washington, DC, just to murder and
get away with it. In a sentence:
*if you don't care about life—you
don't care about life.*"

    Lincoln chooses the
succeeding letter of the word.
"G: is <u>government</u>....

    "The government proposes
capital punishment because
politically; you, the voter,
believes this means they are tough
on crime. We're all against
crime! The death penalty is the
government's way of making the
taxpayer feel safer. With fees
and appeals, did you know it costs
more to administer the death
penalty than it does to give a
person life? There are more than
3,500 people on death row; if they
were to all die tomorrow—would you

feel any safer today? Would we become a less violent person or society because of it? Would the government make your life any more peaceful?

"It is always evil that kills. If you are for the death penalty you want to kill, if you are not: you don't. Justice my ass; justice is just an evil excuse. Just as if you condemn a killer to die, evil lives on—the evil lives on in you. If the government says, 'don't kill' and then they kill—who's going to convict them? I'd like to see another attorney file murder charges against the state the next time the state puts someone to death. I'd like to see the judge and jury brought up on charges of conspiracy. If no one is above the law, and all men are created equal, and the government is just a body of men—then when they murder—aren't they breaking the law they've sworn to uphold? And when they find themselves guilty; I'd say, 'You're forgiven—just abolish the death penalty.'

"This is why it should be *entirely unlawful* to kill anybody. The government now has supreme authority and power over the life and death of all humans: 1776-2000, 224 years this has been 'the system,' and for 224 consecutive years, there have been ten times ten has many murders, killings and deaths." He tears the Constitution. "I'm fed up with people who say, 'until someone finds a better system, it's the only system we've got.' Isn't it time we gave someone else, gave ourselves a chance?"

He appeals to the jury. "There is not one among us who should be asked to, or is qualified to, declare who should live and die." He addresses the media people. "Perhaps you sir, you created Heaven and Earth?" He asks a woman member of the press corps, "Or you, you made Adam and Eve?" He continues, "The government is not perfect, nor are we. The majority of people; are at times: good, and at times: evil." He points a finger upward. "But I must admit; only one is perfect and mistake-free. So when the government and the people learn how not to copy, but create, an egg or a seed—then talk to me."

Lincoln chooses the following letter of the word. "E: E equals equal—equal justice."

He refers to a 'stat' sheet. "On death row, over one half the prisoners are minorities. And while only thirteen percent of the American population is black—close to fifty percent of death row is

African-American. The fact is:
every statistic points out the
death penalty does not work.
Bryan Stevenson, a fellow
attorney, believes the death
penalty has a subconscious
attraction to the middle class,
and I quote, 'By symbolically
communicating to poor people and
minorities, "We will not let you
terrify us, we will strike back at
you." If the death penalty were
administered fairly, it would lose
this symbolic value and be
abolished.' He says, 'I don't
believe society is capable of
making the judgment that the life
of any person, even a guilty
person, no longer has purpose or
value.' I agree.

"If you are a proponent of
the death penalty, there are so
many questions as to its fairness:
rich versus poor, black versus
white, guilty versus innocent.
Rather than go on forever debating
how to murder fairly, why don't we
just outlaw it once and for all
and get on with our lives? Let
the guilty rot in prison and be
done with it."

Lincoln chooses the last
letter of the word. "L: Long live
<u>life</u>. L, L is <u>life</u>. As was in
the beginning, let it be in the
end.

"I hearken the defender of
life: Saint Michael, the deliverer
of immortality, who shall lead the
souls of the faithful into the
eternal light and truth. Saint
Michael: the benevolent,
charitable, angel over death; the
chief of the order of morals and
virtues; the Prince of the
presence; the angel of repentance,
righteousness, mercy and holiness.
Saint Michael: the angel of the
final judgment and reckoning, the
weigher of souls, who holds in his
hand the scale of justice! The
greatest of all angels: God's
number one! Who, at the end of
the age, will lead the angels of
light into war against the angels
of darkness! God versus the
devil, good versus evil, life over
death; in the end—the archangel!"

The faithful love it! The
accusers are shocked to see
Lincoln's apparent transformation.
The cheering supporters fill the
aisle. Lincoln returns to the
defense table. Lesliannas Von
Adolf says to Lincoln, "John 5:24,
The Lord said: 'Most assuredly, I
say to you, he who hears My word
and believes in Him who sent Me
has everlasting life, and shall
not come into judgment, but has
passed from death into life.'"

Camael leaves the Weissman's
with a contract in her hand. She

says to Lincoln, "The Weissman's agreement—sign on the dotted line..." Lincoln holds the pen and begins to sign. She says to him, "I almost forgot, Goldstein said your friend Roman got a producer—someone from his church. His script's value is a million-plus."

Lincoln says to her, "Hold your horses. That's a lot'a Lincoln's." He tells her, "I got an idea. If she's found guilty, I can keep Roman paying to pursue the appeal. I know Roman; he'll see this through to the ends of the earth.... That's the ticket: a million dollars-plus. Harriet, my genius is worth the price of admission."

Camael says, "But at what cost—her life?"

Lincoln replies, "That's a small price to pay." He tells her, "Don't play devil's advocate with me. Whose side are you on? Whoever it was that said, a servant cannot serve two masters knew what they were talking about." He tells the judge, "If it pleases the court, the defense has one bit of business it needs to conclude—a shred of evidence we've been banking on, so to speak."

The judge pronounces, "We stand adjourned until tomorrow, Holy Thursday."

Camael asks Lincoln, "What if it backfires and some supernatural spirit moves them—and guilty or not—their morals refuse to put her to death?"

Lincoln grants, "Then we would've lost one. Okay, one person whose life was spared— there's enough evil out there— there'll be someone to kill again."

SOS – SUICIDE OR SELF-DESTRUCTION
2

ALMOST 9:00 P.M. E.S.T.

Elvis Presley music plays in the religious art shop. A testy, middle-class woman, and her thirteen-year-old, bratty son are browsing. Judy tallies the cash register receipts. Eli, Billy, and Zoe huddle at one end of the counter. At the counter's opposite end; a thirteen-year-old, cute, black, deaf girl is enchanted with a ladybug residing on the open Bible page: Matthew, chapter 18. She is ready to finger-flick it off the page. Aunt Mary unwittingly speaks loudly to her. "Chapter 18: The Greatest in the Kingdom—excellent choice. Wait! da Vinci couldn't

paint the back of that ladybug."
She signs, "I think it's an angel.
It's been here since I found out I
was sick: five days. It must be
an angel." Aunt Mary's sign
language is graceful and
choreographed. Noticeably evident
is the pronounced scar, on her
forearm, from the knifing she took
at Michael's baptism.

The deaf girl cannot
understand 'angel.' She signs
back, "What is angel?"

Aunt Mary signs and says,
"Angels love you through God.
They are God's helpers. Angels
serve and they watch over you.
They tell you things from God. An
angel can be in nature; a star,
the wind, a bright light....
Animals, angels can take the shape
of any animal.... People, angels
can look like people....
Ladybugs, angels appear as
ladybugs."

The ladybug has flown off.
The deaf girl looks warmly to Aunt
Mary. In a muzzled, non-distinct
tone; she vocalizes loudly,
"Angel...Angel." Aunt Mary
doesn't understand; the girl
points directly at *her* and signs,
"Angel."

Aunt Mary nears tears. She
signs in reply, "I love you." She
kisses the youngster's forehead.
Instinctively a giver, Aunt Mary

yanks out the plug and presents
the child with the portable,
ladybug radio.

The girl signs, "I love you."
Running out, she joyously waves
good-bye.

Aunt Mary, Bible in hand,
walks to her entourage. Her
emotional balloon pops when Judy
needles her as she passes, saying
incredulously, "Stars?"

Aunt Mary informs her, "God
enlightened me with the knowledge
that intense, bright, points of
light seen on Earth may be
angels." She poses, "When you hit
your head and you 'see stars,' how
do you know those aren't angels
sent to protect you when you're
hurt? You don't."

Judy says relatively, *"You
don't know what you don't know."*

Aunt Mary theorizes, "If your
mind can admit it's possible—then
you have the insight to actually
see various angels." She
maintains, "Scientists say
'stars'—the spirited say 'angels.'
Prove to me, beyond a shadow of a
doubt, that stars in the sky are
celestial bodies visible as points
of light. Think, the possibility
exists these stars may be angels.
"Luke too, saw angels. Matthew
too, 'inquiring, "where is the
newborn King of the Jews? We

observed His star at its rising and have come to pay Him homage...

After their audience with the king they set out. The star which they had observed at its rising went ahead of them, until it came to a standstill over the place where the child was."'" She wonders, "How good do you think you'd feel in Heaven when God says you're right? How bad would you feel if God says: See what you were missing?"

Judy asks, "Enlighten me? Why on Earth, for God's sakes, do angels appear so only you can see them? Why is it, when people have an angel sighting, no one else is ever around to see it?"

"Because Judy...the angel Raphael once landed on my head, healed and enlightened me with the answer. The incredible reason why angels appear alone is—not because I, myself, wouldn't believe it, but because human hearts and minds are weak and angels are aware that the viewer of the angel might end up believing you, the non-believer. God's angels know some people believe other people, instead of believing angels—that's why."

Judy says cynically, "Amazing."

"That's the truth. God never lies. He would not send them to us to believe in, if they were not for real."

Aunt Mary reads from the Bible as she approaches her friends. "'For where two or three are gathered together in my name, there am I in their midst.'" The group holds hands in a preparation for prayer.

The middle-class woman, her son in tow, storms over with a possessed look in her eyes. He's reviewing his expensive sports trading cards, as she yells, "Stop that in public! There ought'a be a law. What right do you have to influence my child's life like that?! He doesn't know better at his age!" She almost yanks her son's arm out of the socket in leaving. He nearly falls from his $150, untied sneakers.

Initially stunned, the group prays in silence.

Aunt Mary cringes in pain. She prays aloud, "God: I know I am created body, mind, and soul—physical, mental, and spiritual. The body is earth. The mind is sky. The soul is Heaven. I live in physical pain, mental pain, and spiritual pain. God: my body is dead, my mind is dying, my soul is alive. I pray my mind heal my body. I pray my soul heal my mind. Good God: You created life, the evil devil suicide. Suicide kills my body and mind—save my soul from death. The question is not: Why? Is the answer, suicide?"

Rabbi Eli prays aloud, "Yahweh, God: We know the soul is first. Spiritually, if we are not healthy, we will die. Doctors agree terminal illness leading to depression is normal. It is the depression, not the disease that leads to suicide. Yahweh, God: We know depression is clinically treatable. Hopelessness is the number one cause of suicide. We pray the hopeless get the care they need, and for angels to lead the way—now this is the life."

Reverend Billy prays aloud, "'Brother Lord': We know the mind is second. Mentally, our behavior triggers us to decide. When we are in pain, none of us thinks straight. It's psychological problems, followed by hopelessness, that lead to suicide. 'Brother Lord': We know mental illness is curable. Our mental health is suicide cause number two. We pray the Bible is the cure we've detected—while the psychologist looks for clues."

Sister Zoe prays aloud, "Father: We know the body matters least. Physically, it's the defected and disabled part of our life. For the handicapped, it's not the pain that hurts but the lack of respect. We have no right to destroy the disabled by assisting in suicide. Father: We know disabilities are not the end of life. Without the spiritual, and mental, there would be no body. We pray love begins to heal. Suicide always terminates a miraculous recovery."

Aunt Mary petitions, "Christ: We know suicide is a cry for help. Body, mind, or soul; who cares if we live or die? You do Lord—our pain You bore on the cross. We're challenged to hear the call not to help in committing suicide. Christ: We know the attempts vanish after they're first prevented. We pray, after counseling, we seek your divine intervention. We have seen science search for the answers— but, we have never seen an angel ask a question."

Judy says loudly, "Closing up! Another day, another $66."

Aunt Mary asks, "Intercessory prayers? Special personal intentions anyone?"

Rabbi Eli says, "I pray for the upcoming remembrance of Yom Hashoah and the murder of 6 million Jews and 5 million Gentiles."

Aunt Mary intercedes, "For Holocaust Memorial Day—we pray."

Reverend Billy offers, "I pray for the people of Europe and the trip my church is taking to The Netherlands; a country where euthanasia, physician-assisted suicide, mercy-killing, doctor-assisted suicide, whatever you call it—it's death by any other name—there it's legal. I pray we in the United States learn from a country where this evil spreads like a wildfire. Don't they know how Satan operates?" He explains, "At first, they all but legalized the murder of the terminally-ill; then the killing of those with incurable disabilities, like multiple sclerosis; then the death of the healthy, but depressed, by their own request; then infants born, not only abortions, but children born with disabling diseases, like Down Syndrome and Spina Bifida; then people in comas—without any consent. God save the world!"

"Amen," says Aunt Mary.

Judy says sympathetically, "Spina Bifida? I've got a relative with S.B.... G-D, I can't imagine her not being alive and kicking. Where's this, the *Neverlands*?"

Sister Zoe says rhetorically, "This is the same country where doctors risked their lives defending people against Hitler

263

when he ordered these types of defenseless people killed?"

Aunt Mary instructs them, "It's the parable of the unforgiving servant." She pleads, "God: We know you hate suicide: self-inflicted or physician assisted. God: There is only one truth: life. But there are many evil ways to treat a lie: the terminally ill, incurable diseases, competent or guardians and surrogates for the incompetent, physical pain or psychological pain, voluntary or involuntary, disabilities or non-disabled, to save money or to make money. God: The devil knows suicide will spread like a disease, like a wildfire, like a cancer—God we pray..."

On that note, the threesome exits in orderly fashion. The conversation continues...Rabbi Eli says to Reverend Billy, "All that murder. All God's chosen people. New suicide houses will be a Second Coming. It reminds me of that demon-possessed Hitler trying to create a master race."

Reverend Billy tells him, "Thank God, defeating death, Christ exists so that antichrist Hitler didn't one day destroy life as we know it."

Sister Zoe asks, "Brother Eli what's wrong with adopting Christ

as the Messiah? If God was to
send another, wouldn't He have
come when Hitler was alive? Who
of perfection could follow the Son
that would make this existence any
better?"

Aunt Mary tells them,
"Children don't fight. God is
God, and this is life." From Aunt
Mary's vantage point, down the
sidewalk they go. She pokes her
head back in the door. She locks
it behind them and displays the
"CLOSED" sign. Walking toward
Judy, Aunt Mary cringes in pain.
She almost falls. As the pain
increases, she contemplates the
use of drugs and suicide. Aunt
Mary begs, "God, in Matthew you
said: 'Whatever you ask for in
prayer with faith, you will
receive.' I pray I make it to
Easter."

Judy reminds her, "God never
says, 'No,' right? Either, 'Not
now,' or 'I have something better
for you.'" From her handbag, Judy
unscrews an airline bottle of
booze. She offers it to Aunt
Mary. "Here. I'm taking you to
the doctor."

Aunt Mary pours the liquid
spirit to the floor. "No. My
time is here. Please, water...my
body is in trouble, because my
mind is troubled. Man on Earth
caused much disease, so man tries

to remedy it. But before man and disease, was God."

Judy hands her a glass of water and offers some prescription pills. "At least take something for the pain."

"No, it's useless. I believe pain and suffering are spiritual—and not of the reality of this earth. On Earth, science saves you. If you live in the Spirit, the Spirit saves you. The Spirit on Earth prepares me for the Spirit World—nothing else on Earth can claim to do that. You may depend on man's earthly remedies, but I will only be healed by my spirituality." Aunt Mary returns the cup. She points out a plaque on the wall; "THE EAGLE WHO SOARS ABOVE THE CLOUDS—IS NOT CONCERNED WITH THE RAGING RIVER BELOW."

Judy tells her, "For Christ's sake, stop quoting me bullshit clichés on plaques. What's it say if the eagle is a dumb old hen and is too busy squawking half the time to get help for herself? We're talking about medical science, not some shot in the dark."

Aunt Mary says to her, "My only shot is to pray for the pain to pass. Medical science is human work—and human nature needs to see and have an explanation—but people and doctors can't explain everything. In the Spirit World, faith is the science of God—and God can explain everything—so God's work is greater. Miracles are how He explains it." She cries out: "But oh: 'the spirit is willing, but the flesh weak.' God will it, please let me sleep in peace tonight. Please do not betray me in my hour of need."

Judy embraces a weakened and pleading Aunt Mary, and kisses her cheek. Poignantly, Aunt Mary knowingly turns her other cheek. Judy balks. Temporarily merciful, Judy whispers, "I love you, Aunt Mary Frances, but forget miracle, forget angels. Think 'Princess Fatima.' Think Elvis. We'll play games...'Lost Wages' is calling... I swear, I'm doing this for you—not me."

Aunt Mary is injected with a dose of doubt and despair. She breaks the bond. "Judy, I love you, but your words cut me like a sword. You know what it says at the end of Matthew: 'Put back your sword where it belongs. Those who use the sword are sooner or later destroyed by it.' Like a drug addict, who lives by the needle will die by the needle—that is God's prediction, not permission."

Judy tells her, "Don't you want to have some power over your

life? Don't you want to have a
say in the way you die? This way,
you can write a final stanza in
your own poetic life story."

    "But Judy, I've always known
God is in control. He's always
healed my mortal body. I just
look in His direction, and all
that I don't see between He and I
has saved me." She relates, "If
the stars were healing angels and
God were the moon—whether you see
the moon as full or partially lit—
the stars still watch over you."
She says, steadfastly, "This is
the only time I will die."

    Judy is rank. "For Christ's
sake, Aunt Mary, what the hell,
you only die once. Holy shit, I
can't believe we're even in the
same family. I swear if it were
me, I'd die with some pride."
Judy gets teary-eyed at her own
lashing out.

    Aunt Mary too, is emotionally
hurt. She seeks comfort from an
Elvis doll she picks up. "Sing to
me, 'King.'"

    Judy closes the register.
"You're killing me Mary Frances.
Here, here's your $66. I'm sorry,
you're sick. I'm sorry, your life
is ending. I'm sorry, but if you
need to be put out of your misery—
good luck trying to find someone
else who'll help you kill
yourself." Judy says to her, "You

always told me the meaning of life—is death. And the meaning of one's life was the meaning of one's death. In a sentence—yours is pain." She extorts, "Maybe, I'll go to Vegas without you."

"If you say so."

Judy says, "Before I go—I know you think drugs are drugs. But there's two sides to every coin, and two sides to every human being. I know you believe when you're good and God-like, angels protect and enlighten you. And when you're evil and human, that angel the devil makes you sinful and suicidal; and don't give me that B-S about suicide being the number one cause of death if you factor in: emotions, evil, risks, and health." She tells her, "The bottom line is, what you fail to remember is: that while drugs are drugs—drugs are also medicine— every Pope, person, and president, even a living Elvis Presley used medicine.... Thank you, thank you very much."

Aunt Mary, in her struggle to survive, looks to Judy with false hope.

Judy, faking departure, mocks like a screaming fan. "Elvis...Oh, Elvis! Here, 'King'! Ask yourself, what would the 'King of Rock 'n' Roll' do?"

"I'm not great like 'E.' I'm
me. And what makes me the best
me, is God. God makes me. And I
believe the best act I can perform
is to not kill myself. I don't
want to meet God with my final act
clouded in a haze of drugs.
Assisted-suicide is a double-dose
of the devil. It's a suicidal
drug overdose."

Judy tells her, "I'm giving
you a last chance—they even gave
Christ drugged wine for His pain
on His way to be crucified."

"Right; and God would not
take it."

Judy tries tricking Aunt Mary
into identifying with Elvis'
death. "But Elvis 'The King' did—
and wasn't Elvis the voice of God?
When Elvis sang gospel, wasn't
that how God would sound? And
isn't Elvis the greatest gospel
singer that will ever live?" She
tells her, "You know God doesn't
bless a voice like Elvis' and then
keep it from being heard by
mankind. Elvis' body and mind
went bad, but not his voice, his
soul, not the soul in the gospel
he sang. The evil angels attacked
Elvis, but they could never get to
his voice—that's where God lived.
Like Christ, he did all he could
to change the world—and the voice
he used is immortal."

The ploy weakens Aunt Mary.
She says, "And like Christ's
words, the voice will never die
but truly live forever..." Her
praise, solo, without the choir,
like the sun on a holy sea, is
sinking; *"Eli, Eli, my God...maybe
your right."*

Aunt Mary cringes with the
most pain yet. She almost falls.
But, be it her will, she might,
she would, worship her idol.
"Elvis too was a sacrifice, a
lesson for us all on the
imperfection of life and the
challenge to remain alive. Elvis
was the perfect example of the
greatness of God and the evil of
the devil. For all the good in
Elvis, the devil had a way to
attack." She expresses and
communicates, "The greater the
gifts God gives you—the greater
the devil tries to destroy you.
The devil attacked Elvis with his
strongest weapon in the war on
life: self-destruction, suicide.
And the devil's favorite
instrument is drugs." She begins
to see, saying forthrightly,
"'E' did not die from drugs.
Elvis died from self-destruction.
Elvis Aron Presley committed
suicide—slow suicide." She
reconciles, "There never has, nor
will there ever be, a greater
sacrificial example of drug-use

and self-destruction than 'The King.'" Walking on, just as if she could fly, she says, "Oh, what I wouldn't do to dance with 'The King.'"

Judy injects her with discord and disharmony. "And Elvis is more revered today than when he was alive. Christ, Pope John Paul II, Elvis, maybe even Billy Graham...these are the most recognizable people dead or alive. Remember, Elvis is also at peace more so than ever before in his life; the angels of Elvis, shining like a sequined, white jumpsuit, keep his memory alive, so we may remember the gift of his song, his life, his death." Judy, helping Aunt Mary rise, triumphantly says, "Let the games begin! Ladies and gentlemen...Las Vegas is proud to present: Aunt Mary Frances and 'The King,' appearing together on stage in fabulous Las Vegas for one night only—with an encore in Heaven.... Imagine."

Aunt Mary abhors her own mortal weakness. Self-pity and shame become her creed. She says ambivalently, "Imagine...imagine the power and will of God in those disciples who never self-destruct—or those who never quit. If you quit, you'll never have a chance to win the game of life. To win the game of life: is to not kill—

kill an unborn child, kill each
other, or kill yourself.
Abortion, the death penalty,
suicide—to win the game of life is
to not have killed, or kill
yourself, when God calls your
name. To save lives, and to be
alive at the end of the game—that
is winning the game of life..."
Aunt Mary is defeated. Duped, she
finds solace in Judy's apparent
victory. Aunt Mary turns to place
an Elvis statue on the top shelf.
Weak and shaky, she knocks one
off. It strikes her near the eye.
Her eye swells up immediately.

Judy yells, "Mary Frances!"
A disciple, who's won in her own
way, she utters, "See what
happened?!"

Aunt Mary dismisses it. "I
see...you don't have to hit me
over the head."

APOCRYPHA

LATE NIGHT

In the Roman's living room, a
psychic's infomercial plays on TV.
Maggie is passed out on the sofa.
The coffee table is aligned with
fruity candy, empty beer cans,
cigarettes and prescription pills.
A nightmare startles her awake.

273

The TV goes dead. She instinctively lights a smoke stick. Morning sickness rushes her into the darkened hallway. She tries flicking on a light. "Where is the light down here?"

She runs into the dark bathroom. She flips the light switch—no light. Her cigarette billows smoke. "Great... where's the power?"

In a dark bathroom, Maggie is knelt praying to the porcelain god. "Why me? Why did you give me this life?" She vomits the candy and looks upward. "Eat me, God!"

BOOM! A hellish explosion breathes fire from the mouth of the toilet bowl. The exploding cellar furnace ravages the floor below. Fire is everywhere.

In that darkened upstairs half-bath, the moonbeam from the skylight catches Maggie's terrified look. She shrieks, "Help! Michael!" A precautionary, panicking Maggie feels the door for heat. "H-o-t." She's trapped.

She's guided by the moonlight—her only escape. She climbs on the toilet. With her fist, she cannot smash the skylight glass. She removes the heavy toilet lid, but musters only a futile heave. She opens the

274

bathroom cabinet. The drawer
holds *Band-Aids* and an aerosol
can. She throws the can in vain
at the skylight. "Michael!"

With a sudden blast of
intellect, a composed Maggie
calculates her escape. From the
drawer, she wraps adhesive *Band-
Aids* around her fingertips. She
unlatches the loose U-shaped
toilet seat with a pair of
tweezers. Standing on the bowl,
she affixes the large toilet
plunger to the tile wall. Like a
horseshoe ringer, she preps to
catapult the toilet seat at the
skylight. "Come on!"

She launches the seat.
Ringer! It loops around the
skylight latch. Maggie hops on
the bowl. She braces her foot on
the plunger and like *Batman* or
Spiderman, clasps onto the U-
shaped seat, and in a cantilever
maneuver crawls out.

The vixen, in red underwear
and a flimsy red gown, prances
across the rooftop of the flaming
structure. She leaps from the
roof. Like a cat that's stuck or
a bird perched in a nest, Maggie
clings to the treetop.

D A Y   E I G H T

JUDGMENT

THURSDAY - APRIL 20, 2000

DAWN

　　In the backyard, the sun
rises over the woods. The lake
glistens. One sees the stable,
the dove gravesite, and the
barbecue pit. Maggie's gown hangs
from the tree. The charred, but
intact, cathedral window and the
fireplace stand like tombstones on
the ashy skeleton of the gutted
house.
　　In the front yard, a fire
engine rests, precariously, in the
collapsed sinkhole. Maggie,
wearily defeated, is huddled alone
against the large, rubber tire of
the truck. She is wrapped in a
blanket hooded over her head. She
clutches her stomach. Maggie, now

276

sporting a nose ring, is spent. She fears having to move from her resting-place.

A colorful array of approaching sirens highlights her, 'too little, too late,' expression. To her surprise, it's a customized, monstrous, bronze and orange tow truck; its sirens like that of a rainbow. Its horn trumpets a melodic blast. The door panel reads: IZZY and ZEKE'S GOOD WILL AUTO SALVAGE AND DELIVERY—"IF YOU CRASH...WE PROPHET."

Inside the tow truck, Zeke, the driver, wears a 'Mr. T' supply of bronze religious jewelry—noticeably the Star of David. He is a gigantic, deep-voiced, black man. "Thank God, the Virgin Mary never had an abortion."

He is teamed with his gun-in-the-rear window, skinny-as-a-rail, long-bearded, hillbilly partner Izzy; who says, "There she is."

Zeke prophesies to Izzy:

"'I saw a windstorm, lightning flashing. I saw what looked like four living creatures in the human form. Two wings of each creature were raised so they touched the tips of the wings of the creatures next to it. As I was looking, I saw four wheels touching the ground. If the creatures rose up from the earth,

so did the wheels. Above was a
figure that looked like a man. It
shone all over with a bright light
that had the colors of the
rainbow.... This was the dazzling
light which shows the presence of
the LORD.... When I saw this, I
fell face down on the ground.
Then God's spirit lifted me up. I
heard the voice that said, "Praise
the glory of the LORD in Heaven
above!" I heard the wings of the
creatures beating together in the
air, and the noise of the wheels
as loud as an earthquake. The
LORD spoke to me. "I am making
you a watchman for the
nation...'''"

Izzy tells Zeke a prophecy:
"'I saw the LORD on His high
throne. Seraphim were stationed
above. "Holy, Holy, Holy!" they
cried. "All the earth is filled
with His glory!" At the sound of
that cry, the frame of the door
shook and the house filled with
smoke. Then one of the seraphim
flew to me. I heard the LORD
saying, "Whom shall I send?"
"Here I am," I said; "send me!"
And He replied: "Go and say to
this people...'''"

The wrecker pulls up to the
crippled fire engine. The men
exit the rig. Maggie growls, "Un-
fuckin-believable."

Izzy warns:

"'A day is coming when the LORD will take away from the women everything they are so proud of— the ornaments they wear on their ankles, necks, and wrists...the rings on their fingers and in their noses; all their fine robes, gowns, and revealing garments. Instead of fine clothes, they will be dressed in rags; their beauty turned to shame!'"

Izzy and Zeke dispense warm milk and an extra blanket to Maggie.

Zeke's message is:

"'The LORD said, "Now, look at the women among your people. You want to possess the power of life and death and use it for your own benefit. You kill people who don't deserve to die." The LORD says: "I hate your attempt to control life and death. By your lies you discourage good people. You prevent evil people from giving up evil and saving their lives. I am rescuing my people from your power, so you will know I am the LORD."'"

Izzy further warns and promises:

"'They say, "God's judgment is like a fire that burns forever. Can any of us survive a fire like that?" You can survive if you say and do what is right. Don't use your power to cheat the poor and

don't accept bribes. Don't join
with those who plan to commit
murder...'"

The woman asks, "All this
because I want an abortion?"

Izzy's message, on the LORD
of Creation, is:

"'Does a clay pot dare argue
with its maker? Does the clay ask
the potter what he is doing? Does
anyone dare say to his parents,
"Why did you make me like this?"
The LORD says, "You have no right
to question me about my children
or to tell me what I ought to do!
I am the one who made the earth
and created mankind to live there.
By my power I stretched out the
heavens; I control the sun, the
moon and the stars."'"

Zeke, speaking for the LORD,
promises:

"'"...The life of every
person belongs to me, the life of
the parent as well as that of the
child. The person who sins is the
one who will die."'"

Izzy condemns the woman:

"'It is your sins that
separate you from God. You are
guilty of lying, violence, and
murder. The evil plots you make
are as deadly as the eggs of a
poisonous snake. Crush an egg,
out comes a snake! You are always
planning something evil and you
can hardly wait to do it. You

never hesitate to murder innocent
people. You leave ruin and
destruction wherever you go.
Everything you do is unjust. You
follow a crooked path, and no one
who walks that path will ever be
safe.'"

The woman tells him, "But the
law says it's okay."

Zeke tells her:

"'The LORD spoke to me again.
"The government officials are like
wolves tearing apart the animals
they have killed. They commit
murder in order to get rich. I
looked for someone who could
defend the land, but I could find
no one. So I will turn my anger
loose on them, and like a fire I
will destroy them." The LORD has
spoken.'"

Izzy tells her:

"'The LORD says, "The people
do as they please. It's all the
same to them whether they
sacrifice a human being, a lamb,
or break a dog's neck. So I will
bring disaster upon them because
no one answered when I called or
listened when I spoke. Do not
think I will bring my people to
the point of birth and not let
them be born."'"

She asks, "Hasn't G-o-d
punished us enough?"

Izzy's judgment is:

"'The people have defiled the
earth by breaking God's laws, by
violating the covenant He made to
last forever. So God pronounced a
curse on the earth. Its people
are paying for what they have
done. Fewer and fewer remain
alive.'"

The woman asks, "What if we
said we're s-o-r-y?"

Zeke speaks on individual
responsibility:

"'"Tell them I, the LORD, the
living God, do not enjoy seeing a
sinner die. I would rather see
him stop sinning and live. I may
warn an evil man he is going to
die, but if he stops sinning and
follows the laws that give life,
he will not die, but live. I will
forgive the sins he has committed,
and he will live because he has
done what is right and good."'"

Izzy is in a trance. He's
sensing some thoughts:

"'But this is what the holy
God says: "You ignore what I tell
you and rely on violence and
deceit. You are guilty. You are
like a high wall with a crack
running down it; suddenly you will
collapse. You will be shattered
like a clay pot." The Sovereign
LORD says, "Come back and trust in
me. Then you will be strong and
secure." Instead, you plan to
escape by riding fast horses.'"

Zeke tunes in.

Maggie comes clean, telling them, "I'm going to California. California, here I come."

Izzy warns and promises:

"'O God, their land is full of silver and gold, horses and chariots, idols and objects made with their own hands. Everyone will be disgraced. They will hide in the rocky hills or holes in the ground to escape from the LORD'S power and glory! On that day, the LORD Almighty will humble everyone who is powerful, proud and conceited. He will level the high mountains and every high tower. He will sink the largest and most beautiful ships. Idols will disappear and the LORD alone will be exalted that day.'"

Maggie rises, to allow for the fire engine's extrication. Her emotional roller-coaster begins to stoop to her old self.

Zeke consoles Izzy as they retreat to their truck. The results of the message are: "'People crowd in to hear what you have to say, but they don't do what you tell them to do. Loving words are on their lips, but they continue their greedy ways. To them you are nothing more than an entertainer. But when all your words come true—and they will come

true—then they will know that a
prophet has been among them.'"

To Maggie, over the tow
truck's intercom system; comes the
announcement...Izzy says, "I'm
sorry; your three-day grace period
has expired..."

Zeke says, "You're being
repossessed."

The tow truck backs up (the
driveway) to hitch the red Rover.
Maggie goes ballistic. "I'll kill
you!"

Jeremiel Apocrypha, a
fireman, vaults down from the
engine—frightening Maggie. An
Israeli bodybuilder, he is tan and
extremely handsome. His shoulder-
length, white locks tumble from
beneath his helmet. His striking
eyes and magnetic presence soothe
Maggie. She feels he is
breathtaking—a vision. "Fear," he
says. She's a bit fearful. He
knows her thoughts, before she
knows her own. He thinks—
Magdalene angel, question: Fear
the God of Love? He says,
"Answer: no, never."

Maggie thinks—question—
explain?

He says, "Answer: A child who
breaks a lamp is afraid when the
father comes home. If it was an
accident—accidents happen—the
father understands. But if the
child beats his little brother

284

over the head—then they will be
disciplined, disciplined for their
own good—then forgiven. Life goes
on."

Jeremiel is reading Maggie's
mind. She asks herself, What did
you say?

He says, "Fear God? Never!
Fear the devil forever.... *Out
with the Old, in with the New—
don't fear God, God's not afraid
of you...*"

Magdalene thinks, It would
have been better if we had never
been born then to live in a world
of sin and suffering without
understanding why things happen as
they do.

Having read her thoughts—he
waves his arms like antennae: one
hand up, the other open. Jeremiel
says, "...the people of this world
can understand only what goes on
in this world, and only heavenly
beings can understand what goes on
in heaven." He thinks—Magdalene
angel, question:

She thinks, What is Heaven?

He says, "Answer: Only what
this life is not."

Magdalene thinks—question—why
do we die as quickly as insects?
Why doesn't God do something to
help? Maggie wonders, Who are you
again and why am I asking you
this?

285

He says, "Answer: I'm Jeremiel Apocrypha." Jeremiel says, "It will happen as soon as the complete number of those who have suffered as you are here. For God has weighed this age, measured the years, and numbered the days."

He thinks—question...

Magdalene asks, "Can a pregnant woman keep her child from being born?"

Jeremiel says, "Answer: No, she cannot.... In the world of the dead, the place where God has stored the souls is like a womb. It is as eager to return the souls entrusted to it, as a woman is to end her labor pains."

He thinks, Magdalene angel: In birth, God gives, *gives* a woman, the greatest pain she will ever endure short of her death, and rewards her with the greatest miracle and blessing—the gift of life. This is how God treats everyone with pain. How could you tell what sweet tasted like if you did not know bitter also? The pain and suffering on this earth, the Lord allows the devil to inflict—is the bitter. Life in Heaven is the sweet. Have you not heard: life is bittersweet?

She nods a sympathetic, yes. She asks a question, she believes he will not be able to answer.

Magdalene thinks—question—why was I born? Why didn't I die?

Wisely, Jeremiel says, "I will answer you if you can do the following things: Tell me how many people are yet to be born; make dead flowers bloom again; open the rooms where the winds are locked up and make them blow; show me the picture of a sound."

She is obviously confounded.

Jeremiel says, "How can you expect to understand God's judgments or why God has promised His love to his people?" He thinks—Magdalene angel: Every mother who gives birth—gives birth to the will of God....

She thinks—question—if I abort now and have a child later; will the quality be less? Are all eggs not the same? Is your first attempt the best?

Jeremiel says, "Answer: You can learn from any woman who has given birth to several children. She will tell you that those born while she was young and healthy are stronger than those born when she was getting old and becoming weak.... You will notice creation is already getting old and losing the strength of her youth."

Maggie is inwardly upset. She doesn't get the answers she wants.

Jeremiel says, "Why are you upset by the thought that you are mortal and must die? Why don't you think about the age to come? The present age is not the end of everything. Even in this age, the glorious presence of God is not always seen." He thinks—question—what good is it for any of us to have life in the present age, when all we can look forward to after death is punishment?...

Maggie asks, "...What g-o-d is the hope of eternity, when we find ourselves in such a completely hopeless situation?"

Jeremiel says, "Answer: Here is the meaning of the conflict that every person on earth must endure: If he is defeated, he must suffer the things you have just told me about, but if he is victorious, he will receive the rewards I have just mentioned. That is why Moses urged the people to choose life so that they might live. But they did not believe him or the prophets who came after him, and did not believe me when I spoke." He asks, "Magdalene angel, question?"

Maggie asks, "For a woman thinking about having an abortion—technically, when does life begin?"

He says, "Magdalene angel, answer: Life begins at the

creation—from the beginning of time—man thinks, breathes, and believes. This is why we are alive—to sacrifice our lives for God and man—each in our own way. You live, you love, you die—end of story—ashes to ashes, dust to dust."

Like a husband, Jeremiel carries Maggie to the threshold of the burned-out home. Jeremiel whispers in her ear. She repeats after him...Maggie says, "I must search for wisdom and try to understand. I was brought into this world without my consent, and I will leave it against my will..." He sets her down. She is tranquil again. They speak in unison, "Why? We're only human." She begins her trek over the ashes.

Jeremiel departs. Arms high, he prays for Maggie:

> "O Lord above,
> permit me,
> your humble
> servant, to
> offer this
> prayer: Plant
> a seed within
> us, and let it
> grow until it
> produces new
> hearts and
> minds, so that

sinful
humanity may
have life.
For you alone
are God, and
you created
all of us, as
the scripture
says. You
give life and
provide arms
and legs to
the body
formed in the
womb, where it
is kept safe
in the
elements of
fire and
water. The
body which you
form is
carried in the
womb for nine
months, and
you alone
provide safety
for the
protecting
womb and the
protected
body. Then
when the womb
delivers what
was created in
it, your
command

produces milk
from the
breasts of the
human body.
The infant you
created is fed
in this way
for a while,
and then you
continue to
provide your
mercy. You
raise the
person on your
righteousness,
teach him your
law, and
discipline him
with your
wisdom. You
are his
Creator and,
as you wish,
you can take
away his life
or allow him
to live."

    Maggie strolls the hollow
home. In what was the living
room, she uses a poker to unearth
the fireplace remains. The
magazine she tossed there days
ago—and Michael's birthday bumper
stickers—together read: LIFE/READ
THIS/YOU DIE.

Like Moses with a staff, she
moves to the burned-out rear
window. She clears away the
singed rug. "What do I do? What
do I do?"

On the blackened earthen
floor, like a neon sign against a
pitch-black night, she spots the
colorful dove egg that secretly
rolled there days earlier. She
cups it in her palm. Incubated by
the rug and fire, the shell cracks
open. The vulnerable, newborn
dove sees the light for the first
time. Maggie, herself, looks up
to Heaven for the first time.

The spirit of the baby bird
appears to descend on an angel
statuette, as the religious art
shop opens this Holy Thursday,
about 9:00 A.M. Eastern Standard
Time.

The angels are aligned
leading from the curtain that
separates Aunt Mary's back room
living quarters. Aunt Mary has
her second wind. She swings open
the curtain. Black eye and all,
she performs her best, karate
kick, Elvis impersonation. An
intense cringe of pain briefly
thwarts her. Drug free, she
recoups. She uses an Elvis doll
for a microphone and sings a
contrasting Presley gospel verse.
She struts to the register in
song:

"I awakened this morning,
I was filled with despair.
All my dreams turned to ashes
and gall. Whoa, yeah. As I
looked at my life, it was
barren and bare. Without
love, I had nothing at all."

With an oversized, single,
key on a ring in hand; she walks
to the front of the store. She
flips the sign to "OPEN," and
unlocks the door. Outside, cars
commute to work, but not a soul
walks the sidewalk. Mary opens
the door a bit, forgetting to
remove the key. As the door
closes automatically, she starts
the walk back. A gust of wind
lodges a gift-wrapped box at the
door's base. The wind and chimes
alert Mary. Intrigued, she picks
up the box. It's sized like a
bottle of liquor, but shaped like
a cross. With no one in sight,
and a blank card attached, she
wonders about her life. She
reasons: this must be angelic.

Poetically inspired, she
meanders to the register. She
recites to herself, "Life is like
a Christmas present: The box is
the body. The bow is the mind.
Writing on the card is what you
think. But more than the thought
that counts, is the gift of your

293

soul inside; in return, the soul
is the gift you give—flesh and
bone in wrapping paper.
Discarding the box and the bow is
suicide. Don't throw it away, now
or in the end. When God opens the
box, all that remains—is the
present that brings His Christmas
to life."

Behind the register, the same
spot she's stood forty years, she
cringes in intense pain. She
drops the box behind the counter,
then struggles to write a poetic
suicide note.

> *God why me?*
> *Why is there pain and*
> *suffering?*
> *Why is there life?*
> *Why do I think of pain*
> *and suffering,*
> *when I think of life?*
> *Why is there pain and*
> *suffering?*
> *Why is there death?*
> *Why do I speak of pain*
> *and suffering, when I*
> *speak of death?...*

In an odd sight—Mary sees the
priest, Bible crooked in his arm,
purposefully pacing by outside the
store. A rush of inner
tranquility overwhelms her. She's
guided, almost possessed, to
encounter him. Striding quickly,

she opens the door. She searches
intently, combing the sidewalk,
but he is gone—nowhere to be
found. She doubts her own sanity.
Was it a ghost? An angelic
seizure overwhelms her. Her right
hand and left leg mysteriously
cripple. Her body withers like a
flag in the wind. She cries. Her
lips quiver, she's unable to
speak. She hobbles back inside
the store. She turns the sign to
"CLOSED," and locks the door,
purposely leaving the keys behind.
Trying to grasp reality, and her
sense of touch, she lays her left
hand on a Bible. On her knees,
she crawls to the register and
reads, in a magnanimous and
hallowed voice that consumes her,
a verse from the Book of Job:
"'Where were you when I founded
the earth? Tell me, if you have
understanding. Who determined its
size; do you know? Who stretched
out the measuring line for it?
Into what were its pedestals sunk,
and who laid the cornerstone,
while the morning stars sang in
chorus and all the sons of God
shouted for joy?'"

　　Pain free, in the presence of
an angel of God; Mary humbly
succumbs to the Inner Light and
peace that exudes from within her.
Standing, she completes penning
her note in a joy all her own.

Why?...
Why is there a God?
Why is there a Son?
Why angels?
Why a Heaven?
Why is there a
light of day?
Why is there a dark
of night?
Why an Earth?
Why a sky?
Why is there love?
Why is there
laughter?
Why a before?
Why an after?
Why are there plants?
Why are there creatures?
Why nature?
Why people?
Why are there
words? Why is
there song?
Why belief?
Why thought?
Why must I go on?

Like a lightning bolt, Mary
is struck with the most intense
cringe of pain she's ever known.
She's rocked back against the
shelf. Angels and Elvis'
avalanche her. She covers her
head. With the angels around her,
from her knees, arms stretched
wide, at the top of her lungs, she

screams, "Oh God!" She silently
mouths to God above: "I love you.
I'd die for you!" Tears stream
from her eyes.

The salt water, dissolving
over the light inside the
courtroom, on this pacific
morning, appears to create an arc:
The A-R-C-H-A-N-G-E-L sign.

At the defense table,
Lesliannas prays to herself:
"12:24 'Most assuredly, I say to
you, unless a grain of wheat falls
into the ground and dies, it
remains alone; but if it dies, it
produces much grain. He who loves
his life will lose it, and he who
hates his life in this world will
keep it for eternal life.'"

Lincoln confers with Camael
about the jury. "What are we
looking at now?"

Camael says, "Right now:
fifty-fifty. Those filled with
fear and hatred, who need to get
even—the lost sheep who follow the
herd and the government's law—
they'll vote to kill her." She
advocates, "On the other side,
those who are fearless, loving,
and forgiving—they'll be leaders
and intelligent enough to
understand how to make the world a
better place."

Judge DePilate instructs
Counselor Peters to proceed.

Lincoln ratifies, "Your Honor, members of the jury, those in attendance...I present...no...I call to the stand Lesliannas Von Adolf." The courtroom is stunned. Lesliannas had no idea she'd be called to testify. The guard unchains her. She sets aside her drawing.

Camael tells Lincoln, "It'll be suicide for her up there. She'll have to fight for her life with nothing but the soul behind the words she speaks."

Lincoln hammers out his injunction. "It'll be the nail in the coffin that's driftin' up the river."

Lesliannas tells the guard, "Our Lord said: 'You could have no power at all against me unless it had been given you from above. Therefore the one who delivered me to you has the greater sin.' John 19:11. I say, 'What can man do to me that He and I together can't handle?'"

Lincoln, ever the emancipator, proclaims to his confederate, Camael, "It's their decision now. It all begins and ends with whose life is more important—their own or somebody else's. If they forgive—she lives. If it's revenge—she's dead.... If she dies, they can

298

live with that the rest of their lives."

Lesliannas walks freely for the first time in many years— perhaps, into a deathtrap. She makes the Sign of the Cross and prays to herself: "'For God did not send His Son into the world to condemn the world, but that the world might be saved through Him. Whoever believes in Him will not be condemned, but whoever does not believe has already been condemned, because he has not believed in the name of the only Son of God.'"

The bailiff asks her, "Do you swear to tell the truth, the whole truth, and nothing but the truth?"

With the back of Lesliannas' left hand on the Bible, she raises her unscathed, right palm, saying, "I will not swear."

The judge advises, "The Constitution declares you may practice religion freely."

Lesliannas collates, "God declares you may form governments freely."

The judge asks, "Do you affirm to tell the truth?"

Lesliannas takes a firm grasp of the Bible, the bailiff holds, saying, "I always do." She amends, "As a re-christened, true believer of God, I too, shall call

on the archangel and the Word of
the Gospel according to John.
'If you remain in my word, you
will truly be my disciples, and
you will know the truth, and the
truth will set you free'; chapter
8, verses 31 and 32."

The bailiff tells her, "State
your complete name and date of
birth for the record."

"Lesliannas Suriel," saying
apologetically, "it's a family
name, Von Adolf. August 23,
1949."

The judge tells her, "Be
seated."

Lincoln Peters, ever the
conjuror, standing before his
witness, tells the judge, "I have
one question, then I will let my
client speak solely for
herself.... Did you kill this
child, or attempt to kill the
plaintiff Hillary Paul?"

Lesliannas, billing herself
as a defendant united against
injustice, states, "If you accuse
me of the human rights violation
against only one of those human
beings—then the people might as
well have killed that baby
yourselves—they are one in the
same. No, I did not." She
constitutes, *"Capital punishment
is the death penalty for those who
have been born—abortion is the*

death penalty for those who have not."

Lincoln, wedded with Lesliannas' testimony, proposes to her, "Speak now or forever hold your peace."

Lesliannas is thinking.... She patterns her self-defense, after Lincoln's, by spelling out: "A-R-C-H-A-N-G-E-L, archangel."

She avows, "A: is <u>accused</u>—meaning damnable.

"In this case, the innocent, aborted child has gone to Heaven. I cannot speak for all victims in a homicide as to where they may eternally go; but if you kill, pray for Christ's forgiveness, because you are damned to Hell. If you ever hope to see a slain loved one in eternity—do not murder in the name of justice. Murder in the highest degree is murder committed in your heart. First John 3:20 'For if our heart condemns us, God is greater than our heart, and knows all things.' I for one, in the end, hope like Hell, I go to Heaven."

Lincoln asks her, "What does the R mean?"

Lesliannas responds, "<u>Revenge</u> or forgiveness: these are the only two choices in the death penalty debate.

"In a death penalty murder, revenge is just another bullet in

the devil's gun. Forgive and let
live. Be glorified in God's eyes.
He will justly, justly I swear to
you, give you peace of mind. Tell
the killer you are not as they
are; you are for eternity
infinitely greater. In killing—
you battle, but lose a war. I
swear to you, if you forgive and
show mercy—you and your guardian
angel win the war on peace—have
faith. Without forgiveness for
one another, without a willingness
to allow a chance at repentance,
the hopelessness of unresolve will
ultimately prevail. Unforgiving
leads to revenge and retaliation,
and each of those knows no limit,
but always come to a timeless end.
*Revenge: is a weed from a seed of
hatred—forgiveness: a leaf from
the tree of life.*"

Lincoln asks, "Miss Von
Adolf, what if you are judged
guilty by this jury and condemned
to die?"

Lesliannas replies, "So be
it. The dark angels controlled
the minds."

He asks, "Won't you seek
revenge?"

She retaliates: "'Vengeance
is mine sayeth the Lord.'" She
rejoins, "No. I will forgive
them. Who will forgive me, if I
don't forgive? Between God and I,
if He can forgive me—then I can

forgive myself. And if I can
forgive myself—who am I not to
forgive everyone else?"

Lincoln asks, "C?"

Lesliannas chides, "<u>Children</u>
of Christ. We murder the <u>children</u>
of Christ.

"Abortion kills life at the
beginning. The death penalty
kills life in the middle.
Euthanasia kills life at its
end...start to finish. If the
wheels of justice, on the cycle of
violence, keep going around—we
will one day put to death a ten-
year-old bred from the violent
society we've grown to become."

She confirms, "Long, long,
ago in the old days, the lawmakers
used to kill for no less than
twenty-five crimes.... Number
Five: committing sins. Four:
contempt of court. Three: cursing
your parents. Two: consulting a
psychic. And Number One: holy cow
is right—having a cow that kills!
If we can give the death penalty
to a perfectly innocent teacher
for teaching—the only person dead
and alive who can free us from the
death penalty—who, what, where,
when, and why, will we kill come
the next generation, the
millennium, come tomorrow?"

Lincoln is befuddled that his
client is presenting her argument
so well, before he can ask—

Lesliannas hails, "H: is hypocritical. Defined as: that which makes no intelligent sense."

She hallows, "This existence is based on certain principles and laws of nature. Never quitting is one of these. Think about it: no one ever achieves a thing if they quit—it's physically impossible. Hypocrisy is another principle. You cannot kill a killer and expect it to work—it's like lying to a liar: you don't know who to believe. Ever since God forgave the third human being, Cain, for killing the fourth human being, his brother Abel—mankind has punished death with death. And ever since then—civilization has become worse and worse. Let's try a final principle—if it is not working—fix it. Two wrongs don't make a right. *Creation is a long time to go without a change for the better.*"

Lesliannas orates another angle in her interpretation of Lincoln's archangelic, orthographical discourse. "A: is apply—apply to oneself.

"'I loved my brother or sister until they were wrongfully murdered—so to express my love—I'd love to see the guilty dead.'" She argues, "What if a family member, friend, or someone you know is the person facing the

death penalty? How then would
execution appeal to you?" She
ascribes, "In that case: 'Do unto
others?'" She asks, "Honestly,
tell the truth—if you criminally
killed someone, would you think it
just and fair if their loved ones
wanted to execute you? Would *you*,
you yourself, scream for revenge
or beg for forgiveness? Would
you, *you* yourself, *you* want to be
sentenced to die?" She pauses to
allow for their self-examination.
She adjures, "Don't say you
wouldn't try to kill someone...
you're trying to kill someone
right now."

Courtroom objectors lash out.
A male objector hollers, "You're
anti-death penalty to save your
own skin! Even if it doesn't
deter crime—fact is, it'll stop—"

A female objector hollers,
"Yeah. It'll sure as Hell stop
you from killing!"

The judge hollers, "Order in
the court!"

Lesliannas attests, "Yes.
But it won't stop you."

Lincoln says to her, "Miss
Von Adolf, we know experts agree
the death penalty will only
exterminate you—but your
condemners will still be running
around loose—so is your N: non-
deterrent?" Lesliannas
contemplates.

Urim Af-Thummim grows enraged. He tells prosecutor Stone, "Object; he's leading the witness."

Stone's beliefs sway. He says quietly to his partner, "No. No. She's right. It doesn't deter—stop. It doesn't. It propagates, gives birth to, a new killer."

Lesliannas notes, "N: is nature—laws of nature....

"The first and foremost law of nature: every life created one day dies. I do not need to be God-like to understand this. What I don't understand, is why we people believe we are superior to nature. Can anyone present stop an earthquake or the rainfall? When people dominate nature—we kill it: the plants, the animals, people. We are all going to die by the hand of nature—let 'Mother Nature' take her course."

She says necessitously, "To kill an animal is to give it the death penalty—continue to kill and the animal becomes extinct, no longer existent. Mankind is no different. Don't expect God to make another man after we've killed ourselves off. The laws of nature do not exclude the animal man from extinction."

She says notably, "If revenge and hatred are bullets in the

devil's gun—then self-destruction
points the gun at our own head.
Suicide, abortion, the death
penalty; one way or another, self-
destruction will forever be the
number one cause of death."

Lincoln says to her,
"Question, would you consider
suicide if you were sentenced to
death?"

Lesliannas says to him, "God
no. You see: ever since Eve
partook of the apple—we were all
sentenced to death—and just as
life is life, death is death.
Whether by your hand or my own, it
is by the devil we shall die and
by God we shall live." She tells
him, "Besides, why would I kill
myself before the people can?
It's like the old movies we see
where the supposed good-guys go to
the ends of the earth to keep the
bad guy alive, just so they can
stand him before the firing squad.
Do they seem like the type of
films I'd like to see?"

Lincoln checks his watch, the
second-hand stops. Strange. It's
8:22. Lincoln grows angry,
asking, "Is G: government?"

Lesliannas, ever the good-
natured judge of people, says,
"Infinitely more meaningful—G: is
God," saying greatheartedly,
"Forgiveness or revenge, love or
hate, good or evil, God or the

devil, life or death—the choices
are only two. If you are for one—
you are against the other."

Lesliannas Von Adolf lets her
gnostic side speak. "The Bible:
In the beginning God made
creation; He made Adam, a man in
God's own image. In creation's
first natural birth, Adam had a
son: Cain. In inheriting the
earth's evil, Cain committed the
first murder—he killed his own
brother Abel. Cain himself became
fearful for his life among the
people. But, God forgave Cain.
He wanted Cain to remain alive,
not die. God told mankind: Let
Cain live, no death penalty.
However, God needed to act on the
murder so that the murderer would
understand he did wrong. So, God
disciplined Cain by taking from
him the freedom of Paradise, just
as if he were sending him to a
prison."

Von Adolf germanely says,
"Remember: 'In the day that God
created man, He made him in the
likeness of God.' Next chapter:
before the devil's murderous evil
would self-destroy the man of the
world and man become extinct—God
sent an angel and saved a holy man
named Noah from man's downfall and
disaster. God forgave man. God
gave man another chance. God,
with Noah, saved us from

ourselves. Were it not for God, man would self-destruct and die. The moral of the story: The death penalty does not forgive and never gives a second chance, and were it not for God—no one would be alive today."

Lesliannas galvanizes: "Genesis 9:6 'Whoever sheds mans blood, by man his blood shall be shed. For in the image of God He made man.' Next sentence, 9:7: 'And as for you, be fruitful and multiply.' God knowing man murders—*does not give man permission to murder in 9:6*—the perfect God knows killing is evil and leads to extinction. With man made as if he were God, God commanding man to kill—would be like God commanding man to kill God. It would be God committing suicide!"

She gleans, "God promises to man and the animals, I will not destroy you. But the dark fallen angel, that prideful spirit in man—that man himself believes is right—it sentences man to die on this earth. The perfect God knows this devilish spirit possesses man to be self-destructive. Why else would God create life on Earth, if Earth were not to have life on it?" gainsaying, "The moral of the story in Genesis 9:6 'kill a man, and by man you shall die,' is: *God*

*does not give permission, God
makes a prediction!* Kill and you
will be killed! And an all-
powerful, all-knowing God is right
and true because that is just what
we do."

She genteelly says, "I once
had a dream..."

Urim calls out, "Object; not
relevant."

The judge declares,
"Overruled."

Lesliannas tells the court,
"...in it I had an adopted, not
aborted, brother Mo. I loved him
as if he were my God. Once, my
brother murdered a man. God
bless, he escaped the death
penalty having never been brought
to trial. One day, my brother,
thankful for his life, found God.
God, like an angel, found my
brother. My brother then became
the leader of his neighborhood.
But, he lived in a violent society
where gang wars and murder were
commonplace. People were fearful.
Through prayer, my brother knew
God was the God of love and was
against killing, yet my brother
was for the death penalty; life
then death, fear of dying, kill or
be killed, death begets death,
these were all the people knew.
In my dream, my brother Mo always
wanted a baby brother; only, he
had to die to ever see Him. In

Heaven, where they join together,
Mo's brother taught him how in
death, they, we, shall all live
again and how God alone knows the
truest meaning of life."

Urim yells out, "I object!
Mo is Moses isn't it?! And you
want us to believe the evil spirit
that just once possessed Moses,
the deliverer of those faithful,
is the same evil spirit that once
possessed you?! And if God can
love and forgive someone who
worships Him like Moses, and then
give Moses the law—why can't the
people, and the same law, forgive
you and grant you parole?"

Lesliannas tells him, "I love
Moses. I'm just thankful Moses
didn't get the death penalty."

Urim, searing, exclaims, "I
hope you burn like a desert bush
struck by lightning!"

The judge denounces,
"Counselor, you're out of order!
Objection overruled. One more
outburst and I will find you in
contempt of court." He tells
Lesliannas, "Go on."

Lesliannas quotes: "7:19 'Did
not Moses give you the law, yet
none of you keeps the law? Why do
you seek to kill me?'"

Lincoln, resuming, asks,
"Miss Von Adolf, is your E: equal
justice?"

Lesliannas exonerates,
"Fairness is: I came into this
world against my will and I will
leave against my will. God gives
life and God takes life away—
that's what is fair," exhuming,
"E: is <u>eye for an eye</u>."
    She explicates, "In the
second of the first, five Books of
the Holy Bible, Moses, the man,
receives the Ten Commandments of
God. In the third Book,
specifically chapter 18, he writes
Commandments against certain sins.
In 19, Moses writes: 'worship no
other Gods and love thy neighbor
as yourself.' Later in 19, he
also reports: 'nor shall you take
a stand against the life of your
neighbor.' He writes on: 'you
shall not bear hatred for your
brother in your heart,' and:
'though you may reprove your
fellow man, do not incur sin
because of him,' there is more:
'do not take revenge on anyone or
continue to hate him, but love
your neighbor as you love
yourself—I am the LORD.' *However*,
in the following chapter 20, these
divine Commandments when written
by mortal man as law, laws if
broken, now include the phrase:
'shall surely be put to death.'"
    Lesliannas expurgates, "If
God were to speak of death—He
speaks from Heaven on eternal

death. When man thinks of death,
he thinks of an earthly death."

She says exemplarily, "When
God appears on Earth in the body
of Christ that Moses so often
noted when he wrote about 'man
formed in God's own image.'
Christ Himself spoke these words:
'If I have told you earthly things
and you do not believe, how will
you believe if I tell you heavenly
things? No one has ascended to
heaven but He who came down from
heaven, that is, the Son of Man
who is in heaven.' And: 'Do not
think I shall accuse you to the
Father; there is one who accuses
you—Moses, in whom you trust. For
if you believed Moses, you would
believe Me; for he wrote about Me.
But if you do not believe his
writings, how will you believe My
words?'" She exalts, "The moral
of the story: Adam and Eve; Cain
and Abel; Noah and the ark;
Abraham, Isaac, and Jacob; Moses
and the Commandments—not BC,
before Christ; or AD, after His
death; *has 'eye for an eye' ever
been one of the Ten Commandments!*"

Lincoln says, "Last but not
least. L is law."

Lesliannas lobbies, "Law?
The very rule we live by is
<u>life</u>...<u>life</u>, love, and <u>life</u>."

She lectures, "If you grew up
on a farm, and you wanted to teach

313

all the animals to love life—it
would take time for that love to
grow. When the cows give birth to
the calves, the sheep to the
lambs, and the horses to the
foals—they too, would learn to
love life. But, if you the farmer
were to kill just one of the
animals—all the animals would know
fear and hate. You would want to
kill them, and they would want to
kill you. Until the one day, when
the farmer, alone in the barn,
discovers: the farmer wasn't
killing off the animals—he was
killing off the farm."

The death penalty advocate's
cheer rises slowly. A pro to con
transformation has begun.

Lesliannas lauds, "With God
as my witness, may the archangel
and all the angels show you the
one person, dead and alive, who
frees man from the death penalty.
May the hand of God give you..."
She holds her right palm up in
prayer. "...*vie, vida, vita,
Leben, liv, zycie, zivot, zhisn,
zo-í, haya, chayim, inochi,
sheng*...life!"

The crowd is uproarious.
Those speaking French, Spanish,
German, Russian and English
harmonically chant "life" in their
native tongue.

The judge beats his gavel.
"Order! Order in the court!"

Judge DePilate asks the defense if they have concluded.

Lincoln says loathingly, "The defense rests."

The judge asks the prosecution for their rebuttal.

Thurgood Stone responds, "No questions." He says to the judge, "The government and the people request to see the drawing."

The judge says to Lesliannas Von Adolf, "You may relinquish the chair. You are still under your oath to God."

Lesliannas advances to retrieve the drawing. She speaks to herself: "John: 'Let the one among you who is without sin be the first to throw a stone at her. Woman, where are they? Has no one condemned you? Neither do I condemn you. Go, from now on do not sin.'"

Everyone is in anticipation: the nun, the weeping woman, the Muslim leader, the Cardinal, the bailiff and judge, Urim and Stone, the Weissman's, Hillary Paul, Camael and Lincoln. In the center of court, Lesliannas holds the drawing high above her head in her right hand. It is a sketch of Christ crucified on the cross. Below it reads: EX. 20:13.

The jury cannot see, but upon close inspection, her telltale, left palm reveals no cuts or markings.

She mutters, "Exodus, chapter 20, verse 13...read it in the Bible."

Urim Af-Thummim says cantankerously, "Let the court note we are dealing with a hostile witness!"

Thurgood U. Stone states, "The prosecution rests."

The stirring discourse and personable nature of the accused has visibly altered the mindset of many who have witnessed the trial.

The judge instructs the jury. "Members of the jury, the fate of the accused rests solely in your hands. It is my duty, as justice, to instruct you to survey the facts and evidence you have seen presented in these proceedings and to render, upon your deliberation, a verdict of guilty or accept the defense's plea of innocence. The prosecution's case for the government is representative of our society and the rules of law that you, the people, have dictated to govern over your lives. This government was given birth to by the people of this nation. She was born of your very own values and ideas. And since the separation of church and state, in the 200-plus years since her inception, she has grown to

rule as the daughter of our
nation. This government, of the
people, for the people, and by the
people—is the embodiment of the
laws you believe in and have
declared independently for
yourselves. These rules outlaw
murder and killing, unless
authorized by the state. Whether
it be: the senior citizen, the
adult, the youth, or in this case
the unborn fetus; each of us, and
our crimes, is protected and
punished by yourself, the society
of people greater than oneself,
and by the politicians whom you've
elected, as well as by the
President who presides over our
entire body which is the
government. In the name of
justice, it is the duty of this
court to persecute and prosecute
one of us for the betterment of
all of us.... For we pledge of
allegiance to the flag of the
United States of America, and to
the republic for which it
stands....

"On the other hand...
"We are one nation under God.
We are indivisible; for united we
stand, and just as Christ said: 'A
kingdom divided against itself
will fall.' So, may we look upon
ourselves as He—with love and
justice for all. I ask you now,
to welcome your instincts and the

natural presence to receive
guidance by your conscience or
created Spirit. Justice is
seeking the truth, and in truth
you will find righteousness.
Reflective of the defendant's
plea, is the belief that the truth
will set us free. Therefore, let
the testimony you've witnessed in
this trial be a tribute to your
choice for the righteous.
Conceived in His own image,
created as one, in all our beliefs
and dreams, for nearly 2,000
years, God has shown like the sun—
He is Father of our nation. The
law Moses passed down, and the
Commandments that govern us, were,
from our birth, implanted in our
life as a part of our nature to
perpetuate our existence.
Therefore, it is in God we trust
and in His Spirit within us that
we demand of ourselves not to
murder, kill, or put to death, be
it: the elderly, the man or woman,
the child; or in this moment, the
unborn baby. Each of our sins are
not to go undisciplined, nor are
they to be mercilessly unforgiven;
for each of us needs to plead to
our God before we must answer to
ourselves; only then, may we
appear before our neighbor; for in
eternity, will we finally be
judged. In the name of God the
Father and of the One persecuted

in our defense, I pray...God bless
America, land that I love, stand
beside her and guide her with the
light that shines from above."
...His Honor slams the gavel. He
rises to exit.

The bailiff announces, "All
rise." The religious faithful
choose to kneel instead. "By
decree of the court, the jurors
are free, for three days, to
return to their lives and loved
ones to worship and celebrate the
feasts of Passover, Holy Thursday,
Good Friday, and Easter. The
defendant, Lesliannas Von Adolf,
will be remanded to custody and
remain imprisoned until the jury
of the people passes judgment and
reaches a verdict on her living or
dying. Court is adjourned."

The letters, and the word, in
the A-R-C-H-A-N-G-E-L sign—would
cross the land to the U.C.A. Life
+ God, and the presence of Mark
Anthony, if *he* had *his* way. (He's
always looking for one.)

SERVICE - PART III
"Enlighten"

APPX: 7:00 P.M.

Inside the Universal Church
of Angels, Life and God this

Thursday evening; truly looking
like a preacher for the first
time, the Reverend Mark Anthony
stands at the lectern. Now,
ninety-six people of varied races
and religions are seated. They're
arranged in a dozen respective
groups of fours and/or eight's.
From the vantage point of the
single listener in the last row,
Reverend Mark Anthony opens the
Bible. "This is the prophet
Isaiah—around 700 years before
Christ...."

     To the pacing and tone of
"The Night Before Christmas," he
rhythmically reads, verbatim, a
series of verses:

> " '*Here is my
> servant whom I uphold,
> my chosen one with whom
> I am pleased, upon whom
> I have put my spirit.
> Until He establishes
> justice on the earth,
> the coastlands will wait
> for His teaching.*
>
> *Hear me, O
> coastlands, listen O
> distant peoples. The
> LORD called me from
> birth, from my mother's
> womb He gave me my name.
> He made of me a sharp-
> edged sword and*

concealed me in the
shadow of His arm. You
are my servant, He said
to me, through whom I
show my glory.

And I am made
glorious in the sight of
the LORD, and my God is
now my strength! It is
too little, He says, for
you to be my servant; I
will make you a light to
the nations, that my
salvation may reach to
the ends of the earth.

The LORD God has
given me a well-trained
tongue, that I might
know how to speak to the
weary a word that will
rouse them. Morning
after morning He opens
my ear that I may hear,
and I have not rebelled.

I gave my back to
those who beat me, my
cheeks to those who
plucked my beard; my
face I did not shield
from buffets and
spitting.

The LORD God is my
help, therefore I am not
disgraced; I have set my
face like flint, knowing
that I shall not be put
to shame.

*See, my servant
shall prosper, He shall
be raised high and
greatly exalted. Even
as many were amazed at
Him—so marred was His
look beyond that of man,
and His appearance
beyond that of mortals.*

*Because of Him
kings shall stand
speechless; for those
who have not been told
shall see. Who would
believe what we have
heard? To whom has the
arm of the LORD been
revealed?*

*He was spurned and
avoided by men, a man of
suffering, accustomed to
infirmity; one of those
from whom men hide their
faces, spurned, and we
held Him in no esteem.*

*Yet it was our
infirmities that He
bore, our sufferings
that he endured, while
we thought of Him as
stricken, as one smitten
by God and afflicted.
We had all gone astray
like sheep, each
following his own way;
but the LORD laid upon
Him the guilt of us all.*

Though He was harshly treated, He submitted and opened not His mouth, like a lamb led to the slaughter.

Oppressed and condemned, He was taken away, and who would have thought any more of His destiny? When He was cut off from the land of the living, and smitten for the sin of His people, a grave was assigned him among the wicked.

If He gives his life as an offering for sin, He shall see His descendants in a long life, and the will of the LORD shall be accomplished through Him.

Because of his affliction He shall see the light in fullness of days; through His suffering, my servant shall justify many. Therefore I will give Him His portion among the great, and He shall divide the spoils with the mighty.

Because He surrendered Himself to

*death and was counted
among the wicked, He
shall take away the sins
of many, and win pardon
for their offenses.'"*

The Reverend Mark Anthony
closes the Bible. The
congregation claps with approval.
The Reverend Mark Anthony remarks,
"God bless the Book of the Prophet
Isaiah."

Reverend Mark Anthony
proffers, "I'm often asked: 'What,
or who is God?' And I preach:
God, *God is believing in love*. He
philosophizes, "Every human being,
every soul on Earth, no
exceptions, needs to believe and
needs to love. And the unknown,
invisible, whatever it is, thing,
to believe and to love—that is
God. God is the invisible
combination of believing and
loving."

The Reverend Mark Anthony
queries, "What does God look like?
What do believing and loving look
like? Man cannot even imagine how
any of these things appear. God
gave us belief so we could *believe
in love*." Reverend Mark Anthony
reasons, "If every human being
needs love—and God is love—then
everyone needs God." He
concludes, "Listen, every human

324

knows love and every human believes in something. God gave us belief; then He gave us love. As creatures, not spirits, we believe in that which we see. Faith is believing in that which we do not. Because of a universal lack of faith, God sent His Son so we could *believe in love* without faith. So, as a human, we could see what love in a human being looked like. Through Christ, we now can continue *believing in love.* But we need faith again, because, He, Christ, is here in Spirit. Faith, so we may better *believe in love.*"

The Reverend Mark Anthony's powerfully poignant philosophy is plastered on the faces of the faithful. The vantage point from the last row listener reveals their attentiveness.

The Reverend Mark Anthony unceasingly bombards them with rhetoric. "All of humanity shares four things. From the four directions of the wind, to the Four Corners of the Earth, the only four things mankind shares are: God, beliefs, love and life."

Reverend Mark Anthony explains, "God: There is only one God. Belief: We all believe in something, as I said. Even atheists tragically *believe* there isn't a God. Love: We all need to

love and to be loved. And last
but not least, is life. Life: We
are all alive." He radically
tells them, "And there are only
two, two kinds of people in this
world: those who believe in God
and those who don't. If you
believe in love and life, you
believe in God. If you don't—then
you don't. And those who believe
in God, in love and life, because
they believe in God—never lose for
doing so. They know a life with
God is perfect and the rest of
life is imperfect. And to those
who believe—never let anyone who
doesn't put you down or change
you. The born again especially,
have seen both sides of life.
You have experienced the
difference between right and
wrong, good and evil, what works
and what doesn't. The people who
don't know God—how can they
understand or comment on something
they know nothing about?
Remember, those who believe in
love and life—believe in God.
Those who don't believe in love
and life, those who believe in
hate and death—don't believe in
God."

The Reverend Mark Anthony,
commenting, says, "I believe one
of the greatest, if not the
greatest, philosophers of all
time, was Confucius. I truly

believe God too, thought the same. Confucius once said, 'No doubt there are those who find it possible to act without first understanding the situation, but I am not one of them. To hear much, select what is good and follow it; to see much and take careful note of it; these are the steps by which one ascends to understanding.'" Reverend Mark Anthony fundamentally concludes, "Now Confucianism is not a religion, but Confucius knew and understood beyond all else: there is truth in life...."

The Reverend Mark Anthony instructs, "The gift of life is not just your physical life. The gift you can give to people is to give of the life within you, to give of yourself, not material gifts, but priceless gifts, gifts of actions and words; a good deed for the day, a kind word, gifts of meaning and thought. The greatest of these gifts is love. Give each other love; love, laughter, hope, I can name a million of them. Whether you know it or not, we each have at least one; the one gift given to us by God that we can give to each other. Give the true gift that keeps on giving— give each other the gift of your love and the gift of your *life*!" Again, there is rousing applause.

He hypothesizes, "With that in mind...there are four things we share, there are two kinds of people, and there is one religion. *The only religion—is the one you believe in.*"

Reverend Mark Anthony raises the question, "God did not create religion when He created man. God loves man and man's?"

The church voices, "Life!"

He harmonizes, "Remember: this church, this ministry, is not about religion, but God's words on the meaning of?"

The church voices out, "Life!"

The Reverend Mark Anthony raises his Bible. "I hold in my hands the Book of?"

The church raises their voices. "Life!"

Reverend Mark Anthony encourages, "I ask that the original disciples in the audience please stand now and introduce themselves, and share with us your religious background, and a spiritual or biblical message or passage: your, 'words to live by.' Remember: *the greatest knowledge a person can have is to know God and know thyself.* He hollers out, "This is the Universal Church of Angels, Life and God—you are all welcome here!"

Six members are on each side of the center aisle. They are seated alternately between the first and second row. Similar in religious and ethnic background guests are seated with them. Reverend Mark Anthony acknowledges, "Helen, the last shall be first."

CHURCHES: CHAPTER 1

Helen Theotokos stands. She is the antithesis of Maggie.

"My name is Helen Theotokos, even though the people at work call me 'Helen from Troy.' I am an aids and drug counselor. I'm a single mother and this is my daughter." She cradles the baby.

"I have a favorite passage I'd like to share from Sacred Greek Scripture. This passage was written, after the disciple Paul was called to be an apostle and set apart for the Gospel of God, which He promised previously through His prophets in the Holy Scriptures." She recites the first line of Scripture: "This is the Letter of Paul to the Romans: chapter 1, verse 27. It reads: '...and the males likewise gave up natural relations with females and burned with lust for one another.'"

Before reading the remainder, she points out the proof of the passage to the male AIDS patient seated beside her. She reads: "'Males did shameful things with males and thus received in their own persons the due penalty for their perversity. And since they did not see fit to acknowledge God, God handed them over to their discerning mind to do what was improper.'"

Helen says obdurately, "That was recorded nearly 3,500 years ago. From leprosy and the earliest of time, to AIDS and beyond—there have been plagues, diseases, and epidemics that have wiped out entire populations. Make record, there comes a day when AIDS will destroy hundreds of millions in a short span of time— then maybe we'll regret all the killing we're doing, especially abortion. Without this flock of newborns, who'll repopulate our species? May the Holy Trinity: Father, Son and Holy Ghost be with us all."

Mark Anthony says obligingly, "Bless you, Helen. Bless you for all the work you've done—for accepting me, and the angelic guidance that has been with you from the start." Applause

follows. Mark is almost in tears
himself.

CHURCHES: CHAPTER 2

Dan Mazda stands. An
admiring young lady is seated
beside him. He speaks
confidently. "My name is Dan
'Zoro' Mazda. My friends call me
'Zoro' because I'm swift and
because of my religion. I
practice Zoroastrianism."
He tells Reverend Mark
Anthony, "Right now, I'm training
for the Olympic decathlon."
He tells the church, "What I
like best about my religion is
that it began in an age of idol
worship and polytheism—that's the
belief in more than one god. But
my religion preached the first
monotheistic religion of the one
supreme God. What I also like is
that the loftiest ideal for man is
to be like God. With the
cultivation of the good mind, and
by following the path of
righteousness and with devotion,
man can eradicate all evil and can
hope to attain the twin rewards of
perfection and immortality,
thereby attaining ultimate
communion with God."

He tells them, "See, Reverend
Mark Anthony reminded me that he
once heard, the body is just
something that carries the brain
around; and to be a world-class
athlete, I need a sound mind; and
to be a world-class person, a good
soul. He told me I need to
practice my religion with the same
dedication I have to sport. It'll
keep me free from sin."

Self-revealing, he tells
Reverend Mark Anthony, "My problem
is: I'm physically strong, but
sexually weak. I raped a couple
of girls when I was younger—so I
really need God in my life to
remind me of good thoughts, words,
and deeds. I'm really against
abortion too, because I may have
tempted one of the two girls to
fight evil with evil."

The Reverend Mark Anthony
relays, "Dan, my brother, read
your 'words to live by.'"

Dan tells Reverend Mark
Anthony, "Life is not a race to
the start, but a race to the
finish."

He tells the church, "In the
Bible though, the words are from
Paul's First Letter to the
Corinthians, check this out." He
reads: "'Do you not know that the
runners in the stadium all run in
the race, but only one wins the
prize? Run so as to win. Every

332

athlete exercises discipline in every way. They do it to win a perishable crown, but we an imperishable one. Thus I do not run aimlessly; I do not fight as if I were shadowboxing. No, I drive my body and train it, for fear that, after having preached to others, I myself should be disqualified.'...That's golden huh?" He tells them, "Then I like to read one of these books that helps translate, because sometimes I have a hard time understanding the Bible. One said, 'the rules of the Christian "game" are strict and call for consistent self-discipline. We cannot lose our salvation. But we can lose the prizes our dedication to the Lord might otherwise win.'"

Reverend Mark Anthony concedes, "Thanks Dan. Godspeed as they say." As with every testimony, the congregation applauds. Dan sits.

CHURCHES: CHAPTER 3

Dr. Parkinson rises. "Hello. My name is Dr. Solomon Parkinson. I am honored to be here, and to speak. As a psychologist, it's a rare opportunity for me to be counseled. But that is what I

find most rewarding about the
power of God. It's a motivational
tool for me involving the power of
positive thinking. In my work and
in my studies, I've never
encountered Freudian doctrine, or
contemporary concept, that has
succeeded with the perfectibility
of the power of God. I'm not a
religious man, quite the contrary.
But in my case, the redemptive
power of God is infallible.
Strictly speaking as a
psychologist, the power of the
mind is immeasurable, and yet, the
power of the Spirit immeasurably
outweighs the powers of the mind.
Frankly it behooves me; how even a
non-religious human being would
not endeavor to use such a
powerful force to radically
improve the condition of their
life. I don't think of it as
religion, I think of it as a
personal program or plan for
positive thinking. If it succeeds
in serving its purpose, which it
does; to improve or save your
life, why not use it? Why not
give it a try? Absolutely, what
has one got to lose?"

The Reverend Mark Anthony
replies, "Doctor Parkinson, I
concur." He suggests, "But, I
know a greater dilemma weighs on
your mind. Go ahead and share
your testimony with us."

Dr. Parkinson tells Reverend Mark Anthony, "If I may, I'd like to first read some of the literature that has positively influenced me." Reading his Bible, he tells the church, "This is an excerpt from the Letter to the Galatians: 'For you heard of my former way of life in Judaism.' This is Paul speaking: '...how I persecuted the church of God beyond measure and tried to destroy it, and progressed in Judaism beyond many of my contemporaries among my race, since I was even more a zealot for my ancestral traditions. But when God, who from my mother's womb had set me apart and called me through His grace, was pleased to reveal His Son to me, so that I might proclaim him to the Gentiles, I did not immediately consult flesh and blood...' and it continues on in that vein."

He tells them, "As of present, I am experiencing conflicting thoughts. My wife and I, being the most recent victims of violent crime, immediately responded by lashing out; by temporarily seeking relief in the retributive justice of corporal punishment. But, I've succumbed to what I believe is the longer lasting positive reinforcement of this chapter, here is a segment:

335

'For through the law I died to the law, that I might live for God. I have been crucified with Christ; yet I live, no longer I, but Christ lives in me; insofar as I now live in the flesh, I live by faith in the Son of God who has loved me and given Himself up for me. I do not nullify the grace of God; for if justification comes through the law, then Christ died for nothing.' It continues, next chapter: 'Why, then the law? It was added for transgressions, until the descendent came to whom the promise had been made; it was promulgated by angels at the hand of a mediator. Now there is no mediator when only one party is involved, and God is one. Is the law then opposed to the promises of God? Of course not! For if a law had been given that could bring life, then righteousness would in reality come from the law.'"

He tells the people, "The result for me has been twofold: whereby, I was perplexed, I am at peace; where I was left powerless, I remain positive. I am now positively convinced—in what I've termed, 'the self-contained trinity of synopses'—the death penalty solves nothing." The congregation approves.

Dr. Parkinson is overcome by their receptiveness. Oddly, he gets carried away. He tells Reverend Mark Anthony, "Again, if I may, in the next chapter: 'Tell me, you who want to be under the law, do you not listen to the law? For it is written that Abraham had two sons, one by the slave woman and the other by the freeborn woman. The son of the slave woman was born naturally, the son of the freeborn through a promise.'

He tells the church, "Of the multi-faceted meaning to this—for me, the semantics are the coalescence of the covenants of life. What was the loss of one son has changed our outlook and led to the adoption of another son. I'm pleased to announce, June 9th, my wife and I are expecting the adoption of a newborn son." He tells them, "God has forgiven us for the transgressions of our youth, for the other son or daughter we never had." The congregation cheers.

The doctor holds hands with his wife. He tells the people, "Finally, I'd like to close this dissertation by imploring my colleagues in the medical community: I am a physician of the mind, I cannot condone my fellow physicians assisting in suicide. My behavioral patterns these last

days had led me to suicidal
tendencies. I thank God for
renewing a positive outlook on
life. The glass is full. We all
have something to live for!" He
tattles, "I apologize, but my wife
never lets me speak." He breaks
down. He gives Mrs. Parkinson a
huge hug. She now—will take some
convincing.

CHURCHES: CHAPTER 4

　　Kara Kesh stands. Kara is
between twenty-five and thirty-
five-years-old. She has sandy,
long, sun-streaked hair. She
wears a large steel bracelet and a
matching emergency medical
bracelet. She is big-boned,
similar to Judy in appearance,
only younger, and delightfully
more colorful.
　　Hi, I'm Kara Kesh. I feel
bad. I don't have any problems.
What I do have is a lot of
terrific friends here in this
ministry and at work. I'm a
lifeguard and an instructor on the
island. Maybe that's why my
friends call me 'Guru.' I also
have a lot of terrific friends
where I study the religion of my
birth, Sikhism. Sikh's have this
real cool mantra, it goes: 'One

338

Supreme Being; Truth Eternal is
the Name; Creator of All;
Fearless; Without Rancour;
Timeless Form; Beyond
Incarnation...' sorry teacher,
'Self-Existent'...sorry Swami;
'Revealed through Divine Grace.'
Isn't that terrific?! But what
really floats my boat, is this
message in the Bible; this is
Ephesians 4:11—"

        She reads: "'And He gave some
as apostles, others as prophets,
others as evangelists, others as
pastors and teachers, to equip the
holy ones for the work of
ministry, for building up the body
of Christ, until we all attain to
the unity of faith and knowledge
of the Son of God, to mature
manhood, to the extent of the full
stature of Christ, so that we may
no longer be infants, tossed by
waves and swept along by every
wind of teaching arising from
human trickery, from their cunning
in the interests of deceitful
scheming. Rather, living the
truth in love, we should grow in
every way into Him who is the
head, Christ.' Isn't that
terrific? I know it's been a real
saving grace for a lot of my
friends. I know by reading that,
Christ doesn't want anybody
believing in cults and killing
themselves. It's one thing to be

bad yourself, but it's a real sin to drag other people down with you." She felicitates, "That's it. I hope everybody watches to see *Lots of Promise* after he wins the Kentucky Derby."

The Reverend Mark Anthony, smiling, says kindly, "Thanks Guru. You're a real lifesaver."

CHURCHES: CHAPTER 5

The Reverend Mark Anthony nods, and cradles his hands, inviting Jairus to speak.

Jairus, in fellowship, says, "I love God. I'm a widow. My Gerard would be here with me, but he's passed on. He was Methodist, a constant source of leadership and support in the fight for equal rights in his church; a true slave of the Lord for the Protestant peoples, if there ever was one— shame, shame, shame," saying formidably, "The Good Book was central to the formation of his faith and life. Lordy, Lordy, Lordy..."

She reads faithfully: "'My eager expectation and hope is that I shall not be put to shame in any way, but that with all boldness, now as always, Christ will be magnified in my body, whether by life or by death. For to me life is Christ, and death is gain. If I go on living in the flesh, that means fruitful labor for me. And I do not know which I shall choose. I am caught between the two. I long to depart this life and be with Christ, for that is far better. Yet that I remain in the flesh is more necessary for your benefit.'"

Jairus says fruitlessly, "People ought practice what they preach," following, "I'spect I always felt the same way 'bout the Good Book, seeing I was raised Catholic an'all." She says forthrightly, "My daddy was a proud and lovin' man. His religious roots ran deep. He didn't deny the ultimate authority of the Catholic Church, but that didn't mean he wouldn't pull out the switch none, and spank my bottom 'lest I deserved it. I best remember the time we went'a fishin' by the railroad, and I dropped the fish on d'ground—shame, shame, shame," floundering, "Daddy too, done died on me at a young age."

Jairus says fortifyingly, "That's what I like 'bout church goin' with these here folks—all the stories of what God has done. The doctor's story, or when Mr. Goldstein, like my

husband, sees The God of Scripture
as One who delivered oppressed
people—freedom, freedom, freedom.
Catholic to me as always meant
universal or worldwide. That's
what I like very best 'bout this
here Church of Life—the freedom of
all the races, religions, colors
and creeds to be one with the life
of Christ. Lordy, Lordy, Lordy,"
saying freely, "I remember my
daddy tellin' me when I was knee
high to a stork, that my grand-
daddy was an abolitionist and the
Lord was the only man that could
free the enslaved. With Him, we
would never be abandoned. Daddy
would say, the heart of the
religion for Catholic Christians
is, 'it's not only possible to
know God's will, but to know God
personally. The followers of
Christ the Man, feast on this
grace in the good works she or he
performs,'" ferreting out,
"Freedom, freedom, freedom, but
still I feel like a slave—shame,
shame, shame." Jairus,
foreordained, says, "My deceased
Gerard, 'fore he passed, told me I
could always read the Good Book by
myself—Lordy, Lordy, Lordy."
    She says fearfully: "'So then
my beloved, obedient as you have
always been, not only when I am
present but all the more now when
I am absent, work out your

salvation with fear and trembling.
For God is the one who, for His
good purpose, works in you both to
desire and to work. Do everything
without grumbling or questioning,
that you may be blameless and
innocent, children of God without
blemish in the midst of a crooked
and perverse generation, among
whom you shine like lights in the
world, as you hold on to the word
of life, so that my boast for the
day of Christ may be that I did
not run in vain or labor in
vain.'"

    She says futilely, "Shame,
shame, shame! I remember my daddy
telling me, when they wasn't
workin', how the Good Book helped
to free the slaves. And my
husband used to tell me when I
read 'bout slavery in the Good
Book, I might relate it to bein'
an employee, that the lessons that
freed the slaves might free me.
Lordy, Lordy, Lordy, I done feel
like a slave. I keep readin', but
I can barely read past the end of
this part—" She opens the Bible:
"'Join with others in being
imitators of me, brothers, and
observe those who thus conduct
themselves according to the model
you have in us. For many, as I
have often told you and now tell
you even in tears, conduct
themselves as enemies of the cross

343

of Christ. Their end is
destruction. Their God is their
stomach; their glory is in their
"shame." Their minds are occupied
with earthly things.'"

Jairus says faintheartedly,
"Shame, shame, shame! 'Cause now
even the doctors is gone. I can't
do any nursin'. I got no people.
I got no patients left. All's I
wanted to do was be a real-life
nurse. To belong to..." The
congregation collectively sighs at
Jairus' apparent misfortune. She
exorcises her deep-seated grief.
Her guest, Miss Norma, puts her
hand on the distraught woman's
thigh. Jairus says foresakingly,
"No, no, no! Shame, shame, shame!
I wasn't that kind'a nurse. No,
no, no! I'm down right shamed to
call myself a nurse. Shame,
shame, shame! God make me whole
again. No, No! I'm not a nurse.
I'm retiring for shame, shame!"
Miss Norma seeks to console
Jairus, but Jairus is bitterly
angry and sobbing uncontrollably.
Face-to-face, she says, "No!
Don't talk to me. I'm so shamed.
Shame. Don't touch me. Leave me
be."

The Reverend Mark Anthony,
entrusting Miss Norma, says, "It's
okay. Let her alone. She's not
alone. Let her let it out. It'll
be okay." Reverend Mark Anthony

344

empathetically asks, "Go ahead Cally." He avows, "God loves you Jairus."

CHURCHES: CHAPTER 6

Cally too, is weak in the knees. She rises however, brokenhearted in camaraderie, saying, "God forgives you Mrs. Martin-King. We all love you. I'm Protestant myself, and I carry with you the cross you must bear. But your husband and father, alive in the spirit, will tell you: of the many crosses Protestant Christians bear, the crucified Christ represents suffering and death, but the empty, 'risen,' cross symbolizes the resurrection of Christ and the promise of salvation and eternal life. Our Christian family's prayers are with you."

Cally says self-assuredly, "I empathize with you Jairus. My husband also is Catholic. For me, my life, my world, revolves around he and my family. That's why I'm privileged to read all of you this paragraph: "'Wives, be subordinate to your husbands, as is proper in the Lord. Husbands, love your wives, and avoid any bitterness toward them. Children, obey your

345

parents in everything, for this is
pleasing to the Lord. Fathers,
do not provoke your children, so
they may not become discouraged.'"

She says, "With me today is
my husband, P.J. Pope Jr. I am
Mrs. Cally Pope, and these are our
children." P.J. Pope Jr. is a
perfect match for his wife. They
look like twins. He possesses a
dominant presence. Their adorable
daughter is Ann; their son, P.J.

Cally sermonizes, "As a
female, I'm not ashamed to say, my
place is in the home. But this is
how I hope I've ministered to you
today. In my church, I disagree
with the role women play in the
ministry. In my husband's
Catholic church, they too, much to
my disagreement, are becoming
politically 'de-gendered' and
biblically incorrect. I follow my
husband's and God's teachings,
beliefs, and will. My husband
even jokes to me, 'When he came
into the world, he himself was no
more than a child; it was his
father who taught him how to be.
And it's my job to raise him too,
when he comes off acting like a
child, because he himself said,
"If it wasn't for his mother—where
would he be?"'" Cally goes to
comfort Jairus. She places her
hands on Jairus' shoulders.

346

Jairus, relieved, opens up. "I didn't feel like a minority, weak or powerless. Often times it's the woman that must serve to help carry the man, while the man carries the cross."

Cally, addressing the church, says, soft-heartedly, "If I may..." she says to Jairus, "Mrs. Martin-King, the children don't have a grandmother, we'd like to adopt you to be Ann and little P.J.'s grandma." She says to her husband, "P.J.?"

P.J. Jr. says to his wife, "By all means, Honey." He asks, "Jairus?"

Jairus says fosteringly, "Bless your heart, Son."

Mark Anthony weeps, as are many at the sight of the union. He becomes markedly less serious, "Before I lose it again. Chief..."

CHURCHES: CHAPTER 7

Chief Spirit of Life rises from his seat near the aisle. "'For the Lord Himself, with a word of command, with the voice of an archangel and with the trumpet of God, will come down from heaven, and the dead in Christ will rise first...4:16.'"

He says soberly, "My name is Spirit of Life. I am an alcoholic," sincerely saying, "Truth, no lie; I believe I was as good as dead. The sacred Spirit of Christianity saved my life. When I drank, I smoked. I was addicted not only to strong spirits, but tobacco nicotine. The drinking and smoking only tempted me with greater evil. Truth, no lie, I stepped into a dozen programs, but Christianity freed me from the dark side. Believing all things are interconnected, descended from the Great and Holy Mystery—I find it no accident, I was sworn my post as Tribal Leader, and casino Executive Officer, the very day I stopped. I've been 'off the wagon,' as people say, since."

Applause interrupts the speech. The Reverend Mark Anthony intervenes. He confides, "God bless you, Chief. I don't want to say I was an alcoholic too—but I haven't had a drink in nine years, one month and seven days," jokes Pastor Mark. He marches on. "The Chief doesn't have two minutes to rub together, but he is also the head volunteer at the 'ARC in the Park.' I'm sorry, go ahead Chief..."

The Chief says sagaciously, "I take stand against all

murderous loss of life, from the youngest life to the eldest life. Look at the plant family, a tree; sever the root, and the oldest living branch will soon be dismembered. In the nation, we disregard the elderly. But in the Native American nation, the elders of my people are most sacred. By their nature, they are nearer to the heavenly sky world. That is why men of medicine are to heal— not release to death. That is a hypocritical oath."

The Chief's elderly, decrepit, alcoholic, Native American father: 'Prism of Promise in the Sky,' whispers to him. The Chief signifies, "Thank you, Father"; saying, "My father, Prism of Promise in the Sky, and I welcome you to ceremony; to give testimony and sing traditional songs as a sacrament for healing and spiritual well-being. Come, I have acreage I call Handsome Lake. Come and celebrate your individual freedom as Jairus did in her trance. Come and I will show you how to love and worship Grandmother Earth; how to preserve her and her wildlife for her own survival."

The Chief says soulfully, "We also have a religion which was given to our ancestors and has been handed down to us their

349

children. We worship in that way.
It teaches us to be thankful for
all the favors we receive, to love
each other and to be united. For
my people, God the Great and Holy
Mystery, religious traditions, and
ceremonies like these, we call:
The Sacred Life-Ways. These ways
of living maintain a balance with
the spiritual world and all of
creation. Our Sacred Life-Ways
are great religious ceremonies.
We pray as a means of direct
communication with God the Great
and Holy Mystery. We fast, dance,
chant and tell stories to restore
harmony and balance into the lives
of the people. At the core of
Grandmother Earth, and the heart
of the Sacred Life-Ways, are both
the words: sacred, life. That is
truth, no lie. Come. Come all.
Come Sunday, the casino is
closed."

Reading the Bible, he says:
"'For all of you are children of
the light and children of the day.
We are not of the night or of
darkness. Therefore, let us not
sleep as the rest do, but let us
stay alert and sober. Those who
sleep go to sleep at night, and
those who are drunk get drunk at
night.'" He takes his seat.

The Reverend Mark Anthony
says consentingly, "Thank you
Chief for the invite. We accept.

350

And thank you for bringing your
father, who I understand hiked
half the country from Sangre
DeCristo just to be with us." The
crowd applauds the Herculean
effort.

CHURCHES: CHAPTER 8

Gabe rises. He is a thirty
or thirty-five-year-old Irishman
with reddish-brown hair. He looks
just as he did at Aqueduct: a
pleasing in appearance, warm-
faced, sturdy guy. His male guest
is a hard-core, gum-chewing, Nazi-
like cop.

"How are you today? I'm
Officer, no; I'm, um, Gabe St.
Patrick. I'm Episcopalian. Ah,
the, um, the Episcopal Church is a
self-governing church of the
Anglican Communion. Our Church
upholds the laws of the Catholic
and Apostolic faith, based on the
creeds and Scriptures, interpreted
in the light of Christian
tradition, scholarship, and
reason." He enlists, "By baptism,
in the name of the Father, Son and
Holy Spirit, a person is made one
with Christ, and received into the
Church. In the celebration of
Holy Communion, in this offering
of prayer and praise, are recalled

the life, death and Resurrection of Christ, through the proclamation of the Word and celebration of the Sacrament."

Gabe enjoins, "I'm of the opinion there is no longer reason to carry out other death penalties. I'm an officer of the law, a cop. But because of my beliefs, as a person first, cop second, my hands are gladly tied. I must oppose capital punishment."

He enforces, "Ah, the, um, the biblical creed I follow, is from the Second Letter, last chapter, to the Thessalonians. It talks about the conduct of disorderly people, not the indigent per se, but those who are more or less freeloaders because the devil keeps them from being productive during their self-destruction. It, ah, it, um, talks about how even though churches have the right to remain fed by the fruits of their labors, ministries work better when they work out of love, and love for those outside the ministry, like the homeless."

Gabe elicits, "At the station I work out of, I have a sign posted on my locker I wish the other cops would read and respect, then adhere to, it goes:

'Give the
homeless work,
there is no
vagrancy.
Give the
homeless
money, there
is no debtor's
prison. Give
the homeless
clothing,
there is no
indecent
exposure.
Give the
homeless
shelter, there
is no
trespassing.
Give the
homeless food,
there is no
shoplifting.
But always
give a godly
word, if you
want'a
book'em—throw
the Good Book
at em'.'"

He evokes, "Also, I have the
right to remain silent, but the
words I live by are a sort of
policeman's guiding oath. A
reformed cop at St. Matthew's
heard this. Legend has it; it was

inspired by St. Michael, the
patron saint of policeman. To the
best of my knowledge, there are
only two kinds of cops: the so-
called good cops and the bad cops—
as personified by the way we treat
or mistreat the homeless. So here
it goes:

'The good
cops—are those
who possess
strength of
character and
enforce a
moral code of
ethics whereby
human rights
rule; and the
belief in the
power of the
One God, means
protecting and
serving like
the Son of God
might if He
were a peace
officer. The
bad cops—who
use their job
and limited
authority to
cover their
weaknesses in
character;
corrupt
themselves by

enforcing a
code of ethics
whereby
constitutional
civil rights
are primary to
human rights,
and misuse
human power
protecting and
serving their
own self-
interests: to
think and act
as if we were
some kind of a
god, when all
we are is an
officer of the
law.'"

Gabe echoes, "I, Officer St. Patrick, when I go home tonight, must look in the mirror and ask myself, 'What kind of cop am I?' That's it. Have a nice day."

The Reverend Mark Anthony warrants, "Thank you, Officer St. Patrick."

CHURCHES: CHAPTER 9

Before Gabe can be seated, J. Bartholomew Gautama IV is up and prepared to speak. He is pale-skinned, with brown hair. He is outfitted like a highly sponsored pro golfer; casually elegant. He is his usual classy and powerful self.

The natty one says, "Good evening. May I present myself? I am J. Bartholomew Gautama IV, Chairman of the Board of this areas nuclear power plant."

The nonviolent one says, "By the conclusion of the week, I will be forty-five years of age. By the close of business Thursday, I will resign my position at the plant, and retire. I will begin two new ventures. The first, mind you, will be the continued research and development of my calling on Earth: harnessing the use of solar energy. At least with solar power, when the lights go out—half the planet won't be left in the dark—hopefully we'll all be in Heaven, praise the Son of God.

"My second, mind you, will be my calling in Heaven: my work as a philanthropist traveling the country in my only luxury, my vintage Lotus. Mind you, the rich man who lives modestly will never be poor. I will be distributing the one hundred million dollars worth of trust funds from my foundation."

The nomadic one says, "I tell you this, not to enhance my own status, but to pay homage to the man the Holy One enlightened as the world's, the world mind you, the world's first billionaire: John David Rockefeller. John D. Rockefeller, whose work in the energy field as founder of Standard Oil, netted him worth in excess of one billion dollars; who once remarked, in indebtedness to his Lord, 'God gave me my money.' A man, who felt every rock and flower, and plant, was a manifestation of the divine; mind you, every *rock and flower*. Who, alone, asleep on his death bed, at a tender age of just over fifty, death bed mind you, hated by man, suffering from physical disease and mental breakdown was visited by an angel of God."

The noteworthy one says, "Keeping in mind suffering is universal, caused by ignorance; and ignorance can be overcome by the right ways. Mr. Rockefeller was told by the Divine, to give to the poor and learn how to live. Mind you, the fortune in life is not money: it's to be alive. J.D. Rockefeller, an Awakened One, awoke the next day to spend more than forty-five years doing just that; living to give to the poor. So too, mind you, did his only son, J.D. Rockefeller II; a man born with it in his blood, mind you, to give to the poor. It has been said, the only difference between the rich and the poor—is the rich find out first—money can't buy you love. That leads me, not by coincidence, to the divine words in the First Letter to Timothy, chapter six. Mind you, when I first ventured to open the Bible, this is the page I randomly opened."

The newborn one reads: "'Tell the rich in the present age not to be proud and not to rely on so uncertain a thing as wealth but rather on God, who richly provides us with all things for our enjoyment. Tell them to do good, to be rich in good works, to be generous, ready to share, thus accumulating as treasure a good foundation for the future, so as to win the life that is true life.'"

The Nepalese one says, "I too, am in agreement. My religious teaching, Buddhism, believes in the dignity and worth of each living being, in respect and compassion for all life and in the need for each person to find their own path to enlightenment and to an understanding of the nature of life. Keep in mind, the right ways of Buddhism's Noble

Eightfold Path: Right
Understanding. Right Thought.
Speech. Conduct. Livelihood.
Effort. Right Mindfulness. Right
Concentration."

The noble one says, "Keep in
mind, I find it no less than
divine, that the circumstances of
Rockefeller's life, my life, and
that of Buddha, are so strikingly
similar—as if they were
predestined. The wheel of truth,
like life, is always in motion.
As I travel, I will look for and
keep you in mind. Mind you, life
is not about one of many
religions—life is one way to live.
I must go. Good evening." The
nabob taps the leg of the twenty-
nine-year-old, male, junior
executive that was his guest. As
he promptly exits for the rear, he
places his hand on the shoulder of
the unseen listener in the last
row; the listener's head bowed in
prayerful concealment.

The Reverend Mark Anthony
advises, "Remember, J.
Bartholomew, anyone along your
path who tells you your life's a
journey not a destination—is lost.
They don't know where in Hell
they're going. God bless you....
Swami Mahabharata..."

The Swami is as personable as
he was at the racetrack. He tells
Reverend Mark Anthony, "I wish to
introduce myself." He tells the
church, "I am Swami Oscar
Mahabharata. Please call me O.M.,
all my friends do." He tells
them, "I, I'm sorry, we are movie
producers. This is my friend
Yogi." He tags, "Yogi..."

Yogi is a tiny man with a
squeaky voice. He speaks the only
words in English he knows. He
tells the members, "Yogi says,
make it happen."

The Reverend Mark Anthony
informally asks, "Mr. Mahabharata,
O.M., I've always been interested
in things like reincarnation and
déjà vu. I didn't know, but I
just saw on a calendar, that's a
Hindu thing isn't it?"

He tells Reverend Mark
Anthony, "You are correct. In
Hinduism, we believe through
reincarnation or repeated births,
the soul tries to realize its
oneness with God.

He tells the church, "We
believe in the Hindu teaching,
there is one ultimate reality
behind the universe, which is
called Brahman, God. We believe
this reality is manifested in

different symbols and levels of God in the universe, on Earth, and the inner soul of man. The symbolic worship should not replace God, but again, as with other religions, is merely human thought that man utilizes to rationalize, imagine, and envision a belief and a faith in the One God that is incomprehensible to the human mind. This should be wholly acceptable since the spirit and soul are attainable through the reincarnate beliefs that we are the creation of Almighty God, and created in His own image—a devoutly Old Testament belief. That is why, I, we two, as my dear friend Helen Theotokos, do not believe in abortion. The common bond is; our God is a God of life.

"Before the teacher asks—" He tells them, "Our problem, no, my difficulty, when I came here, is: I must not think of myself as an icon. I must tell myself; the stories we select to produce are divine. I need to remember: Heaven-sent. I, we, are not to be idolized. Everybody has a story; and a great, incarnate story of life will never die. God, He is the most creative mind in Hollywood." He tells the members, "I remind myself; to live by the Hindu belief that man attains peace who lives devoid of longing,

freed from all desires and without
the feeling of 'I' and 'mine.'

"Before the teacher must ask
again—" He tacks on, "Here is a
favorite Book passage. This is
Paul's Second Letter to Timothy:
'All scripture is inspired by God
and is useful for teaching, for
refutation, for correction, and
for training in righteousness, so
that one who belongs to God may be
competent, equipped for every good
work.' That is all. Good day."
Swami O.M. sits after exchanging a
complex handshake with Mlaykiki
Hâyat-Alláh.

CHURCHES: CHAPTER 11

"I'm Mlaykiki Hâyat-Alláh. I
grew up in a town outside of
Orlando, Florida," expressing, "I
recall as a child, being
fascinated by the technological
space exploration work being done
at NASA." He explains, "That's
when I knew I wanted to work with
computers. Now I'm currently
employed as video game computer
programmer and operator. My
company makes combat and violence-
oriented games and software."
He entertains a thought.
"I'm no genius, but let me
download some logic on you, on the

greatness and meaning of life,
technically speaking."

He educates on the thought.
"Now, think of the inventive
miracle of the computer. The
computer is man-made. God, in His
infinite wisdom, could not invent
a computer. Now think, in the
less than fifty years, how the
computer has grown from the
development of its invention.
Still, a computer cannot believe,
love, or have life. Answer me,
which is greater—the computer or
the man who invented it?

"Now, think of the creative
miracle of a lake. A lake can be
man-made, if man digs the cup that
is the earth. But a God-made lake
was created with fish. Can man
create a fish? Can man create
water? Or soil? Artificial dirt,
someday maybe. But how does man
create water? Now, lakes and
oceans, and bodies of water—how
have they changed in millions of
years? Still, a lake cannot
believe or love. Answer me, which
is greater—a man-made lake or a
God-made lake?

"Now, think of the creative,
inventive, miracle of man. God
made man from the soil of the
earth. In His infinite wisdom,
God even made man alike. We call
them twins. Can man make man from
the ground up? Now, in those

363

thousands of years, man has not
changed. He has a mind, a heart,
and a soul. He thinks, breathes,
and believes. Still, to this day,
only man can believe, and love,
and have life. Answer me, which
is greater: the man or the God who
made him?"

He enlightens them on the
thought. "Man made the computer.
Man even made a lake. And man
will try to make a man. But only
God—first created, invented, and
made the man. You don't need to
be a genius to know man is made of
life. The point is: *life* makes
the *life* in the man, greater than
the man himself—and God the
greatest."

Mlaykiki says esoterically,
"Personally speaking, my love of
the Word of the Lord began at work
one day, when a co-worker called
me a 'Cretan.' I never knew this
expression was in the Bible. I
know it doesn't really constitute
much today, people are people
wherever they're from and evil is
everywhere," explaining, "but, I
was surprised to learn how many
commonplace names, terms, phrases
and words are derived from the
Bible. Technologically oriented,
it was the first bit of literature
I'd browsed through, whereby, I
was held captive by the subtext,
and spiritual true meaning of

randomly selected phraseologies. From that point, I've slaved to read the Bible daily. It's better than a morning cup of coffee. I focus on the points in one of Paul's letters in particular." He expresses, "I've been so desensitized by the violence in my work and personal life. Even my hobby of communicating on the Internet was becoming an overindulged, violent, sexual obsession. The New Testament, for me, has served to delete my violent nature." Mlaykiki Hâyat-Alláh clears his throat. "'For the grace of God has appeared, saving all and training us to reject godless ways and worldly desires and to live temperately, justly, and devoutly in this age.'"

Mlaykiki says ecclesiastically, "I don't wish to renounce my Islamic upbringing. I just deplore all forms of violence and disrespect for life," expressing, "As a Muslim, and now a Christian, I've worshiped the identical One God, the Creator and Sustainer of the Universe. And I believe in the covenant with the children of Adam, that throughout history, prophets have been sent to every country to guide humanity. I have respect for the Islamic duty to build a just

social order and the invitation
for all humanity to submit to one
Lord and become one family."
He explains, "But my violent
nature, respect for life, and the
level of forgiveness and mercy I
need to achieve for a personal
peace—I've located by adapting to
Christianity. I like to focus on
the good in people of all faiths
rather than be zealous as some
Christians might be. I love my
brothers and sisters of Islam.
Christ was sent here to bring us
closer to God so the human heart
and mind could realize what was
beyond people's faith and belief
at the time. I'm certain Christ
would love Muhammad for wanting to
bring mankind to the Father. I'm
hopeful Muhammad would've felt the
same about Christ."

He says entertainingly,
"Personally speaking, I love
believing in a Son of God." He
says educationally,
"Problematically, the question for
any or all religious peoples is:
Are you willing to lie down and
die—or must you fight back, even
if it means taking a life?" He
says enlighteningly, "Life's
solution for me: is to die—never
having taken a life." He sits.
His female, analyst, guest is
wearing sunglasses and her hair in

a bun. She is uptight and
fearful. She analyzes his words.

CHURCHES: CHAPTER 12

     Baháullá "Blood" Christopher
the eighteen-year-old, bald,
black, gang leader—rises.
Onesimus, his guest, is fifteen-
years-old and is also black.
Onesimus is under house arrest.
He has a tracking device mounted
to his ankle. Blood tells
Reverend Mark Anthony, "'Yo,
what's up? You said the goal of
this church was for everyone to
bring just one brother or sister
and the world would be saved. You
know?"
     He tells the church, "This is
my main man Onesimus, he's out on
behalf of all my blood brothers,
all the bloods kickin' it in the
gangs. You know what I'm sayin'?"
He tells them, "Not all the
brothers can shoot the rock. For
those that don't play B-ball, we
need outreach programs and
ministries like these. You know?"
     He says, tipping off, "So
what's up? I'm the Baháullá
"Blood" Christopher you been
readin' 'bout in the papers. I'm
against the death penalty for
obvious reasons, 'cause even those

with a bad rap get busted. You
know what I'm sayin'?"

He tells the congregation,
"'Yo, if the government,
politicians, cops and voters start
cappin' or smokin', shootin'
people up—the 'bloods' on the
street gonna win that war baby.
Cappin' 'bloods' out there for the
gang bangers ain't no big thing.
But livin' that life in the joint
to you an old man, that's gotta'
sting baby. You make that prison
on the inside, like the prison on
the outside world, on the streets—
criminals won't know the crime
when they're doin' the time. You
know what I'm saying? We gots to
have peace in the world. You
know?"

He tells Reverend Mark
Anthony, "When I was in the joint,
one of the 'bloods' dropped this
Bahá'í faith on me. He said, 'The
earth is but one country and mankind
its citizens.' You know what I'm
sayin'?"

He tells the church, "This
Bahá'í faith is a world religion
whose purpose is the unity of
mankind and world peace. You
know? The brothers were usin' it
on the inside to maintain unity
and peace. You know what I'm
sayin'? The principles were the
same: equality of the brothers and
sisters, education, harmony

between science and religion, the
elimination of all prejudice...You
know?...the recognition of the
divine origin and the unity of all
the major religions of the world
and the recognition of each
person's right to independent
investigation of truth. You know
what I'm sayin'?"

He tells them, "Listen up,
the brother dropped this word;
'This is the changeless Faith of
God, eternal in the past, eternal
in the future. Let him that
seeketh, attain it.' You know
this faith is talkin' 'bout
spiritual solutions to economic
problems with elimination of
extremes of wealth and poverty.
This was a brother who was
stripped of his wealth, tortured,
beaten and imprisoned, poisoned
three times for setting forth a
plan to establish a new world
civilization based on peace and
justice. You know what I'm
sayin'?"

He tells the congregation,
"Word up, I urge you on behalf of
my child Onesimus whose father I
have become in my imprisonment,"
talking it up, he reads the Bible,
addressing the words in regard to
Onesimus: "Verse 11, of Paul's
letter of Philemon: '...who was
once useless to you but is now
useful to both you and me. I am

369

sending him, that is, my own
heart, back to you. I should have
liked to retain him for myself, so
that he might serve me on your
behalf in my imprisonment for the
gospel, but I did not want to do
anything without your consent, so
that the good you do might not be
forced but voluntary. Perhaps
this is why he was away from you
for a while, that you might have
him back forever, no longer as a
slave but more than a slave, a
brother, beloved especially to me,
but even more so to you, as a man
and in the Lord. So if you regard
me as a partner, welcome him as
you would me. And if he has done
you any injustice or owes you
anything, charge it to me. I,
Paul, write this in my own hand: I
will pay. May I not tell you that
you owe me your very self. Yes,
brother, may I profit from you in
the Lord. Refresh my heart in
Christ.' Amen. You know what I'm
sayin'?!" Enthusiastically
trolling, "Amen, Amen, brothers
and sisters!! God is cool. You
know?! Amen. Amen. Amen!!" He
continues to speak with unabashed
enthusiasm over the energetically
contagious, uproarious crowd.

The Reverend Mark Anthony
stops in his tracks. "You know
what your problem is Baháulláh?"
Mark answers himself satirically;

"You need to cheer up." He
comedically proceeds. "God bless
you, 'Brother.'"

<u>CHURCHES: CHAPTER 13</u>

    Reverend Mark was prepared
introduce...however, a hand is
raised. "Yes, Sir. What can we;
I, do for you?"
    The man stands. "How do you
do?" The man, in a variety of
both suburban and urban greetings
and gestures, greets and
handshakes many seated near him.
    The man is a successful-
looking, handsome, athletic, 54-
year-old with salt and pepper
short hair. He wears a black and
white suit and a rainbow tie. His
four-person entourage or family of
guests wears identically colored-
schemed uniformed clothing. One
person is African; the second is
Asian; the third is Indian and the
fourth is Latin.
    Reverend Mark replies, "I'm;
we're blessed." Mark and the man
appear to have a personal
relationship.
    "Deal; we are in agreement.
I know I am not one of the
original twelve disciples; but the
Bible records, after the suicidal
death of Judas; that another

disciple, from a choice of two, was added to the original dozen; making it basically, thirteen, a baker's dozen."

Reverend Mark: "True."

"Deal; we agree. Reverend, ladies and gentleman; I am just visiting; in fact, I was on a recruiting trip of my own. It was 14-years ago I went on my mission. Now, 14-years later, I find myself adding this story to my story."

Reverend Mark: "Maybe you unknowingly or unwittingly, or even satanically, forgot or failed to add something."

"Deal; agree. May I introduce myself; I am Coach Smith, Bill Smith. My staff calls me 'Sandy' or 'Smitty'; I am originally from Sandy, Utah. My players and team call me, 'Sir' or 'Coach.' I live in Salt Lake City and just completed recruiting trips to LA 'The City of Angels'; the OC; NYC the 'New Babylon'; Las Vegas 'Sin City,' the 'New Sodom and Gomorrah'; and now the Island; all in this 'New Unholy Roman Empire.'"

Reverend Mark: "Coach..."

"I am the AD, head ball coach, and manager at MSI: Mormon State Institute."

"Yes, Sir..."

"We, Mormons, are a religious and cultural group related to

Mormonism, the principal branch of the Latter Day Saints, or LDS, which began with Joseph Smith in upstate, New York.

"We, Mormons, self-identify as Christian though some of our beliefs differ from mainstream Christianity. We, Mormons, believe in the Bible, as well as the *Book of Mormon*. We believe that all people are spirit-children of God. We, Mormons, believe that returning to God requires following the example of Christ and accepting his atonement through ordinances such as baptism. We believe that Christ's church was restored through Joseph Smith and is guided by living prophets and apostles. Central to Mormon faith is the belief that God speaks to his children and answers their prayers."

Reverend Mark theorizes, "Coach Smith, to me, personally, Mormonism is like the new Judaism; only they believe in the Christ. It's almost like this new 'Prosperity Gospel'; where everything is prosperous, productive and positive. In my enlightenment, education and life experience Mormons can be too materialistic and wealthy; while Christ was homeless and penniless; but Adam, Abraham, Job, David, Solomon, even John, Peter, and maybe even Paul had made for a wealthy club; so one never knows."

"We are in agreement. It's up to Heavenly Father. In my career or business; sports and entertainment are synonymous. My players or I can earn letters; and oddly, I can even be prophetic and predictive; and I can work or deal with acronyms like ESP, NFL and PSI. Do you know that math is a language of God's?" It's been said, 'numbers never lie.'" But spiritually and strategically, there's only a ten-percent chance I will be a success because the networking in both businesses is fraternally Jewish, or even minority and female biased; and the Mormon in me has a better chance to succeed because of my business background than does the Christian in me who spends most of his time, energy and talents talking to God and preaching football or sports."

Reverend Mark reports, "I love sports. To me, it's a game of math and men. And as noted, math is God's language."

"We agree. In Jewish culture the number seven is blessed, or as Americans would say, 'Lucky.'"

"Don't believe in 'luck.'"

"Agree."

"Don't even believe in 'good luck.'"

"Deal; we are in agreement."

"Would rather say, 'God Bless.'"

"Deal; we agree."

"We all know '10': 'The Ten Commandments.' Forty: Noah and it rained for 40-days and nights. Moses 40-years in the desert; Christ, 40-days and nights He was tempted by the devil; and women, a woman's gestation period is 40-weeks or 9-months. Turn nine upside down and we all know, 'the Devil's number' of 6-6-6."

"Deal; agree."

"Coach Smith, I imagine you have a Bible and the *Book of Mormon*; with all due respect, would you please read?"

"We..." Smith refers to the four in his entourage or family with him, "We agree to share four verses all from First Timothy, chapter 6, NIV."

He reads, "Verses 1+2: 'All who are under the yoke of slavery should consider their masters worthy of full respect, so that God's name and our teaching may not be slandered. Those who have believing masters should not show them disrespect just because they are fellow believers. Instead, they should serve them even better because their masters are dear to them as fellow believers and are devoted to the welfare of their slaves.'"

The four in his entourage nod in agreement.

He reads, "The chapter: False Teachers and the Love of Money, verses 6-10: 'But godliness with contentment is great gain. For we brought nothing into the world, and we can take nothing out of it. But if we have food and clothing, we will be content with that. Those who want to get rich fall into temptation and a trap and into many foolish and harmful desires that plunge people into ruin and destruction. For the love of money is a root of all kinds of evil. Some people, eager for money, have wandered from the faith and pierced themselves with many griefs.'"

The four in his entourage nod in agreement.

He reads, "Verses 11+12: 'But you, man of God, flee from all this, and pursue righteousness, godliness, faith, love, endurance and gentleness. Fight the good fight of the faith. Take hold of the eternal life to which you were called when you made your good confession in the presence of many witnesses.'"

The four in his entourage nod in agreement.

He reads, "Verses 20+21: 'Timothy, guard what has been entrusted to your care. Turn away from godless chatter and the opposing ideas of what is falsely called knowledge, which some have professed and in so doing have departed from the faith. Grace be with you all.'"

The four in his entourage nod in agreement.

Reverend Mark offers, "Coach, billions watch sports and show business; and billions and billionaires are invested in sports; that just about covers the world?"

"We are in agreement."

"That's why you're the best."

"I am at MSI now, but one day, I hope and pray; I am an owner, co-owner, Managing General Partner, coach, or even strategist or analyst for a team in LA, 'The City of Angels.' They could be called 'The Archangels'; because of all the sports or animal team nicknames; that is the most powerful of all the sports; more powerful than the California Angels or the Jersey Devils. One could even have prophetically predicted after God sent a hurricane; the Saints would win the Super Bowl and one day, LA; 'The Big One.'"

"Coach Smith, do Mormons believe in angels?"

"The Angel Moroni is, in Mormonism, an angel that visited Joseph Smith. The angel was the guardian of the golden plates, which Latter Day Saints believe were the source material for the *Book of Mormon*."

"I could make a joke, here, saying Angel Moroni is the Italian baker who cooked-up something; but I know religion is no joke. The Lord God didn't make jokes in the Bible..."

"We agree."

"...Salvation is serious business."

"Agree."

"Coach, final words..."

"The team that wins is the team that wants to win."

"Thanks, Coach."

"Ps. No game means more than 'the game of life.' Go Archangels!"

Reverend Mark: "Peace and God bless you."

CHURCHES: CHAPTER 14

A vacant chair is on The Reverend Mark Anthony's left. Designed symbolically, in a triangle, Ernie is seated acutely to Reverend Mark Anthony's right. The Reverend Mark Anthony lays Ernie out, saying, "If Christ is seated at the right hand of The Father—then Mr. Ernie Goldstein is our right-hand man."

Ernie takes a microphone and addresses the masses. He tells Reverend Mark Anthony, "What can I say? I study the Torah, Scripture, and the Talmud. But unlike the tradition, wisdom, and law, I read the New Testament!... I just love the Universal Church!...

"This is the letter to the Hebrews." The Talmudist reads: "'In times past, God spoke in partial and various ways to our ancestors through the prophets; in these last days, He spoke to us through a Son, whom He made heir of all things and through whom He created the universe...'" The audience applauds.

He tells the church: "'...Who is the refulgence of His glory, the very imprint of His being, and who sustains all things by His mighty Word. When He had accomplished purification from sins, He took His seat at the right hand of the Majesty on high, as far superior to the angels as the name He has inherited is more excellent than theirs.'"

He tells them, "What can I
say? I presently practice my
first love, Judaism, as I said.
Although, I often quip with the
Pastor, I'm still a practicing
Jew, because I'm hoping to get it
perfect.... What else? I just
love angels! 'For to which of the
angels did God ever say: "You are
my Son; this day I have begotten
You?" And again, when He leads
the first born into the world, He
says: "Let all the angels of God
worship Him." Of the angels, He
says: "He makes His angels winds
and His ministers a fiery flame."
But to which of the angels has He
ever said: "Sit at my right hand
until I make your enemies your
footstool"? Are they not all
ministering spirits sent to serve,
for the sake of those who are to
inherit salvation?'"

    The transfuser reads:
"'Therefore, we must attend all
the more to what we have so that
we may not be carried away. For
if the word announced through
angels proved firm, and every
transgression and disobedience
received its just recompense, how
shall we escape if we ignore so
great a salvation? Announced
originally through the Lord, it
was confirmed for us by those who
had heard. God added His
testimony by signs, wonders,

various acts of power, and
distribution of the gifts of the
Holy Spirit according to His will.
For it was not to angels that He
subjected the world to come, of
which we are speaking. Instead,
someone has testified somewhere:
"What is man that you are mindful
of Him, or the Son of Man that you
care for Him? You made Him for a
little while lower than the
angels; You crowned Him with glory
and honor, subjecting all things
under His feet." In "subjecting"
all things, He left nothing not
"subject to Him." Yet at present
we do not see "all things subject
to Him...."'"

　　　He tells the group, "What can
I say? I once told a teacher in
temple, 'I love the Son of God.'
And he said words I'll never
forget, 'Without a Jew like me,
there would be no Christianity.'
I just love angels! I love
life!...'"'According to the law
almost everything is purified by
blood, and without the shedding of
blood there is no forgiveness.
Therefore, it was necessary for
the copies of the heavenly things
to be purified by these rites, but
the heavenly things themselves by
better sacrifices than these. For
Christ did not enter into a
sanctuary made by hands, a copy of
the true one, but heaven itself,

that He might now appear before
God on our behalf. Not that He
might offer Himself repeatedly, as
the high priest enters each year
into the sanctuary with blood that
is not his own; if that were so,
He would have had to suffer
repeatedly from the foundation of
the world. But now once for all
He has appeared at the end of the
ages to take away sin by His
sacrifice. Just as it is
appointed that human beings die
once, and after this judgment, so
also Christ, offered once to take
away the sins of many, will appear
a second time, not to take away
sin but to bring salvation to
those who eagerly await Him.'"

He tells Reverend Mark
Anthony, "What can I say? Judaism
is a civilization emphasizing the
peoplehood of all its adherents,
based on the belief in one God,
coveted with the land of Israel
promised by God from the time of
the patriarchs.... What else? I
just love life! I love God!

"'Since the law has only a
shadow of the good things to come,
and not the very image of them, it
can never make perfect those who
come to worship by the same
sacrifices that have ceased to be
offered, since the worshipers,
once cleansed, would no longer
have had any consciousness of

sins? But in those sacrifices
there is only a yearly remembrance
of sins, for it is impossible that
the blood of bulls and goats take
away sins. For this reason, when
He came into the world, He said:
"Sacrifice and offering You did
not desire, but a body You
prepared for Me; holocausts and
sin offerings You took no delight
in." Then I said, "As is written
of Me in the scroll, behold, I
come to do Your will, O God."
...Every priest stands daily at
his ministry, offering frequently
those same sacrifices that can
never take away sins. But this
One offered one sacrifice for
sins, and took His seat forever at
the right hand of God; now He
waits until His enemies are made
His footstool. For by one
offering He has made perfect
forever those who are being
consecrated. The Holy Spirit also
testifies to us, for after saying:
"This is the covenant I will
establish with them after those
days, says the LORD: I will put
my laws in their hearts, and I
will write them upon their minds,"
He also says: "Their sins and
their evil doing I will remember
no more." Where there is
forgiveness of these, there is no
longer offering for sin.'"

He tells the church, "What
can I say? My obligation to God
is carried out through the
observance of *mitzvoth*, the
Commandments or Divine
expectations that are both of a
ritual nature, and an ethical
nature.... I just love God!
'Consider how He endured such
opposition from sinners, in order
that you may not grow weary or
lose heart. In your struggle
against sin you have not resisted
to the point of shedding blood.
You have also forgotten the
exhortation addressed to you as
sons: "My son, do not disdain the
discipline of the LORD or lose
heart when reproved by Him; for
whom the LORD loves, He
disciplines; He scourges every son
He acknowledges." Endure your
trials as "discipline"; God treats
you as sons. For what "son" is
there whom his father does not
discipline?'"
　　　He tells them, "What can I
say? God does not work the way we
work. Human nature and mortal
weakness control our being. To
disciple ourselves with God, we
need to trust in the way He
disciplines us for our own well
being, even in ways most of us
fail to understand. Like the
father who removes his child's
hand from a flaming oven without

explaining before doing so, if the father reasoned then reacted, the child would burn. React first, then let the child listen as the father explains why it was done for the child's own good.... What else? I just love angels! I love life! I love God!

 "'Besides this, we have had our earthly fathers to discipline us, and we respected them. Should we not submit all the more to the Father of spirits and live? They disciplined us for a short time as seemed right to them, but He does so for our benefit, in order that we may share His holiness. At the time, all discipline seems a cause not for joy but for pain, yet later it brings the peaceful fruit of righteousness to those who are trained by it.'"

The listener at the utmost rear of the congregation shows their attentiveness.

The trainman continues from memory: "'So strengthen your drooping hands and your weak knees. Make straight paths for your feet, that what is lame may not be dislocated but healed.'"

The Reverend Mark Anthony, the empty chair, Ernie, the original members and the audience all vicariously unite.

Ernie tells the group, "What can I say? I'm not certain that

I'm a Messianic Jew; I just love the Universal Church of Angels, Life and God!"

The theologian reads: "'Let mutual love continue. Do not neglect hospitality, for through it some have unknowingly entertained angels. Be mindful of prisoners as if sharing their imprisonment, and of the ill-treated as of yourselves, for you also are in the body. Let marriage be honored among all and the marriage bed be kept undefiled, for God will judge the immoral and adulterers. Let your life be free from love of money but be content with what you have, for He has said, "I will never forsake you or abandon you." Thus we may say with confidence: "The Lord is my helper, I will not be afraid. What can anyone do to me?" Remember your leaders who spoke the word of God to you. Consider the outcome of their way of life and imitate their faith...Christ is the same yesterday, today, and forever!'

"My people, God love them; have waited thousands of years for the Messiah. I'm ready to celebrate right now! Why wait any longer? I read the New Testament and God's Chosen One has arrived!...*How many times do people wait for the train only to*

miss it? It's not that it hasn't
come yet—it's that we didn't know
it when it passed by!"

Ernie receives his warranted
applause.

TESTAMENT

The Reverend Mark Anthony
acknowledges Ernie before taking
over the lectern. The Reverend
Mark Anthony enlightens them. "I
love sports, so sport inspires me.
I love movies, so a movie inspires
me. I am a person, so you people
inspire me!"

Mark Anthony, in oneness,
reveals, "My words to live by are
from the disciple Paul's Second
Letter to the Corinthians: 'I
must boast; not that it is
profitable, but I will go on to
visions and revelations of the
Lord. I know someone in Christ
who, fourteen years ago [whether
in the body or out of the body I
do not know, God knows], was
caught up to the third heaven.
And I know that this person
[whether in the body or out of the
body I do not know, God knows] was
caught up into Paradise and heard
ineffable things, which no one may
utter. About this person I will
boast, but about myself I will not

boast, except about my weaknesses. Although if I should wish to boast, I would not be foolish, for I would be telling the truth. But I refrain, so that no one may think more of me than what he sees in me or hears from me because of the abundance of the revelations. Therefore, that I might not become too elated, a thorn in the flesh was given to me, an angel of Satan, to beat me, to keep me from being too elated. Three times I begged the Lord about this, that it might leave me, but He said to me, "My grace is sufficient for you, for power is made perfect in weakness." I will rather boast most gladly of my weaknesses, in order that the power of Christ may dwell with me. Therefore, I am content with weaknesses, insults, hardships, persecutions, and constraints, for the sake of Christ; for when I am weak, then I am strong.'" He confesses, "*I am a Roman Catholic Christian and addiction is against my religion!*" He discloses, "My body is full of life! My mind is free to dream, free to dream of life—that's what dreams are made of! My soul is alive! My Lord and my mother loved me to death—I am alive with life!"

The Reverend Mark Anthony contests, "Because of life,

I am against abortion, suicide and the death penalty. Do you know: There are as many movie theaters that you do see, as there are abortion clinics that you don't see? Think about that every time you go to see a movie.... Do you know: My life is like a roller coaster? The highest I go, is the lowest I go—up and down, high and low. And once my life has reached its peak—then I will die. But I will not commit suicide. I'm telling you God's honest truth—if you're escorted by God's angels, then it's not a suicide.... Do you know: It's worse in God's eyes when you say, 'He killed first, so it's okay for me to kill.' He's an evil criminal; you're supposed to be good and just. It's like the two players who get into a fight during a football game. God, the referee, always sees the second guy who retaliates, and he's the one who gets the penalty." He tackles the point. "Don't trade evil for evil—trade evil for good."

Mark Anthony contends, "Remember, this church has one divine plan: follow the religion you were born into believing, and follow Christ. Share your religion with Christianity. You don't need to give up your religion to believe in Christ. If

you believe in both your religion
and Christ—Christ believes in your
religion and you. Every religion
on Earth was created by a person—
and Christ loves all people. If
you believe in Christ—Christ
believes in you," saying
circumspectively, "As I said
earlier, the only religion—is the
one *you* believe in. But that
doesn't mean I can't ask you to
adopt another religion."

He shares with them, "Imagine
a father and his family; he has
one child of his own, and he later
adopts a son. Both children will
not be the same. They may have
been born with different inherent
beliefs. But as they grow, the
two learn to understand one
another's teachings and beliefs.
But all the while, what holds the
family together—is the love the
father feels for the both of
them."

The Reverend Mark Anthony
prophetically tells them, "I'll
play my part, but this ministry is
like a great movie—it depends on
good word of mouth...so spread the
Word.... No one else is, but try
to act like Christ. It's time
for, as Christ said; action to
speak louder than words—I have
spoken enough.... For when I
speak, and I sense greatness in
something I've said—I sense the

Word of God. For I don't believe,
I can even imagine saying such a
thing. I don't believe I have it
in me. At best, I can only lay
claim to having been there—when
God revealed his greatness to me!"

The seated congregation
cheers, waiting to explode. From
the vantage point of the last row
listener, mud-stained Bible in his
hands, the Reverend Mark Anthony
concludes. "God bless you! Give
yourselves a hand!"

The last row listener stands,
giving himself a rousing standing
ovation. The loud and long
clapping actually makes a scene.
The congregation grows silent.
It's Michael, standing alone.
"I'm sorry people. I love you."

The Reverend Mark Anthony,
himself, wonders about Michael's
eccentric behavior. "Mr. Roman?"

Michael steps into the aisle,
his briefcase in his seat. "I'm
giving myself a standing
ovation..." He praises, "God
loves me! My name is Michael—and
I love God!!" He proceeds
forward, cradling his briefcase.
His appearance epitomizes that of
an itinerant homeless person.

The entire congregation
explodes in ovation—never knowing
it was Michael who financed the
church revival—they're just joyful
he's found God. The band plays

the theme music. The service has
ended.

The Reverend Mark Anthony
sings out, "I love you!! God
bless you!!!"

Michael is hoisted through
the swarming crowd. The Reverend
Mark Anthony jumps down from the
stage and greets him in a huge
hug. Like a Super Bowl
celebration, the duo is mobbed.
The silver briefcase is hoisted
like a trophy. The men appear
spiritually and visually as one.

D A Y   N I N E
―――――――
SALVATION

GOOD FRIDAY - APRIL 21, 2000

8:01 A.M. E.S.T.

    Spinning and spinning
unceasingly, silver bladed
propellers shine like the silver
briefcase Michael holds close to
his heart. He enters the security
checkpoint inside John F. Kennedy
Memorial Airport, New York.
    A tall, male, Centurion
Company security guard checks
baggage onto the x-ray conveyer
belt. The other security checkers
cruelly leer at an indigent
Michael. Michael protectively
sets the case on the belt. He
proceeds to set off the alarm
walking beneath the metal
detector. A disrespectful, mean
guard commands Michael, "Empty
your pockets." Michael pulls out
the lone item in his pockets. His

393

hand releases the metal object.
It clangs into the tray. Michael
holds open his empty hands; his
pants pocket lining pulled out
like rabbit ears. The guard asks,
"That's it?" He is shocked to see
this is all Michael owns. He
tells Michael, "Pass through
again." Michael sets off the
alarm again. The guard prods and
fleeces Michael with the detector
wand. The device sounds when
waved over Michael's chest. "Your
shirt..."

Michael undoes a middle shirt
button. He's sporting his silver
medal. He speaks meekly. "That's
the last time I fired a weapon at
something I wasn't trying to
kill."

"Move out."

Michael picks up the object
he dropped in the tray. He turns
to the conveyer belt. The tall
Centurion security guard is
concerned over the contents of the
briefcase. Upon a quick
inspection, that guard's demeanor
changes from caution to comfort
and confidence. "Wow! You must
be a true believer?"

"I am."

The Centurion guard
considerately asks, "Will you
please say a prayer and help my
brother be healed?"

Michael nods yes, saying, "A person is never so touched, as when they're asked to pray for someone. Keep the faith. Peace." With the words, not even a touch, the guard is contented.

Michael walks away under the watchful eye of someone.

From God's Heaven, high in the sky, in the midst of the lining of shapeless, scattered clouds; the silver briefcase is in flight. From the cloud formation, the case crosses back to Earth descending from cloudland back to an airport.

Inside the airport, at concourse Gate-A, it is almost 10:07 A.M. Mountain Standard Time. Michael, once again, holds the briefcase tightly. He emerges from the A-Gate jet-bridge into the redesigned, uniquely 12-sided concourse. He is bewildered and introspective, puzzled at the archangelic meaning of his presence here. Even the city he's in remains a mystery for him. Michael's appearance earns him either dirty or indifferent looks from the 550 travelers congregated here.

Rhoda, a comely, redheaded, airport hostess converses with a black, cynical, airplane mechanic. Rhoda reminds him, "The airport

chapel is having Good Friday
Stations of the Cross at noon."

The mechanic says to her,
"Rhoda, let me *aks* you, I thought
you was a born again? Ain't
Stations a Catholic thing?"

Rhoda replies, "It's a God
thing."

Michael presents her his
ticket. The mechanic gives
Michael a mortified look. She
reads the ticket. "Ah, the city
of...Los Angeles, LAX. Your
flight departs at 12:07 from right
here at Gate-A, so you've got just
about a two-hour layover.... God
bless, enjoy your flight."

"God bless you." Michael
leaves for the bay of seats in the
A-Gate area.

Rhoda remarks, "Poor guy."

Michael sits in a secluded
seat. He places his briefcase in
an adjacent seat. Palms joined,
he prayerfully wonders what the
conclusion of his story may be. A
thought quickly comes to his mind.
He places the case on his lap,
using it as a desktop. He pops
its locks open. He removes and
snaps open the rings of a thin,
tattered, black binder. He
withdraws a blank piece of loose-
leaf paper. Forgetful, he
neglects to snap together the
rings as he folds the binder
closed. He removes his Bible.

Reflective, he surveys what he can see of the dozen-gated concourse. In clear view, he visually identifies the activities at each of the six Gates: F through A. As well as: 275 of the travelers situated across the way at Gates K and L.

Oddly, he focuses in on the procession of a family of septuplets traveling from Gate-B to Gate-K. They pass by a radio station's promotional Volkswagen van, near Gate-K. Michael notices the last child carrying a toy trumpet. Michael's look of amazement is brought on by the voice he mysteriously hears in his head. The sound emanates from his soul—it's his own:

"'At the time when you hear the seventh angel blow his trumpet, the mysterious plan of God shall be fulfilled, as He promised to His servants the prophets.'"

Questioning if he heard something, Michael looks to the television speaker and to the large digital clock above it which reads—10:07. Below the speaker, is the flight information television. He glimpses the screen. His flight from New York is listed first. He watches as it's deleted from the screen. Included among the color-coded listings are Flight #2321, an arrival diverted from Chicago; and arrival Flights #1915 and #2722. As Michael quickly glances at the screen, the A-Gate agent announces over the intercom—"Revelation Air would like to remind its Flight 1513 passengers from New York of the Mountain Standard time zone change to 10:07 A.M. Thank you."

The long gaze of someone's watchful eye checks out Michael.

Michael writes, in black marking pen, a page entry in manuscript format: Denver International Airport...Friday... 11:07 A.M.... His writing times perfectly with the voice of the airport public address announcer— "Denver International Airport apologizes for any remodeling inconveniences. Today is Friday, April 21, 2000. Local time: 11:07 A.M. Denver temperature: 33 degrees. Thank you, and welcome to Colorado—'*Nil Sine Numine*.'"

Michael withdraws into a trance. Backtracking, he says to himself, "On the way to a *city of angels*..." Unlike someone who may twiddle their thumbs when they're bored, Michael concentrates deeply. He clasps his hands together in a prayerful pose. He then folds them together. Now, he clenches his fingers and knuckles together. Coming to his mind, as

he initiates the motions, are the
modified words to that childlike
three-part hand rhyme. The view
of the mountains; the air-traffic
control tower; the gates and doors
within Michael's vantage point,
and the overflow of the 160
travelers from B-Gate, parallel
with the rhyme. *"Here's the
earth—there's a tower—open the
doors then save the people."*

Out of Michael's view, at H-
Gate, preparations are made for an
arrival. The methodic, female, H-
Gate attendant is positioned at
the stand at the intersection of
the jet-bridge. She utilizes the
hand-held microphone, saying,
"Denver International Airport
welcomes the unscheduled arrival
of Flight 2321 from Chicago,
Midway."

Maggie, in a snippety mood,
steps into the concourse. She
comments to the attendant, "'Windy
City'?! Blow it out your ass.
I'm not good with geology, but
Denver better be on the way to San
Francisco."

Back at A-Gate, Michael
visually searches the K-Gate area
for the trumpet player. The
family is gone. He focuses in on
the windshield of the van. In
large blue numerals, he sees the
time—11:15. The classical disc
jockey's voice can be heard from

the multiple sets of speakers
perched atop the VW van. The DJ
distinctively says, "...Mile High
Radio. It's 11:15."

Michael's prompted to open
his Bible. Randomly, he's
selected a verse from Revelation
11:15. Michael reads: "Then the
seventh angel blew his trumpet.
There were loud voices in heaven,
saying...'The kingdom of the world
now belongs to our Lord and to His
Anointed, and He will reign
forever and ever.'" Michael truly
believes the archangel has
revealed the finale to him. His
time is at hand. Michael grips
his knuckles together in the first
position of the hand rhyme.

From Michael's vantage point
of Gate-C, where the church is
located—the quaint triangular
steeple juts out of the facade.
It gives the chapel a doll house
quality. It's distinctively-
shaped, triangularly-inverted door
also lends itself to the look of a
contemporary synagogue. The sign
above the door reads:

COLORADO—*NIL SINE NUMINE*—NOTHING
WITHOUT THE DEITY

There are 80 people gathered
here.

Out of Michael's view, at L-
Gate; Lincoln, in a huff, is first

400

off his plane to enter the concourse. An L-Gate agent addresses the microphone. He says, "Will the passengers arriving on outbound Flight #2321 to JFK, New York—please temporarily remain at Gate-L for further instructions. Thank you."

At the boarding counter, Lincoln approaches a pious, no-nonsense, beautiful, light-skinned, African, L-Gate agent. Her uniform is decorated with religious buttons. She readies for this flight's re-routing. Lincoln says to her, "Lightning?! Ben Franklin's spinning in his grave. You didn't hear his mother tell him to stop flying his kite and come inside 'cause of some thunder." He tells her, "A little electricity never killed anyone. I'm willing to risk it."

She leniently says to him, "We need to consider the welfare of all the passengers, not just yourself sir."

A flustered Lincoln reaches for his cigarettes. Bud Beetré, an unkempt, 'red neck,' autograph seeker pats Lincoln on the back. Bud wears a T-shirt that reads: KILL VON ADOLF DEAD, as well as a worn out Joe Camel cap. "Mr. Peters, sign my shirt...To Bud..."

Lincoln obliges while he fumbles for his lighter. He

inquires of Bud, "You got a light?"

The lovely, L-Gate agent legislatively says, "This is a public place sir. There is no smoking."

Lincoln lashes out, "Zip it lady! I'll sue your ass off!"

She lashes back, saying, "Pardon me, 'Mr. I'm so self-centered I could care a less about the rights of the innocent people my second-hand smoke kills'... How'd you like to fly out of here by the seat of your pants?!"

Lincoln is set back. Detained, he checks his watch. He asks Bud, "You got the right time?"

Bud answers, "It's a minute after 11:15."

Back at A-Gate, Michael reads the following Bible verse: "The twenty-four elders who sat on their thrones before God prostrated themselves and worshipped God and said..."

From Michael's angle, at C-Gate, a group of 24 senior citizens recite a prayer outside the closed door of the chapel, sovereignly praying: "'We give thanks to you, Lord God Almighty, who are and who were. For you have assumed your great power and have established your reign...'"

Michael's fingers are fixed in the second position of the hand rhyme. His pointing fingers make a triangular, star-shape.

Outside the window, Michael sees the gray tarmac and its painted white semi-circle. And again, he sees the air-traffic control <u>tower</u>; the outer wall and its inverted triangle <u>doors</u> to the adjacent B-Gate; and lastly, the 20 riders in the AGABUS <u>people</u> mover, which hovers by like a spider zipping over a web. Again, Michael recites the increasingly memorable words, *"Here's the earth—there's a tower—open the doors—then save the people."*

Out of Michael's view, at E-Gate, a plane is docked at the bowels of the jet-bridge. A friendly, young, black skycap waits. The airplane door opens. From the initial first class seat, Judy signals to the skycap to roll a parked wheelchair to Aunt Mary Frances. With her Bible in hand, a weakened Aunt Mary crawls into the chair. The skycap rolls her off the plane. Judy is drunk, impatient, and appalled. She hollers into the cockpit, "Hail?! Hail Caesars! I've seen *less* ice in my drink!"

The girls lead 10 passengers off the aircraft. The skycap wheels Aunt Mary. They trek the jet-bridge leading to the concourse gate. Judy is buzzing with anticipation. Aunt Mary is shameful and despondent. She reads her Bible aloud to herself, remorsefully questioning her own actions: "'I know that You can do all things, and that no purpose of Yours can be hindered. I have dealt with great things that I do not understand; things too wonderful for me, which I cannot know.'"

Judy pays little attention to Aunt Mary. She speaks over her, questioning the skycap, "'Night cap,' she wants to know if this place has a chapel close-by?"

The skycap satisfyingly answers, "Yes, we do, a non-denominational: Gate-C. It's to our right as we enter the concourse. I'll be baptized a Christian there tomorrow myself."

Judy doesn't care. "Come on Aunt Mary Frances; let's get you a shot of fresh air."

The skycap follows Judy's lead. Aunt Mary continues to read aloud: "'I had heard of You by word of mouth, but now my eye has seen You. Therefore I disown what I have said and repent in dust and ashes.'"

The trek is over; the end of the gangplank. They've reached the concourse. The E-Gate agent

404

speaks over the microphone, "We will momentarily be boarding passengers for the 11:18 departure at Gate-E...Flight 2722, the continuation of non-stop service to Las Vegas."

Each of the ladies is dressed in their best Las Vegas fashions. Mary wears a lovely, feminine, Elvis jumpsuit ensemble. She says to Judy, "It's my bowels." The skycap rolls Aunt Mary through the additional ten travelers waiting to board. Judy sees the ladies room symbol located in the center of the concourse. Aunt Mary sees the chapel as the seniors continue their vigil.

The seniors group spiritedly prays: "'...The nations raged, but your wrath has come, and the time for the dead to be judged, and to recompense your servants, the prophets, and the holy ones and those who fear your name, the small and the great alike, and to destroy those who destroy the earth.'"

Back at A-Gate, Michael, with his fingers fixed in the hand rhyme's second position, further solves the intricate puzzle. He wiggles each of his four digits individually. The triangular, star-shape of his hand approximates the concourse's configuration. His wiggling

fingers correlate with the gate
letters. "A...H...L...E."

Michael begins a simplistic
drawing. The figures he sketches
are descriptive with his dialogue.
He starts with a professionally
drawn, well-rounded circle—"_Here's
the earth_..." Within the circle,
he outlines a triangle—"_There's a
tower_..." He overlaps it with an
inverted triangle—"_Open the
doors...then save the people_."

His completed drawing is the
Star of David enclosed within a
circle. The 6-point star is the
exact design of the airport. Each
side matches a gate letter.

Michael shines with
enlightenment as he applies
letters, names, and initials to
the angelic puzzle. "A-angel,
Angelo...H-Hagar...L-Lincoln...
E?...E?...E—"

He's looking to the E-Gate.
He sees and hears an airport
oddity, a barking dog. Suddenly,
he catches a quick glimpse of Aunt
Mary and Judy. Instantly, he
loses sight of them. They duck
into the bathroom. The skycap
waits outside the door.

In a blaze of revelation,
Michael unravels the mystery of
the divine drawing. "L-A-H-E...L-
A: Los Angeles." Michael checks
the flight information TV. The
screen has malfunctioned. All the

406

listed cities read: LOS ANGELES.
"Los Angeles: *'The City of
Angels!'*"

Looking at the drawing, he
says, "H-E...He, He..."
Affirming his own calling, he
says, "God."

Michael looks back to the
clock above the TV. It reads—
11:19. He hurriedly double-checks
that next verse from the Book of
Revelation. He drops the
briefcase at his feet. He falls
to his knees in reverence.
"11:19...'Then God's temple in
heaven was opened, and the ark of
the covenant could be seen in the
temple..." Michael is in the midst
of a heightened, supernatural
experience. He is at the feet of
God. He lays his right hand on
the glimmering briefcase; his left
hand on the floor.

Outside the window, he sees
the fluke weather conditions.
There is lightning, thunder, and
the onset of hail. He reads:
"'...There were flashes of
lightning, rumblings, and peals of
thunder, an earthquake, and a
violent hailstorm.'" He shouts,
"An earthquake!"

Michael, like an Indian on
the plain or a Muslim bowed in
prayer position, throws his hands
and head to the floor. He's
trying to feel a tremor. "My God!

There's gonna be an earthquake!
Everybody out! Save your lives!"
Michael hastily tosses the paper,
notebook and Bible into the
briefcase. He lifts himself up.
He clings to the case. He's off!

Michael bolts into the aisle.
He is determined to fulfill God's
prophecy. His mission is to
physically rescue a life from this
apocalyptic vision, at the very
least save one single soul.
Standing in the traffic lane, he
holds his arms high to the sky and
shouts out, "The archangel showed
me! Earthquake! Please everybody
out before the building falls!
Your lives are in grave danger!"

Of all the travelers, only
twelve heed Michael's call; the
majority mocks him. They push and
shove him, remaining indifferent
to his claim. The earth has made
no such abrupt move, neither have
the people. The mockers scoff at
him. One mocker howls, "Drop
dead."

Michael acclaims, "God help
you! Earthquake! Evacuate the
building! I'm here to save you!"

Another mocker howls out,
"I'll save myself if you don't
mind."

Michael hedges in the
direction he presumably saw Aunt
Mary Frances. Before he can even
trot, he's halted. A pair of

tough, unarmed, D.I.A. guards with
the Centurion Company of Denver
International Airport forcibly
detains him. The guards manhandle
Michael. Like sharks and their
feeders drawn to a bloody fish, a
small mob of onlookers gathers to
encourage the security force. The
commotion soon draws a small,
armed corps of Centurions. The
guards have locked onto Michael's
long, purple overcoat at the
elbows. One of the guards
interrogates, "Hold on. Where do
you think you're going?"

He answers, "To save the
people."

The guards shove Michael
against the wall, knocking the
briefcase from his hands.

A well-respected and
decorated pilot, rubbing dry his
hands, emerges from the men's
room. He confronts the situation.
To Michael's defense, he asks of
the guards, "What has he done?"

The first guard answers,
"We're thinking of having him
arrested for inciting a riot."

An onlooker protests, "He's a
barbarian, take him away!"

The pilot looks around at the
jeering travelers circled like
headhunters. He succumbs to the
peer pressure and readily gives up
his defense. He gives an
affirmative nod of the head. The

409

second guard signifies Michael's briefcase. "Pick it up!" Michael clings to the case. He can hardly bear to be without it.

The first guard viciously asks him, "Who do you think you are anyway?"

The second guard says, "Yeah, who does he think he is some kind of lifesaver?"

Michael, giving in with reluctant meekness, answers, "As you say."

The first guard says to him, "Huh? Is that who you think you are? Answer me?!"

Michael says absolutely nothing. The second, demeaning guard smacks him on the forehead.

Lincoln has made his way to the forefront of the crowd. Bud tags along. Lincoln is ashamed to acknowledge his friend. He remains cowardly silent.

The corps of armed guards helps to barricade the onlookers. As Michael is prodded forward, the second guard purposely trips him. The crowd laughs. Michael, holding onto his briefcase for dear life, knocks his head on it when he falls. His lifeblood drips from his forehead. Michael is on his knees. Lincoln remains idle. Veronica, a beautiful college student, lunges forward to intervene. Her gutless boyfriend

and his spineless father reel her
back in. The boyfriend tells her,
"Don't get involved."

Aunt Mary and Judy exit the
lady's room. Judy sees the
commotion and rolls Aunt Mary into
the eye of the hurricane. The
skycap remains close to them.
Judy exclaims, "A fight!"
Breaking her way through, Judy
sees it is Michael. She is
unwilling to proceed further. She
too, is afraid to encounter him.
Uninterested nonetheless, Aunt
Mary's view is blocked. Judy
tells her, "It's nothing."

Aunt Mary's line of vision
opens. She's aghast at the sight.
"What in God's name?! Michael!"

Judy pulls an about face,
acting as if she's happy to see
Michael. They pull forward to
meet him. Judy utters to him,
"Professor!" She kisses his cheek
and addresses the guards, telling
them, "This is his aunt. They
haven't seen each other in years."

The guards acquiesce.
Michael kneels at Aunt Mary's feet
in the chair. Unabashedly, Aunt
Mary Frances acknowledges,
"Michael..."

He begs her forgiveness. "I
am sorry. God loves you."

Aunt Mary gracefully alights,
"I know." She mumblingly says,
"Michael, things happen for a

reason: a divine pre-destiny. The money has not cured or healed the pain, but archangelic intervention has led you to decide to do what you did. The blessing for me is to see you here; God working in you, working in me. The archangel that guides you guided me." She feels: I know Michael sees God; and if Michael sees me, then God Himself is within my reach. An angelic keepsake, she tells him, "Michael, this is the moment in my life that I've lived for—and the reason I am alive today is so I may say to you..." She wails, "Son, I love you."

"Mother, and I you." Michael sets aside the briefcase. Their hands cross and clutch together; at that moment, the chapel facade cracks and splinters giving way to the earth's tremor.

Mary prayerfully reassures Michael: "'Then the sign of the Son of Man will appear in the sky, and the clans of the earth will strike their breasts as they see "the Son of Man coming on the clouds of heaven" with power and great glory.'"

Some of the people gathered are frozen in their tracks.

The first guard yells out, "What was that?!"

The second guard tells him, "It must be a bomb. Earlier, I

heard him yell he'll destroy the place."

Judy blurts out, "It's no bomb. It's the rumble of the jets."

The skycap says, "But all the flights have been grounded."

The bond strengthens between Michael and Mary. She holds his bloody forehead. The shaking chapel indicates the increased measure of a second tremor. Mary mourns: "'He will dispatch His angels with a mighty trumpet blast, and they will assemble His chosen from the four winds, from one end of the heavens to the other.'"

The floor of the concourse, in the area around the men's room, shakes. Typically, in the face of danger, the spiritually faithful become brave, the unfaithful, cowardly; the believer's believe, and the non-believers become doubtful.

Veronica's boyfriend yells, "It's impossible! Go to Hell; an earthquake in the heart of the country?"

Rhoda reverberates, "He's telling the truth! Three times I heard him predict it!"

The skycap shouts, "It's true! God! It must be from here to California!"

Michael rests his head on Mary's lap. Mary fatefully says, "Son...now, I can die in peace."

The earth moves! The chapel quakes! From the steeple, cracks in the shapes of angels map the two-tone black and white ceiling.

The second guard screams, "Run for your lives! The ceiling is going to collapse!"

The first guard screams out, "Earthquake!"

The guards flee. The hundreds of people react like bees in a swarm. Like bulls stampeding in a ring, they run in a circular pattern. A few are completely frozen in their footsteps. Nonetheless, all the travelers are completely unaware of the escape routes. Lincoln makes his way from the back of the pack, bursting out, "Michael!"

Michael raises his head from Mary's bloodstained lap. His arms stretched, a light shining from the Heavens empowers him. From his knees, he reaches for the briefcase. He bellows out, "Follow me!"

Veronica's boyfriend asks, "Why should we follow him?"

A hand lifts the briefcase. Michael rises. He takes the handle like a runner's baton in a relay race. The man handing off answers the boyfriend for all to

hear. It's none other than Ernest
Sy Goldstein, who edifies,
shouting gloriously, "He's the
architect who built this place!"

Michael blasts, "Follow what
I say!"

Michael's command directs the
action. The believers become
followers: there's Mary; the
skycap; Veronica; as well as Rhoda
the gate agent, who has been
following the pack. Also putting
their faith in Michael are a
cowardly Judy and Lincoln.

The airport is cavernous.
It's not the minimal falling
debris that threatens the people;
it's the collapse of the
structurally weak ceiling that
endangers the travelers. Michael
knows the layout of the concourse
well enough to know the emergency
evacuation exit capabilities of
Gate-B.

In the Gate-B area, 160
people need to be saved. An
emergency exit gate, with an
opening door, houses an inflatable
slide ramp. To activate the
system, a certain lever must be
pulled. The L-Gate agent has been
following the events from afar.
In close proximity to the lever
panel, she puts her faith in
Michael's guidance. She yells to
him, "I believe in you! Save us!"

Michael, pointing to the lever, shouts to her, "Over there! The inflatable slide ramp! Pull down on the middle lever!"

The agent yanks the lever, but the red activation siren light doesn't switch on. She hollers, "It's broke! This airport isn't geared for an earthquake!"

Michael shouts, "There needs to be a trip in the wire—a break in the secondary power line."

Judy foolishly screams, "Pull the plug!"

Like a long fuse from a stick of dynamite—Michael visually traces the power wire snaking over the doorframe; but, how to sever the wire? He spots a cleaver, spear-heading a fish, on a sushi food cart. He lunges a couple of quick steps. With dripping blood impairing his vision, he focuses in on the wire. Instinctively, as if he were beheading a snake, he hurls the cleaver. It severs the wire perfectly. Sparks fly and sirens spin. The system is activated.

The ground tremors.

The door hatch automatically opens. The slide ramp inflates extending out to the tarmac; the first of the stranded bounce and slide away. Michael is unable to tell if they reach safety. Like popcorn kernels down a funnel, it

will take moments for the
congested travelers to filter out.
The agent, arms spread wide,
corrals the trapped out of the
hatch.

Veronica has broken free from
her boyfriend. She rushes to
Michael's aide. She flings off
her purple scarf and wraps it over
his bloody forehead wound. She
valiantly says, "Professor! It's
Veronica. I was in your design
class. I've always believed in
you!"

"Bless you, Veronica."

The frightened boyfriend and
his father tug Veronica away
against her will. They all run to
escape.

The remaining faithful rally
around one another. They stay in
a close-knit unit next to Michael.
He directs his attention on the
next gate area, shouting, "Follow
me!"

In the Gate-C area, 80 people
need saving. The crumbling facade
of the church does all but
barricade the opened doorway.
There is not a fiery destruction,
but a Samson and the collapsing
temple type of devastation. Rhoda
runs to assist the effort at the
chapel. She hollers to Michael,
"What can I do?"

He tells her, "God bless you.
Please get those people into the

chapel!" He shouts to them,
"Follow what I say! The chapel
will save you! The crossbeams
give it support! It will not
collapse!"

Rhoda does her best to corral
those congregated. The mortified
mechanic runs from her side and
boroughs his frightened way
through the masses—so much for
"Women and children first"!
However, there is a logjam again.
The chapel capacity is eighty at
best. Rhoda lays her hands on
many shoulders as she guides
people through the door, ringing
out, "Follow what he says! Into
the church, all of you!"

The tremor increases.

In the center of the
concourse, a storage closet is
situated between the bathrooms.
Michael, with a firm hold of the
briefcase, uses it to batter down
the door.

Ernie effusively asks,
"Michael, why the storage closet?"

Michael answers, "...in
case."

Inside the closet, a standing
artificial plant has fallen,
Michael's momentum causes him to
trip over it; janitorial supplies,
tools, and general items are
strewn about. Michael grabs the
first few items he may find
useful: a short piece of rope; two

strands of bungee cord with hooks
at each end; a carpet remnant, the
size of a large doormat; a long
piece of yellow rope; and lastly,
an oversized screwdriver. With
the bungee cord, he harnesses the
remnant on his back. He wraps the
small rope around his wrist and
lassos the long rope over his
shoulders. He sets off like a
mountain hiker. The briefcase
never leaves his hand, but it
causes him to fumble the
screwdriver. The screwdriver
falls behind to the ground.

Inside the concourse, Ernie
says to Lincoln, "Are you okay?"

Lincoln is shocked into
silence. He rattles more than the
quake. Bud has idolized him to
this point. Bud tells Ernie, "Ha!
He's scared shit-less."

Judy says to Aunt Mary, "If
we get separated, I'll meet you at
the hotel."

Mary, holding hands with the
skycap in kinship, prays, "Glory
be..."

The skycap solemnly says,
"...to the Father..."

Michael hollers, "Follow me!"
Michael directs the group to move
toward the next possible exit.
They inch in his direction. He
shouts, "Gate-D! The AGABUS!"

Ernie, concerned, guidingly says to Bud, "Please, go follow him buddy!"

Bud makes a face, thinking: How did he know my name? He acts like he's won something.

In the concourse Gate-D area, 40 people need saving; particularly, the 40 female members of: Mothers Against Drunk Driving—MADD. The women wear an array of rainbow-colored, MADD shirts. The group is aboard the people transporter. The official markings on the transport vehicle read: AIR-GROUND ARRIVAL BUS—AGABUS. The vehicle is docked at the gate.

A stubborn, overly professional, male AGABUS driver sits in the cab. The women are in distress, trapped on a bumpy ride going nowhere. The driver prepares to open the door. A MADD woman cries out, "Good God!"

Michael has made his way to the docking door. A panting Bud closes from behind. Michael hollers, "Follow what I say! Away! Away from the dock!" Michael reaches into the AGABUS cab's open, cockpit window. He cannot reach a large switch.

The seat-belted driver won't budge. The driver yells, "No. Don't touch that! That's the automatic uncoupling switch! I'm unloading. I've got to go by the book"; exclaiming, "It's my job!"

Another MADD member screams into the cab at the driver, "Don't listen to him! Let us out! Look at him! He looks drunker than a skunk!"

Michael shouts to the driver, "Your job or your life? I'll save you, but you have to work with me!"

A mediating MADD member, weeping to the driver; cries out, "Oh my Lord! Please believe him. He's trying to save people!"

The driver tells Michael, "But my boss will fire me from my job!"

Michael shouts to the driver, "If you don't save these people— God will fire you from life!"

Bud points out, to Michael, a ring-like mechanism on the wall panel. He exclaims, "Man, there's the emergency disengagement ring!"

Michael lunges for it. Bud hops aboard the AGABUS to save his own skin. The doors close. The AGABUS pulls away. It beeps and sirens as it reverses itself from the gate. Michael pulls the ring. The people are rescued without him. The ring drops at his feet. Bud waves a sucker's kiss back to Michael. The docking area overhang collapses.

In the concourse, Lincoln;
not smart enough to head off in
his own direction, is still a lost
sheep. Ernie helps tend to him.
The skycap tries to keep a close
grip on Mary's chair. They both
loyally adhere to Michael's plan.
Ernie exhorts, "I asked him to
help keep an eye on Michael—not
sell him out!"

Judy, still tipsy, stays
within reach of the rest of the
pack. She says defiantly, as if
Bud was within his rights, "He can
save himself!"

The skycap straightforwardly
says, "If he's not willing to save
others..."

Mary rolls free from the
skycap. In the chair, she
confronts and counsels Judy. Mary
watchfully says, "Judy," she tells
her, speaking as an example, "Look
at Michael... Remember, Matthew:
'For man it is impossible...
But?...'"

Judy says: "'But for God all
things are possible.'"

A motherly Mary calls out,
"Bingo!"

Michael returns right on
time. "Follow me."

In the Gate-G area, 20 people
need to be saved. With nowhere to
run for escape, the travelers are
huddled around the narrowly
opened, debris-riddled, jet-bridge

entrance. Michael instructs them,
"People! Please get back on the
plane! Tell the attendants to get
everybody back on this flight.
Tell the pilot to bring up the
power and take off for the clouds.
You'll be safe off the ground.
Please follow what I say! Listen
to me! I'm telling you the
truth!"

As the twenty people line-up
to board the plane; Mary wheels
herself closer to the open shaft.
The skycap helps escort an afraid-
to-fly Judy, as well as the other
stranded passengers.

A tall, bearded, creepy,
hardened gambler dressed in a
black and red trench coat, and
sunglasses; streaks from the jet-
bridge like a bat from a cave.
Earth shaking, broken gas pipes
spew fire from the wall heralding
his arrival. Drenched in blood,
he goes right to Judy and embraces
her. From the two, locked, black
briefcases in his hands: black,
clay, gambling chips with no logo
spill from his pockets like coins
from a slot machine. The gambler
says to Judy, "He's lying.
Whatever you do lady, over Hell or
high water, don't think about
getting on that craft. I've been
hot! I gotta' hunch! I'll bet
you $66, at eleven-to-one odds,

there will be a fiery explosion—
you'll be reduced to ashes!"

Meantime, Michael lunges to
push Mary's wheelchair. His hands
fall just shy of the handles. The
skycap takes the reins. Mary
turns and blesses Michael. In
faith, she says, "Hold on, Son."

He says, "Bless you, Mother."

The high-pitched cry of a
feminine voice is faintly heard.
It mixes with loud caterwauling.
Maggie shrieks, "Somebody!"

Michael says to the skycap,
about Mary, "Go with her."

Maggie shrieks again,
"Somebody!"

Mary, knowing Michael must
save others, encourages him as he
starts away. To his kingship, she
shouts, "Run like the wind
Michael!" Mary makes the Sign of
the Cross and gasps to him as he
flees, worshipingly praying, "May
the souls of all the faithful
departed, through the mercy of
God, rest in peace. Amen."

The skycap, arms spread wide,
funnels Mary and a scared-to-death
Judy into the jet-bridge.

Judy sees Michael moving, the
gambler shadowing him from behind.
The earth moves. Judy yells,
"Fire?! Over Hell or high water!"
Without so much as a look to Aunt
Mary, Judy takes off in the

direction of Michael and the gambler.

In the Gate-F area, 9 international tourists and a uniformed, Asian, male baggage handler need saving. At the end of a scattered line of people, the Seeing Eye dog barks. His attention is on a white baggage cage. The dog belongs to Bart Thomasson. Bart is angry and bitter, full of self-pity, a fiercely independent, blind man. He wears an eye patch beneath dark glasses.

Michael jaunts in the direction of the voice. He trips over the unseen, unattended cage. The cat screeches. The dog barks, as does Bart. "Watch it!"

"Sorry."

Michael, on his knees, hears the crying originating from the H-Gate area. Looking...he sees Maggie crying and whimpering like a lost little girl. "Magdalene!"

She spins like a toy ballerina running low on power. "Michael!"

Ernie Goldstein sees he is nearer to her than Michael. He lumbers after her, shouting, "I'll get her Michael!"

Michael, never relinquishing hold of the case, scrambles on his knees to see if the cat is okay. "Sorry, Girl."

The cat owner rushes to her lost cat's cry. Michael reaches for the cage, but the relieved owner snares it away, saying to Michael, "Oh! Bless your heart," and to the cat, "Jag, you're alive!" She champions, "Oh my, I couldn't sacrifice leaving without her. I couldn't live with myself if I wasn't willing to try...I'd have two chances—slim and none—you know what I mean?"

Michael answers, "I do." He instructs, "That's why God won't let anything bad happen to you... all you have to do—is be willing to."

Michael rises to his feet. He hollers, "People! Follow me! What's more valuable, your possessions or your life?"

The people do little to heed his call. They are fighting to identify and claim their belongings. Most cannot even lift or tug their bags from amongst the tossed and discarded others.

Michael rushes to the auxiliary baggage conveyer belt. About thirty feet long, it remains operable amidst the rubble of an alternate, check-in counter. The system is used mainly for passengers who neglect to check-in oversized, oddly-shaped bags and packages. Michael hollers to them, "People! Follow what I have

to say! This is your only way
out!"

Michael grasps a suitcase
handle; like an ancient Olympian,
he hammer throws it just short of
the belt. The baggage handler
places it on the belt. Suitcases,
already on the belt, emerge
periodically from a chute shielded
by plastic strips. The strips,
like those in a car wash, cover
the exit port as well. The
travelers opt for Michael's plan.
He hollers again, "Here! Here,
one at a time! This conveyer belt
unloads into a carrier truck
outside of the airport. Get on a
case, it will cushion the landing.
Leave your baggage behind and
trust in me. This will lead you
to safety!" He says to the
handler, "Please help these
people." Pointing to Bart and the
animals, Michael says, "Make sure
he gets out okay, and please save
those animals!"

The handler tells Michael,
"Way to go 'Bro!'" The handler
takes hold of a male tourist's
arm, telling him, "I'll lend you a
hand 'Brudder.'" He helps to seat
the man on a case.

Michael has yet to physically
touch another person. He says,
"Don't overload it. One at a
time!"

Before the next female
tourist can hop on, the handler
butts in line saving his own ass.
He's pulled out of sight into the
conveyor's corridor.

The quake again increases in
strength.

In the concourse Gate-G area,
Ernie has retrieved Maggie. He
rounds up Lincoln and Judy.
Maggie screams, "We're all going
to Hell!"

Judy tells her, "What do you
mean going? This is Hell!"

Ernie groans, "Hell. I'll
tell you all what Hell is: Hell is
the choice you made not to follow
God and die in a way that pleases
Him. Hell is that death you can't
yet imagine, the dying that makes
you wish you died in a different
way: a peaceful or glorious way.
Hell is that place where you look
back on your death and say, 'I
wish I had it to do over.' God
gave me the chance to do something
special with my life, the chance
to die in the greatest of the
ways: because of something holy
and good I did. 'Now look at me,
now I have to die in some common
way, I wish I had it to do over...
I wish I'd known during my life
that I had the chance to make a
choice about the way I was going
to die and not end up dying like
this.' The second thought; the

'do over'; the regret you can't have until you've gone to the other place and wish you could return from the dead to do it over again—that's Hell!... Let's go!"

Ernie sees a broken sign, above GATE-G, that reads:

TRAIN___ ENGINE

He enigmatically says, "Gate-G, train...A-Abel to G-Goldstein: first to last, last to first." He gallantly hollers out, "The train! This way!" Ernie rallies the three captives. They pat him on the back, thankful he may be right. But Ernie too, is running on increasing fear.

At Gate-G, the gate hatch looks like a gigantic bank vault. A large, spoked wheel, like a valve, opens the hatch. There are hazardous material markings and warning symbols plastered on the door. Signs read:

⊗ DANGER: A.N.G.E.L.
⊗ EXPERIMENTAL FLIGHT TRAIN___/DO NOT ENTER

Michael has painfully made his way here. Judy offers him a shot of booze from an airline bottle she's stolen. Michael

swipes his hand over his mouth,
denying the gesture.

Ernie counts with his
fingers, equating, "A, B, C, D, E,
F, G...seven...Gate-G, the seventh
sign." He says, directly to
Michael, "Your flight leaves at
12:07.... The seven trumpets..."
He grievously asks, "This is it,
isn't it?"

They all look on. Michael
nods his head, positively, in
sorrowful grief. Life's journey
has reached its crossroads.
Michael asks, "Maggie? Judy?
Lincoln?"

Maggie nods her head
affirmatively.

Judy tells him, "You can
count on me."

Michael asks, "Lincoln?"

Lincoln tells him, "I'm not
leaving [you] if my life depended
on it."

Michael gives a look of trust
to Ernie. Ernie gives him one
back, eulogizing: "'You relied on
the LORD—let him deliver you, if
He loves you, let Him rescue
you.'" He says to Michael, "You
helped to save the others—it's
time to save yourself." Michael
and Ernie forge on. They attempt
to turn the valve.

Judy is already looking for
another way out.

Maggie inspires mock heroism from an idle Lincoln. She says, "Lincoln, give him a hand."

Lincoln says, "It's jammed."

Ernie says, "We need some kind of fluid to jar it loose."

Judy points out a fire extinguisher, in a glass encasement, on the wall of the upper level. Along with an ax, they've come loose and rest up against the glass case. The short stretch of second floor walkway has collapsed. It leaves the apparatus virtually impossible to reach. Judy screams, "Michael, the extinguisher!"

Michael positions; verbally commands, and inspires himself, "Think..."

He spots the large, display gate letter F; a banded package beside it. The items are near Bart, who's standing behind the cat owner. They're waiting to board the baggage belt. Michael approaches Bart suddenly. Bart lashes Michael with his walking stick. Michael winces, and asks, "What's your name?"

"Bart Thomasson. What's it to 'ya?! Huh?! You ever been hysterically blind? Do you know what it's like to not see because your mind makes you blind?"

"Bart, I need your eye...your patch, to save others."

"*You* need!"

"Bart, you see yourself in what you look to do for others."

Like he's being mugged, the disgruntled Bart whips off the patch beneath his sunglasses. "Here, take it."

"Bless you. Say a prayer..." Michael handcrafts a slingshot. He connects the package's rubber band between the letter F's horizontal lines. He uses the protective eye patch for the pouch. He looks to the floor for a projectile. He tows in a toy *Matchbox* car. He braces his left arm against the letter's frame. He puts the car in the pouch. He focuses in...asking, "God?..." He pulls back the band and lets the car fly. The toy shatters the glass.

Bart hears it smash. He barks out, "Bull's-eye!"

The ax falls to the rubble. The extinguisher-can drops and rolls on the long planks of debris. The can stops at the feet of Judy. She hands it to Ernie, telling him, "Hurry, I'm dying over here!" He gamely hollers, "Stand back!" Ernie sprays the valve that unlocks the volatile vault. He and Lincoln try opening the door. It won't budge an inch. The men shout out to Michael. An excitable Ernie tells him, "It won't move!"

Lincoln corroboratively tells Michael, "A strong bar or lever will do it!"

Michael shouts out, "The ax!" Looking at the obedient dog, he asks, "Bart, do you think your dog saw where it went?"

Bart touts, "He sees like a hawk." He takes a knee and tells his Shepherd, "You're my best friend, Boy," shouting out, "Rover, fetch!"

Rover is off! Like a Saint Bernard in the Swiss Alps, the gallant dog climbs and scales the debris. He's able to grip the ax handle in his jowls. He carries back the big stick.

Michael yells to his group, "Call him!"

Ernie shouts out, "Here, Boy!"

The cat owner says to Bart, "That took courage."

Bart boasts, "He's the best."

She says, "I meant you."

Michael asks, "Bart, what do you want me to do for you?"

Bart tenders, "Mister, I want to see who you are."

"My name is..."

To identify Michael, the blind man touches Michael's face. He feels a blood drop, trickling down Michael's head. He feels his

433

long hair and beard. Overwhelmed,
Bart starts to sob.

    Michael says to him, "Go...
your faith in me saved these
people...seeing is believing, but
bless you: you believed..."
Michael starts off.

    Bart removes his glasses and
rubs a tear from his eye.
Chivalrously, he grabs the handle
of the woman's cat cage. Thankful
and blind no more, he javelin
throws his aluminum walking cane.
Michael plucks the walking cane
from the air.

    Rover delivers the ax to
Ernie, who in turn, hands it
to Lincoln. Ernie sends Rover
away with a kiss. Lincoln wedges
the ax handle into the valve
spokes. With the girls' help,
they spin the knob. Michael
returns. Michael uses the ax,
like a crowbar, in the handle.
The ax cleaver shears off, almost
slicing his foot. Finally, the
door is swung open. However, a
sliding door now blocks the path.
It has a different variety of
precautionary markings. These
include:

⊗ DANGER: A.N.G.E.L.
⊗ TRACKS TO TERMINAL - HANGAR -
EMERGENCY ABORT

434

⊗ AIR N' GROUND ELEVATION LINK -
A.N.G.E.L. SPIRIT OF ST. LOUIS
EXPERIMENTAL FLIGHT TRAIN<u>ING</u>
ENGINE - DO NOT ENTER:

Judy yells to Ernie, "You
bumbling...it doesn't say train—it
says: train<u>ing</u>! It says: Air N'
Ground, A-N-G-E-L, Angel, you
idiot."
Maggie asks, "What's it
spell?"
Judy tells her, "It spells
Hell! If what's behind there
blows up—this place'll go up like
a mozltov cocktail." From Judy's
vantage point of Gate—K, the radio
station's promotional van rotates
on a display spindle. Only Judy
can see the gambler inside the
van's open panel door. On his
knees, he waves her in.
Ernie holds the ax handle
like a staff. He is fearful and
tense with regards to the sealed,
uncharted door. Ernie garrisons
them, "All aboard that's going
aboard."
Judy, forewarning Maggie and
Lincoln, screams, "No way in Hell!
That'll be suicide. I'll be
damned!" She sees the black van's
open panel door. ~~The gambler is~~
~~no longer there~~. She screams,
"Run for cover! Charge!" Judy
runs for the van. The earth

tremors. Shards of ceiling fall
in her wake but do not strike her.

Michael hollers, "Judy!"

As if she is in slow-motion,
Judy shuts the van door. She
seals it closed and locks the
handle. The door pulls back to
reveal three sets of radio station
call letters painted on the side
panel. She hears the station
identification. It bellows from
the sets of large speakers.
"KIAN, KEVO, KCAJ, Mile High
Radio..."

Judy puts her hands to her
ears as if she's "hearing no
evil." There is no underlying
circumlocution, as Judy, as if she
is in slow-motion again, clearly
mouths these three words—"God, why
me?"

From Michael's vantage point,
the van stares him head on. Its
glowing headlights light his way.
The van seems to have a face of
its own. He hears the disc
jockey's voice. "...This is:
Saint Michael the Archangel..."
The music begins. The
aforementioned masterpiece by
Ottorino Respighi blares its
trumpeted tones.

Michael says to himself, "But
when the seventh...*angel*...blows
his trumpet..."

This is no undermining
coincidence. At Gate-G, Michael

gets hold of the door handle. He
musters all his strength and
slides open the door.
Miraculously, they board. He
screens his eyes from the black,
the trumpeting music continuing to
play in his head.

Fading in slowly...is the
underground rail beneath the
terminal. It is shrouded in
darkness. Slowly, he begins to
see the rolling motion of the
wheels. Ernie was right. It is a
locomotive engine—a shiny, silver
one. The experimental turbine-
electric car, similar to a theme
park monorail, plows its way
through the building wreckage.

Inside, the high-tech train
is extraordinary in design. Ernie
mans the control panel. He
switches and clicks brightly lit,
large, easy-to-read gauges. He
accelerates clear. Lincoln and
Maggie are clenched against the
wall, scared stiff. There are
fuel tanks and complex equipment
on board. The back of the train
is opened like a tractor-trailer.

Michael moves up a central
hatchway to a second level. He
stands inside the A.N.G.E.L: an
experimental, prototype aircraft
that rides atop the train. Its
set-up resembles the space shuttle
on its ground transporter.
A.N.G.E.L. is on display as a

futuristic mode of travel. Two
triangular wings join at the
center point, as does a third
triangular passenger area and a
circular cockpit. From above, the
convertible craft looks like an
angel. The train, beneath,
lumbers through the terminal. The
effect seems to have the
A.N.G.E.L. hovering through the
rubble.

Stranded on an overhead
trestle, partitioned by Plexiglas,
are NBA player Michael Jordan and
his two children.

Michael Angelo hallos:
"'Don't be afraid! From now on
you will be catching men.'"

Jordan holds his kids.
Before Michael can assist, they
jump into the cockpit from the
glass. The train passes beneath
another overhead area in the
abandoned, decimated terminal.

Underground, the train
crashes through debris. It
slithers like a snake in a rock
pile.

Inside the train, Jordan and
kids, then Michael, emerge from
the hatch. Everyone is safe.

Lincoln ballyhoos, "Michael
Jordan!"

Jordan bawls, "God man, this
is a nightmare!"

Ernie throttles the train.
Jordan remains brave. Lincoln

feigns courage to impress Jordan.
Maggie is frightened.

Michael positions himself over Ernie's shoulder. In darkness, the terminal exit nears. Michael guides Ernie; "The hangar, up ahead, might be closed. When we leave this terminal, hit the brakes." In the light, between terminal and hangar—the train exits. Michael shouts out, "Now!"

Ernie pulls the brake handle. Warning lights flash and sound. A fuse singes. Everybody stands still. The train has not stopped. Ernie cries out, "Hold on! The fuse blew. The brakes are...!"

Out of the hangar exit, on the railway tracking atop the mountain, the train/plane combination crashes through the huge hangar door. The world better sees the white A.N.G.E.L.— it's an aeronautical marvel. Its transport train rumbles through building and earthen debris.

Inside the train, Maggie and the children scream. Jordan consoles them. Lincoln is frozen. Ernie works on the tough-to-reach fuse box. Michael oversees. Ernie informs him, "I need to bypass the power connection... a paperclip...metal—"

Michael holds his hands to his chest in meditation...

It takes Spirit to think: The
silver medal around your neck!
Before Michael's into his prayer
mode, he gropes the trinket. He
hands it to Ernie. It fits the
fuse perfectly. Michael asks,
"How's are speed?"

Ernie says optimistically,
"Sixty-six and rising."

Jordan shoots off; "We
clear?"

Michael conducts to Ernie,
"Bring it down slowly."

On the mountaintop tracks,
the train/plane looks like a nymph
as it rolls through beautifully
destructive, earthen landscape.

Inside, Ernie pulls the brake
switch. Warning lights flash.
Ernie is panic stricken. "Hold
on! It didn't work. It's out of
control!"

Panic spreads like a disease.
Jordan, a believer for the most
part, takes his family's matters
into his own hands. He hauls them
up the hatchway.

Maggie and Lincoln cling
together.

Ernie fidgets with the
controls.

Michael goes after Jordan.
The rumbling train stupendously
infuses their actions.

Above, in the A.N.G.E.L.
open-air cockpit, Jordan and his
children emerge, the tree line

blowing by them. Ahead of the vehicle, the broken earth has tilted the monstrous arm of a construction crane. A cargo net dangles a couple of feet above the plane level. In Jordan's eyes, his children are his lone responsibility—not the others. He swoops them up. Like a suicide jumper, he stands at the edge. Michael exits the hatch. Jordan yells out to him, "Man, if I was you—I'd start heading for the exits!"

Michael hallos: "'Will a person gain anything if he wins the whole world but is himself lost or defeated? Of course not! There is nothing he can give to regain his life!'"

Jordan screams, "Hold on kids!" He cries out, "God, you blessed me." He leaps high into the cargo net. Michael lunges but can offer no physical assistance.

From Lincoln's vantage point, out the back of the train, he sees the Jordan's bouncing in the net like a circus act after a high dive. They're entangled in it, like flies in a web. It loops like a jump rope.

Lincoln notices a ski lift. It runs parallel above the railway. The chairs that might normally be on the inverted, T-shaped, guide-way are gone.

Lincoln's got an idea. Fear and
survival motivate him. As he
searches for a piece of equipment—
to help save himself—Michael
returns and realizes his old
friend is deserting him. Lincoln
takes from Michael the long,
yellow rope. Lincoln crouches and
starts tying a lasso. He thinks—
then mugs Michael for the
briefcase. Lincoln pops its
latches. He's shocked to discover
the treasure he's found,
remarking, "Oh my God."

Michael kneels down.

Lincoln removes the large,
iron altar cross. He slams shut
the case's lid. He starts to tie
the rope to the cross.

Michael has a better idea.
He removes the red-white-and-blue
ribbon from around his neck. He
hands it to Lincoln, halloing:
"'If I were to honor myself, that
honor would be worth nothing. The
one who honors me is my Father—the
very one you say is your God.'"

Lincoln's dumbfounded. He
holds the ribbon and the roped
cross.

Michael intervenes and ties
the ribbon to the crux of the
cross, governing, "Here...with the
cross as support—you'll see how
the ribbon works."

Lincoln stands and prepares
to escape.

442

Maggie hoots, "Lincoln!" She hollers, "Your coat, take it off!"

Lincoln does. He removes his billfold from the pocket, and a pistol from the shoulder holster he's sporting.

Michael sees it and comments; "...The religious right?"

Lincoln responds, "Hell no! Death threats! I can't get her killed soon enough."

Michael reminds him, "Your belt..."

Lincoln fumbles to undo his belt. He drops the gun and the wad of hundreds he tries to stuff into his pockets. The money blows out the back of the train. He chases it to the ledge. He's almost suicidal about leaping after it.

Michael questions him resoundingly, "Your money or your life?!"

Ernie, seeing Lincoln in the mirror, advises him resoundingly, "Lincoln, you can't take it with you! Anyone who loses their life over money is never around to spend it!"

Above, in the A.N.G.E.L. cockpit, Michael follows Lincoln out of the hatch. They move to the edge of the craft to see the chairlift. Lincoln screams, "For Pete's sake, it just crossed my mind—if that chairlift power is

on—I'll be electrocuted!" He
yells at Michael, "Some friend you
are—I'd kill for my friends!"

The train horn blows.

Throwing caution to the wind,
Michael boomerangs the cross.
"I'd die for mine!"

It's a strike! The cross
wraps around the track. A
fisherman with a monster catch,
the rope pulls taut.

Lincoln remembers his belt.

Michael ties the rope to the
craft.

Lincoln loops the belt over
the rope.

Michael anchors the rope.

Lincoln slings his arm under
the holster. To brace his chest,
he harnesses the belt to the rope
and holster. He then buckles it.

Ahead, the tree line is
closing in. Michael extends his
hand to bid farewell, but Lincoln
grabs the belt instead. Lincoln
is upside-down. Michael just
misses contact with him.

Lincoln slides safely to the
guide-way. Sparks fly when the
cross rides the metallic rail.
The friction burns the rope.
Lincoln must grab the ribbon or
fall. His hands grasp the ribbon
as the cross sparks. Lincoln,
looking up, sees how right Michael
was.

444

From Michael's vantage point, Lincoln takes the ride of his life. Michael, wind gusting, bravely challenges himself, saying omnisciently: "'Now *my* heart is troubled—and what shall I say? Shall I say, "Father, do not let this hour come upon me?" But that is why I came—so that I might go through this hour of suffering.'"

Inside the train, Michael comes down the hatch. He calls out inspirationally: "'If anyone wants to come with me, he must forget himself, carry his cross, and follow me!'"

Ernie cries, "The emergency abort tunnel's up ahead!"

Maggie, fear also her motivation, makes a quick exodus. She heads for the red, flashing sign that reads:

EMERGENCY ABORT TUNNEL—MANUAL EXPULSION

She hits the red button that automatically slides open the tubular door. A cylinder automatically juts out of the train like a turbine on a jet. It may be equipped for the fuel tanks, or the pilot, one can't tell.

Michael shouts out, "You may be the last people I know on Earth!"

Maggie, neglecting his plea, screeches, "I'm sorry, Michael!"

Michael unfurls the carpet remnant he's been toting. He pokes the bungee cord hooks into it. He's created her a toboggan for the slide. He hands her the rug. Maggie tosses it into the cylinder and adjusts herself on it. The yellow light flashes— VACUUM ON.

Ernie sounds out, "The vacuum tube's ready! Are you?"

Michael presses the yellow button. The clear plastic door seals the compartment. Maggie is hunched like a fetus in a tubular womb. Like a virgin parachutist, she's terrified. Audibly, it's difficult for her and Michael to hear one another. Maggie, panting like she's in labor, cries out loudly, "I'm chicken shit!"

Michael hollers loudly, "Don't touch the button inside!"

"What?!"

"When you see the green light—hold on!"

"For Christ's sake, what do I do?!"

Michael waits for the green— GO—light to flash. He answers loudly, "Don't abort! Don't—"

Maggie mouths the word—"Go!" before Michael can. She prematurely smacks the green button inside.

446

Michael cries loudly, "No!"

Maggie screams like she's giving birth. She spits out of the tube like a deposit into the bank drive-thru.

Michael looks with concern, but has the utmost faith in his prayer: "'Let the children come to me and do not stop them, because the kingdom of heaven belongs to such as these.'"

Outside of the train, exiting from the chamber, Maggie pours out of the spout. Like an amusement park ride, she glides on the carpet in the chute. Like an East Coast, ski slope's alpine slide in spring; the umbilical cord of a chute winds into the station box. The E.A.T.M.E. station box looks like a technically built outhouse or portable john. With the train in the background, Maggie's magical carpet ride ends inside the box. The trap door falls like a guillotine. The evacuation cylinder is sheared off of the train. The train belches a roar passing the back end of the box.

Inside the train, at the control panel, Michael, in perhaps the gravest look of despair ever to overcome a mortal being, walks up slowly behind a seated Ernie Goldstein. He places his hands gently on the shoulders of a hopeless brother, saying: "'For

whoever wants to save his own life
will lose it; but whoever loses
his life for me and for the gospel
will save it.'"

A large, horizontal traffic
light flashes its red—STOP—sign.
Warning sounds alert Ernie. Ernie
shouts, "The automatic track
switcher won't shut off! If we
don't stay on the straight track,
we're doomed! Our only hope is
the manual one!"

"Where is it?"

"Out there! Up ahead! The
Sagittarius Signal Station!"

The Sagittarius Station is a
platform booth next to the track.
Michael sets aside the briefcase.
Searching...he grabs the ax handle
Ernie boarded with. He stamps one
end against a sharp corner on the
floor. He connects the bungee
cord's hooks to the opposite ends
of the handle. He's fashioned
himself a sturdy bow. The
Sagittarius Station gets closer.

Michael shouts out, "I don't
see it!"

He looks around the walls and
the train compartment for some
sort of arrow.... He sees
something. In the swift motion of
a gymnast on a pommel horse, he
mounts a fuel tank. Like a
centaur from Greek mythology, he
leans forward out of the window.

448

Michael is poised. He
reaches behind his shoulder.
He draws the blind man's aluminum
cane. Like an arrow from a
quiver, he positions it. The red,
signal button is the size of an
apple. Michael shouts, "I see
it!" He recoils the arrow, but
his face is haunted by the
recollection of killing his horse.
Ready...aim...he's stoned...he
focuses...he's forgiven...fire!
Bull's-eye again!

Ernie watches the control
panel signals, hollering, "They're
off!"

Out on the rail tracks, the
train speeds past the railway
fork.

At the control panel, the
yellow light flashes, warning
sounds are heard. Michael again
looks over the action. "What is
it?"

Ernie says, "I don't know,
but I'm losing control again!"

"Think; is there any other
way to stop the train?"

"Ohhh!...there is one. Most
trains have a danger aspect
signal. If a train reaches too
fast a speed, it sends a signal
and the power shuts down."

"Can you make it go faster?"

"Ohhh, if I know the right
switches! I've only worked on
model trains! I've only been on a

train once in my life, when my grandfather died!"

Michael instructs him, "I have faith in you."

Head on, Ernie, shifting the controls, almost says it all—"I think I can, I think I can, I think I can."

If this were lightning—and surprise thunder—this is the moment before the thunder sounds.... Splat! A huge gob of mud pastes the windshield.

Inside the train, the splattered windshield blackens the area. Ernie, flicking the wiper switch, hollers, "It's broke...I can't see!" He sees Lincoln's gun on the floor of the train. He yells to Michael, "The gun!... Shoot out the window!"

Michael reaches for it—but he cannot stand to touch it. He takes a knee, propping himself up with the briefcase. Figuratively, he is sweating blood and bullets. In prayer, he cannot lift a finger to the trigger. He looks at the muddied window, thinking, what if there's something outside of it?

Outside the train, the magnificent panorama of the revamped countryside shows "Father Nature" at His finest.

Inside, at the control panel, the green light flashes, warning sounds alarm. Ernie's face

illuminates in green terror. "Oh!
My! God!" He turns to the rear
and sees Michael's arms spread
wide. With the briefcase in hand,
and the earth again beginning to
quake, a magnificent backlight
gives power to Michael's prayerful
pose. Michael is *actually*
sweating blood. Ernie has his
back to the windshield. As if
Michael willed it, an olive branch
shatters the glass wide open.

At the gorge, they see the
awesome span in the earth. The
train trestle is severed in half.
The bridge is out! The river runs
wide. The train barrels for the
ravine like an Evil Kneivel rocket
car.

Michael, beckoning Ernie,
trumpets, "The A.N.G.E.L release!"
At the control panel, the
A.N.G.E.L. release-mechanism is a
green and white, angel-shaped—ON—
signal light and a large, concave
screw/knob. The red and silver
signal—OFF—light is lit. It's
protected by another concave screw
that locks down the clear,
bulletproof container. Michael
holds his hands over the box—
hoping against hope, God will open
it for him. He gives a knock on
it.

Ernie thinks, is he in
trouble or does he have an idea?
Ernie takes a moment...to look

away from the screw...to the
shining—ON—light. The large,
steel release-mechanism screws—
uncouple the aircraft from the
train.

Ernie prays in a sacred pose.
Shaking his head "no," he calls
out for divine guidance.
"Michael?!"

Michael uses the small rope
to strap himself to the landing
gear. He extends his briefcase
hand to Ernie, responding loudly:
"I am, and you will all see the
Son of Man seated at the right
side of the Almighty and coming
with the clouds of heaven!"
Michael is, at this moment,
communicating to God. He spreads
his untied arm wide. He closes
his eyes and lifts his head
upward. The wind gusts through
him.

Boom! Lightning strikes!

A gigantic oak tree lands
across the track. It's braced by
two standing others. The train
rams the fallen oak. Ernie is
ejected out of the window.

On the control panel, there
is a shiny silver dollar next to
the A.N.G.E.L. release-container.

Ernie Goldstein is thrown
toward the last tree at the
gorge's edge.

Michael pleads: "Father, forgive them for they do not know what they do."

Ernie crashes, back first, onto a sturdy branch.

With one arm, Michael holds to the plane. The craft catapults him from the train. As he's ejected, the train's roofing rips the white shirt off his body. The metal leaves bloody tire tracks on his back. In pain, Michael utters not a sound.

The plane flies clear of the crashing, jackknifed train. Fire and black smoke rise as Michael descends. From high overhead and far below, Michael looks like he's riding on angel wings. The plane glides over the gorge.

From the structural wreckage of the bridge, in the center of the geological gap, a large, wooden cross protrudes. With double crossbeams, it resembles a telephone pole. Michael releases the rope. It falls, like a snake, into the train wreckage. He lets go of the case. It drops onto the bridge below. He reaches out for the crossbeam. Like a trapeze artist, he swings onto it.
The crashing plane severs the one crossbeam. A crucifix is formed. A weathered, wooden plaque reads:

FOUNTAIN RIVER

The A.N.G.E.L. continues out
of sight into the waters below.
Blurring by, like a magician's
handkerchief over a top hat, is
the name of the plane: SPIRIT OF
ST. LOUIS.

A voice screams...

"Ijjul'jula!"

It's Noah. Miraculously,
he'd been walking the bridge.

Noah, from his foot to his
hands, clings to Michael's feet.
He sheds Michael's shoes and pants
trying to scale up him. The pants
blow onto the scaffolding.
Michael's left only in his briefs
with Noah holding his feet.
Slowly looking up Michael, Noah
sees blood dripping down Michael's
chest, arms, and face. Michael is
in great pain.

The sign above his head is
more easily read:

FOUNTA **INRI** VER

Noah, fearing his own death
is imminent, screams out, "Save me
a place!"

The cross slowly tilts over—
like a clock's arm from noon to
three.

Michael sees a vision in his
head. He looks up to the ecliptic
sun in a darkened, gray sky; the
rays of light shine down on him.

A powerful backlight reflects the light back skyward. A direct line between Michael and Heaven is opened.

> **"'I, have sent My angel to testify to you these things in the churches. I am the Root and the Offspring of David, the Bright and Morning Star.'"**

Michael moves his torso like a pendulum. He's trying to swing Noah safely onto the scaffolding. It's apparent the only way Michael can—is by himself letting go. He mouths to himself..."Sac-ri-fice."

> **"'Surely I am coming quickly.'"**

Michael is in his greatest agony. His last breath, his final act, is to..."Save a life." He thinks, Will it take his own life from him?...

...*No* angel is *that* omnipotent.

On the bridge, Noah is hunched looking down. He's saved! He's alive!

Michael breathes: "It is finished."

He bows his head.

His hands release from the cross; long, wooden splinters have pierced his palms.

The one man falls, as if in slow-motion. Like a dove to guide him, his bloodstained Bible flutters down after him. Its thin pages rustle free from the binding.

An earthquake rattles the bridge and rocks the ground.

As if in normal speed; he lands, flat on his back, on a concrete slab at the foundation of the bridge. An exposed, iron spike violently spears his abdomen.

The river's splashing water mixes with the gushing blood. His lungs have collapsed. Blood spews from his mouth. The Bible too, lands on its spine on the muddy sandbar.

On the bridge scaffolding; Noah, from his leg to his torso, is pinned beneath the criss-cross of a steel girder—his wrists slashed by two spikes. He is dead. Over Noah's head, the wind frees the written pages from the binder containing Michael's manuscript.

In the tree branch, at the edge of the cliff; Ernie

Goldstein's body is nested there;
compound fractures of both legs
have mixed the gushing blood with
the mire. His eyes closed
forever, he falls dead from the
tree.

Back at the slab, the
anchored body flops about. His
shirt is shrouded over him.

DAY TEN

DEATH

HOLY SATURDAY – APRIL 22, 2000

D A Y   E L E V E N

IN THE END...

EASTER SUNDAY, APRIL 23, 2000

SUNRISE

On the airport land, the white concrete edifice is no more than a junk pile. A bronze sign has fallen. It reads:

ROMAN EMPIRE BUILDERS MCMXCIX

From out of the concrete carnage, a tow truck tows the completely flattened scrap of four-wheeled steel that was the radio promo van. Aunt Mary escorts it like a casket.

At the airport terminal, on the ground transportation level, Joe Arimathea, a respected journalist, reports live from the scene. "It's Easter Sunday. This is Joe Arimathea reporting.... Three days have passed—"

Before he can complete his statement, Mary speaks into the microphone. She's in disbelief. "'Suddenly, there was a mighty earthquake...'"

At the wall of the gorge, in the grated end of the E.A.T.M.E. tunnel, overlooking the site of Michael's death place, Maggie is hunched in the pipe.

Mary continues on, saying: "'...as an angel of the Lord descended from heaven. He came to the stone, rolled it back, and sat on it.'"

In the wall of the gorge, Maggie's covered in sewage and waste, a spot of residue on her forehead. She's in tears. She masks her nose and mouth with her hands. She appears as if she's "speaking no evil."

In a large, rusted out, stilted gas tank on the mountaintop, sawdust fills the emptied, hollowed-out tank; adjectives describing the way Lincoln feels. Hiding his eyes, he's huddled, weeping bitterly. He "sees no evil."

In the identical, pious, bedroom from the beginning of the story; from the TV, Joe Arimathea's voice is heard. "There are three people reported dead and one man known missing."

The TV light creates the silhouette of a man's torso similar in proportion to Michael's. Lying in bed, he reaches to the chair at the bedside. The TV light seems to make a housefly on the chair glow. The fly rests on the identical piece of paper Mark Anthony presented to Roman when Michael endeavored upon writing his story. The hand reaches over and covers the housefly beneath a glass. Mark Anthony, obediently, says to himself: "'Go into all the world and preach the gospel to every creature.'"

A one-time paved road leads from the terminal. On the dirt pathway—with the sun rising—the silhouetted image of a man appears. His back turned, He exhorts a word to a gentleman walking side by side with Jordan. The Jordan children lag behind. The men don't recognize the man; therefore, they listen only casually to Him. As the man's image walks on, the gentleman repeats the message for edification to Jordan. "When you cross the supernatural with God..."

In the bedroom, Mark Anthony's hands remove the glass-encased fly by holding the paper beneath it. The maneuver reveals a shiny, black folder much like a Bible cover. The gold embossed title coincides with the gentleman's words. The gentleman continues on saying, "...the unexplainable becomes *The Archangel*." Mark Anthony pulls back the paper a little further and sees the briefcase under the folder.

At sunset, outside of the terminal, Joe Arimathea is standing alone. He reports: "'...but these are written that you may believe...'"

At the Fountain River Gorge, a hand-written manuscript page is cascading down the river.

Arimathea continues on to say: "'...Jesus is the Messiah, the Son of God and that through this belief you may have life in His name.'"

In the Fountain River, the chapter heading is barely distinguishable: <u>MICHAEL</u>. More easily seen, is the simplistic, two-lined, drawing of a fish. The drawing floats by the cement slab. The man's semi-folded shirt rests where his head no longer does. The man is gone. He has disappeared from the face of the earth.

At the woods, on the other side of the gorge, the rudimentary drawing of a squirrel lays on the snowy ground. In the vicinity, an albino squirrel stands on its haunches. The squirrel then dashes for the woods.

The drawing of a cat blows in the wind. It's swiped and pawed at by a white, mountain lion that roars silently. It too, heads out of sight back into the woods.

The drawing of a dog lay beside the white wolf. The wolf howls, but cannot be heard. It also turns and runs into the woods.

The childlike drawing of a horse gallops in the gust. A magnificent, wild, white horse rises to its hind legs. The horse whinnies in silence.

At the peak of the clouded mountaintop there is snowcapped, white grass; a white flower; the trunk, branch, and leaves of a white tree; there is the face of the moon; the sky; and the prevailing wind, which blows the first line of wispy, angel-shaped clouds away.

And war
broke out
in
heaven:
Michael
and his
angels
fought
with the
dragon;
and the
dragon
and his
angels
fought,
but they
did not
prevail,
nor was a
place
found for
them in
heaven
any
longer.

Rising
in
the
Heavens
is
Jesus
Christ—
The Image of Mankind.
There is a circular rainbow around the
sun...
The
promise
of
the
Son
of
God
to
come.